From Imagining to Understanding the
African American
Experience

Phyllis A. Gray

Kendall Hunt
publishing company

Kendall Hunt
publishing company

www.kendallhunt.com
Send all inquiries to:
4050 Westmark Drive
Dubuque, IA 52004-1840

Printed in the United States of America
10 9 8 7 6 5 4 3 2 1

To my late parents, Charles and Elbertha Gray; my two oldest deceased siblings, Daniel Gray and Vernel Gray Powell; my children, Akeem and Shakenna; my siblings and their families; my Godchildren; my "adopted" children; my students; and, last but not least, my AFRICAN ANCESTORS.

CONTENTS

Preface

The main purpose of this book is to aid individuals in developing their "sociological imaginations" and to broaden their understanding of the "Sociology of the Black Experience," particularly in the United States' multicultural society. Although one book cannot provide the total experience of the black diaspora, this book provides a unique sociological exploration of the African American experience and how it has been specifically impacted by culprits such as slavery and racism. The reality of slavery and racism is deeply threaded throughout the fabric of the current state of African Americans and this threading must be understood. Blacks are still one of the most disadvantaged minority groups in the nation. Because "race" still matters in the United States, every section of this book explores the sociological impact of slavery and racism on the experiences of black Americans.

Moreover, this book provides a solid presentation of the different phases of the "Black Experience" in American society. As the book moves through each phase, beginning with the institution of slavery itself, it explores the impact of slavery and racism on major social institutions and social problems of black life (family, education, crime, etc.), right up to the present, to show how a life of slavery has impacted every aspect of the black experience in America. Understanding slavery provides the foundation for understanding black Americans, and therefore understanding America.

Chapter 1 introduces the main focus of the book, "the Sociology of the Black Experience" and describes **"The Sociological Imagination,"** which is a term coined by sociologist C. Wright Mills. The sociological imagination enables one to understand the events, painful or not, of personal troubles within the larger context of society. It enables one to understand the effect of social forces such as slavery on people's lives, and then allows one to understand how social forces shape people's perspectives and experiences. Historically, this experience has been very excruciatingly painful for black Americans, as is evident in their lives from slavery to the present and everything in-between.

Globally, others are beginning to recognize and appreciate the greatness of Africa. This amazing continent is more than just great wild animals, jungles, deserts, and tribes. It also has a legacy of slavery which has linked it to the most powerful country in the world, The United States of America. Chapter 2 explores this most unique legacy and sets the stage for the remainder of the book. It focuses on slavery, which provides the foundation for understanding black Americans in the United States.

Chapter 3 describes the black experience from the Civil War to civil rights. It briefly explains the significance of the Civil War, and the period in American society known as Reconstruction, or the post slavery era. It concludes with a discussion of the great migration when thousands of Blacks left the South in search of better opportunities and to escape the Jim Crow oppression.

Chapter 4 picks up the black experience through the Civil Rights and Black Power Movements. It examines these two major social movements which challenged the racist fabric of the United States of America. These movements pushed America to a collision with humanity and reality. Together they further served as a turning point in African American history and culture, which, as a result, became the most significant events for African Americans since the Civil War.

Chapter 5 and subsequent chapters examine the American society and its social structure, social institutions, and cultural aspects, as they relate to African Americans' assimilation into a "different" America, which developed after the social movements. It specifically focuses on the black subculture and religion, concluding that the black church is still a dominant force in the black community.

Chapter 6 examines politics and the military. The appointment of General Colin Powell as the Secretary of State by the Republicans in 2001 and the historical election of the nation's first black president and commander-in-chief, President Barack Obama by the Democrats in 2008, show that if given the opportunity, Blacks can serve at the highest levels in America. However, like other social institutions, Blacks have not always enjoyed the freedom of politics and the military in America.

Like other aspects of society, the black community evolved as a response to historical events which led to its very unique cultural development. Some of these events impact the geographical locations, families, and health of black Americans and their communities. Therefore, Chapter 7 examines the geographical locations of the black community, the families within them, and the health conditions of these families.

Chapter 8 examines social class, education, and employment. Just as Blacks developed a burning desire to reunite black families after the end of the Civil War, they also developed an urgent, strong sense of need to become educated, even against all odds. Without a doubt, the major handicap for most newly freed slaves was that most of them were illiterate and could not read, write, or comprehend written materials, since they were forbidden to become educated during slavery.

Chapter 9 explores African American visual artists, literary authors and poets, and entertainers. These individuals have made tremendous contributions in their areas, yet many faced racism in America just like any ordinary African American. Clearly, "race" still matters more in America than social class.

Chapter 10 vividly describes being **"BLACK"** in America. Without a doubt slavery and racism have reinforced each other, and together have unleashed paralytic toxins upon the experiences of Blacks in America since they first set foot on the American soil. Yet, in spite of these toxins, and an excruciatingly painful experience, African Americans still found a way to survive against "all" odds. Therefore, this chapter concludes the book and focuses on the remaining aspects of the "Sociology of the Black Experience" in the United States. It describes what it means to be **"BLACK"** in America by discussing "the good, the bad, the ugly, and the magnificent" in the black culture.

Leroy A. Durant
Claflin University

Foreword and Acknowledgments

There are many individuals who assisted, supported, and sacrificed their time and efforts in the preparation of this book. First, I would like to thank Kendall Hunt Publishing Company; specifically Gregory DeRosa and Linda Chapman for the opportunity to write this book. We developed an incredible working relationship during the preparation of each chapter, and I really appreciate their unwavering support, from beginning to end. As well, I would like to thank Dr. Leroy A. Durant for his critical comments and feedback on each draft of every chapter, and under a very tight and grueling time frame. I sincerely appreciate his endless support. In addition, I am very grateful to my colleagues in the Department of Sociology and Criminal Justice at Florida A&M University for their support and encouragement during the writing process. Likewise, many thanks and appreciation are extended to my siblings and other family members, especially my sister, Aremethia Burnes for her quick turnaround time in assisting me with research and items on spur-of-the-moment requests. In addition, I am very appreciative of my son, Akeem, for the research assistance in finding sources at the library and bringing home tons of heavy classic books. As well, I am forever grateful to him for typing research notes when my fingers occasionally gave out on the keyboard, while at the same time keeping up with his own college courses. To my wonderful 10-year-old daughter, Shakenna, thanks for allowing me to impose upon our precious quality time that we normally spend together while I wrote this book. I am forever grateful for your understanding, patience, sacrifice, and for all of the "why" questions about the contents of the book! Further, I would like to thank my students over the years for encouraging me to complete this book and for allowing me to teach them about the "Black Experience." Their enthusiasm and eagerness to always learn more and more about their African American heritage kept my adrenalin pumping and made me even more passionate about teaching them about "them." Moreover, I would also like to thank two of the greatest Battery Creek High School teachers who taught and prepared me for what later became my lifetime career interest, Mrs. Janie Smalls, who taught my first psychology and sociology courses, and Mrs. Williams, who taught me the first and most significant course on Black Studies. I am forever grateful to the two of them for shaping my future and career while still a teenager in high school. As well, I am also grateful for the professional guidance and teaching of my first major professor at Iowa State University, Dr. Joe Hraba, who was the first to teach me about "race relations," from a white man's perspective. It was such an incredible learning experience working with him in completing my master's thesis research on Buxton,

Iowa: "A Black Utopia in the Midwest." Moreover, I would also like to thank both of my late parents, Charles and Elbertha Gray for all of the love and nurturing they provided me throughout the years, and for being my first teachers. My father taught me how to read and interpret the Bible, and to always be proud of who I am. At the same time, my mother was the first to formally introduce black history and culture to me as a teenager, via the iconic *Ebony* magazine, which she bought monthly, and the Ebony Pictorial History of Black America series, which was the first set of books on black America that I have ever owned, and cherished to this day, which was the greatest gift she could have ever given me, other than birth. Those books were extremely helpful in the preparation of this book. Finally, I would like to acknowledge my African ancestors, of whom I am so very proud to be among their descendants. Likewise, I am just as proud to be the descendant of all of those who have paved the rough road in the long, dreadful journey of the "Black Experience in America," so that I am able to write about theirs and my challenging times. May God continue to bless us for our courage, endurance, and perseverance! Love Thyself…. An African Proverb!

About the Author

Dr. Phyllis A. Gray is currently Professor of Sociology/Social Psychology at Florida A&M University in Tallahassee. She has published numerous scholarly articles in both national and international journals, and has been principal investigator on many grants and contracts. Her research mainly focuses on race related issues and African Americans. Throughout her academic career, she has taught courses on The Sociology of the Black Experience, Intergroup Relations, Race Relations, and Racial Minorities. In addition to being the recipient of many honors and awards, she is also a member of the American Sociological Association, the Association of Black Sociologists, and is the founding Executive Director of the National Black Graduate Student Association, Inc. A native of Beaufort, South Carolina, she received a Bachelor's Degree in Psychology from South Carolina State University and a Master's Degree and Doctorate Degree in Sociology/Social Psychology from Iowa State University.

CHAPTER 1

Sociology of the Black Experience

S ociology is the scientific study of human group behavior and social structure, which refers to recurring patterns of behavior. It focuses on individuals' experiences within their social groups involving cultural roles, norms, and values during social interaction. It has a very unique perspective of its own. This perspective is best explained by understanding **"The Sociological Imagination,"** which is a term introduced by sociologist C. Wright Mills in 1959 and refers to an individual's personal use of sociology through critical thinking and understanding (Shepard, Persaud, and Hughes 2009; Henslin 2011). However, the sociological imagination must be developed through a process which involves cognition and experiences. It is most helpful to the study and understanding of the "Sociology of the Black Experience" in the United States.

C. Wright Mills (1959) stated that many of the things individuals experience are really beyond their control, and that they have to do with the society and the way it is structured, its historical development, and how it is organized and functions. In fact, individuals are affected by the time and place in which they live. Further, the sociological imagination enables one to understand the events, painful or not, of personal troubles within the larger context of society. It enables one to understand the effect of social forces such as slavery

on people's lives, and then allows one to understand how social forces shape people's perspectives.

Thus, sociology allows one to question "taken for granted" assumptions and realities, and then replaces subsequent misconceptions and misinterpretations with more accurate data and explanations (Shepard, et al. 2009). Therefore, it is evident that sociology and the sociological imagination are most useful to the understanding of the "Sociology of the Black Experience," in the United States. Historically, this experience has been very excruciatingly painful for black Americans, as is evident in their lives from slavery to the present and everything in-between.

The sociological imagination or the ability to see one's own life and the lives of others as part of a larger social structure and a larger human condition (Shepard, et al. 2009; Henslin 2011) is the main conceptualization for the "Sociology of the Black Experience." Once an individual develops this critical way of thinking, he/she will be less likely to explain others' behavior through their "race" and will begin to examine the social structures which determine behavior such as race relations.

One will also realize that the solutions to social problems such as racism and bad race relations lie not only in changing individuals' attitudes and behaviors but in changing the social structure of society and its institutions (Shepard, et al. 2009; Henslin 2011). This involves unraveling the established social pattern used in race relations. Of course this is easier said than done, but nonetheless it can be accomplished over time through gradual efforts of individuals during social interaction, and reconstructing social realities. This reconstruction of social reality requires communication, cooperation, and contact, which involves candid, open conversations and activities that will bring different racial and ethnic groups together in exchanges that utilize their sociological imaginations to truly try to "understand" the "race" dilemma in America.

The sociological imagination presents another means to view and to search for solutions to the common social problems and social dilemmas in society (Shepard, et al. 2009). The "race" problem, which is a social creation and not a biological one, can certainly be classified as the "race" dilemma. Americans cannot ignore the fact that "race" matters in this society. However, what is extremely important to note is that until individuals "understand" the problem of "race" and the causes of racism and bad race relations, it will be nearly impossible to work on strategies and possible solutions to this lingering dilemma. It is one thing to "know" what the problem is, but another thing to **understand** what the problem is. Therefore, learning to understand how social structures such as race relations impact behavior is indeed the process of developing the sociological imagination (Shepard, et al. 2009) which is the impetus for understanding the contents of this book.

RACE MATTERS IN AMERICA

Blacks or African Americans, one of America's largest minority groups, share a unique history unlike any other racial or ethnic group in the country and indeed in the world. Most African Americans did not freely immigrate to the United States of America, the land of the free and the home of the brave, instead they entered as involuntary immigrants, or more specifically, as slaves. As slaves, they were given the worst treatment shown to any human race by another. In fact, they were not even treated as humans, but as property owned by white Americans. From the very beginning of slavery

and right up to the present, African Americans have suffered from a social and legally enforced oppression that was even made certain by the U.S. Constitution (Feagin 1989).

Without a doubt, most would argue and many would agree that the African American experience has been the worst, although most unique in the United States. Even in 2011, Blacks are still one of the most disadvantaged minority groups in the nation. Because "race" does matter in the United States, every section of this book explores the sociological impact of slavery on the social structure of black Americans.

The main purpose of this book is to aid individuals in developing their "sociological imaginations" and to heighten individuals' understanding of the "Sociology of the Black Experience," particularly in the United States' multicultural society. Although one book cannot provide the total experience of the black diaspora, this book will provide a unique sociological analysis of African Americans by specifically focusing on the culprit itself, slavery. The reality of slavery is deeply threaded throughout the fabric of the state of African Americans and this thread needs to be exposed and understood.

Many scholars and ordinary people of all races, including Blacks "take slavery for granted" and avoid thinking about it, not to mention talking about it, as the "main" source of African American problems and fate in the United States. Sociologically, everyone knows what the problem is, but not everyone understands what the problem is. Hence, the "black problem" in America is "the problem" in America, and until it is given real and serious consideration and understanding, then it will remain America's problem. Hence, America needs to develop a sociological imagination.

Moreover, this book will provide a solid presentation of the different phases of the "Black Experience" in American society. Each major phase (i.e., Reconstruction, Civil Rights Movement) of the black experience will be sociologically analyzed. As the book moves through each phase, beginning with the institution of slavery itself, it will explore the impact of slavery on major social institutions and social problems of black life (family, education, crime, etc.), right up to the present, to show

how a life of slavery has impacted every aspect of the black experience in America. Understanding slavery provides the foundation for understanding black Americans, and therefore understanding America.

Everyone needs to understand the true American development and not just the sketchy splotches that traditional historical accounts have provided in some early history books, which have practically all but eliminated real discussions of slavery. Sociology is a means for helping all of society to understand this part (slavery) of American culture and social structure that some truly take for granted. Nonetheless, people tend to engage in conversations that they are more comfortable in discussing and avoid those that are more uncomfortable such as race, racism, slavery, and even Africa.

If Americans, Whites, Blacks, and others truly understood Africa and African American history, everyone would be better educated and race relations would greatly improve in the country as a whole. A lot of what African Americans experienced in this society benefitted and had great consequences for all Americans. Whites, too, have been done a misdeed in society and they need to be reeducated on the reality of all of America's citizens. No doubt it is hard to change attitudes and behaviors when they are so much a part of the socialization process, but it is clear that resocialization is needed for Americans, and as a result, perhaps "race would not matter" as much as it does now.

However, until Whites, the powerful majority in America, realize that they, too, need to become better educated on minorities to better understand themselves and their privileged position in America, then America will continue to be undereducated as a country, and racism will continue to be as "American" as "Apple Pie." This book will attempt to stimulate this realization and awareness and hopefully get Americans moving away from pluralism which could then lead to assimilation. As well, Blacks had no other choice but to try to assimilate and acculturate into the American society, as they were thrust into this strange new world through slavery and at the hands and whips of white Americans. As a result, there are no other human creations in the world that are parallel to black Americans. They are a unique creation, created by white Americans and made in America.

BARRIERS TO POSITIVE RACE RELATIONS

This section presents a general overview of barriers to positive race relations, particularly between Blacks and Whites in the United States. It is important to understand these barriers because they affect critical aspects of cooperation and accommodation among the dominant majority and the various minority groups in American society. Although this book focuses specifically on the sociology of the black experience, these barriers affect relations among the powerful majority (Whites) and other minorities as a whole. Unfortunately, these barriers are often learned early in life and continue throughout the socialization process.

Socialization, which is simply the process of learning culture (customs, traditions, and beliefs) differs among racial and ethnic groups. During socialization, each person gradually develops a unique personality, which shapes his/her attitudes in terms of feelings, ways of thinking, and behaviors (Schaefer 1986). Moreover, individuals may develop different views toward others and other cultures during the socialization process. Some of these views may not be favorable, and can contribute to strengthening the barriers to positive race relations.

Antagonistic race relations have always been a barrier to effective communication, coordination, and cooperation between Blacks and Whites in America, particularly in the South. The southern states have been stigmatized for their racial tensions. These racial problems have not only hindered social interactions between Blacks and Whites, but have also stunted economic development in the region. Although much economic development has taken place in the South, it is still one of the poorest regions in the nation. This is due, in part, to its long history of overt racial conflicts between Blacks and Whites, which seems to be a natural part of socialization. However, bad race relations are also present in the North and other regions of the country (Farley 1995).

One of the most exorbitant costs of poor race relations in America has been the failure to use the resources of all individuals, particularly Blacks, which has resulted in economic stagnation and waste (Rose 1951). Racial conflicts have caused the nation's human capital to depreciate significantly. Economic development is made possible only through communication and cooperation between racial and ethnic groups in a nation. To discard the potential and contributions of a large percentage of a nation's human capital, particularly African Americans, is the equivalent of suicide.

Several barriers hinder positive race relations between Blacks and Whites in the United States. These may include ethnocentrism, xenophobia, paternalism, prejudice, discrimination, and racism. First, those who develop ethnocentric attitudes strongly believe that their own culture is superior to all others; they tend to judge other cultures in terms of their own. Until ethnocentric attitudes and myths are dispelled through social interaction in order to develop an understanding and appreciation of other cultures, America will continue to have bad race relations. Whereas xenophobic individuals tend to be afraid of and exhibit an unrealistic fear of people who are perceived to be different from themselves (Parrillo 1985; Kitano 1985), this fear is usually not explained by any logical reasons or plausible explanations. For America to overcome this barrier, cooperation and communication must occur during on-going social interaction among Whites and other minorities, and the mysterious fear would gradually disappear.

Second, individuals who develop paternalistic attitudes have a need to control others who are less powerful. They tend to have a master-servant mentality. Those who are perceived as subordinate are thought to be immature and irresponsible, but are tolerated as long as they remain in their place (Van den Berghe 1967; Kitano 1985). Hence, Whites who have been in dominant or paternal positions might become angry when Blacks "do not appear sufficiently grateful for any [alleged] favors that are given" (Daniels and Kitano 1970, 21).

Paternalistic attitudes are maintained through social distance of etiquette (i.e., segregation). They are often more apparent when at least two racial groups, mostly in terms of skin color, come into contact. During the initial contact, racial caste systems may develop, which limits mobility between races. For them, race remains the major conflicting factor, and the attitudes of superiority and inferiority of races develop and become ingrained into individuals (Van den Berghe 1967; Kitano 1985). As with the previous barriers, real, continuous social interaction must occur between and among racial and ethnic groups so that these paternalistic attitudes can begin to fade away as an understanding and appreciation of cultural diversity is gained.

Third, prejudiced people hold biased beliefs about members of other racial or ethnic groups. These attitudes are expressed through stereotypes, which are negative, mental perceptions of others, and social distance, which refers to the degree of intimacy established in relationships with others. Prejudiced attitudes are also shown through scapegoating, which refers to the tendency to take out one's feelings of frustration and/or aggression on someone other than the true source of the feelings (i.e., the Ku Klux Klan's violence against Blacks). Another way prejudice can be expressed is through projection, which is the tendency to minimize, deny, or forget about certain characteristics of one's own group, while exaggerating these same characteristics within another group (Kitano 1985; Parrillo 1985; Curran and Renzetti 1987).

Stereotypes of Blacks have always been a strong barrier to positive race relations in the United States. Blacks have been stereotyped, humiliated, and insulted in numerous ways. For example, in 1906, during an exhibit by the New York Zoological Society, a small African, Ota Benga, was displayed in a cage among monkeys at the Bronx Park Zoo. He was viewed by thousands of people. Although Blacks protested the inhumane degradation of the young African, Whites thought it was funny, exciting, and great entertainment (Feagin 1989; Henslin 2011).

Blacks were also stereotyped as being mentally and morally inferior to Whites, and had happy-go-lucky sambo attitudes. In addition, their dark skin color was considered unusual and ugly. These stereotypes existed in slavery as well as today (Feagin 1989), and they continue to influence race relations in America.

Prejudiced people may also engage in discrimination, which involves any actions, policies, or practices that deny individuals or groups equal access to a society's resources and rewards. There are two types of racial discrimination: individual and institutional. The former are intentional actions against other ethnic or racial groups by individuals or small groups. The latter, also known as institutional racism, occurs when policies and practices of major institutions (i.e., government, education, economy) discriminate against ethnic and racial groups. This type is harder to identify and eradicate because it is built into the system (Parrillo 1985; Kitano 1985; Curran and Renzetti 1987; Feagin 1989).

There is also a temporal dimension in relations to discrimination; it can be either current or past. Current discrimination may refer to disparities in income and job promotion. Past discrimination refers to behavior enacted in the past that continues to hinder the progress of members of the target group in the present (Schaefer 1979) such as simply not hiring an individual because of his or her race for certain jobs or not allowing minorities to live in certain neighborhoods with Whites. African Americans have always experienced discrimination in America from the time their feet hit the American soil right up to the present.

Robert K. Merton (1949) further described the relationship between prejudice and discrimination through a typology of four different types of individuals. The typology emphasizes that prejudice and discrimination do not always occur together. Type 1 is the unprejudiced nondiscriminator, who is neither prejudiced nor discriminates. Not many people are of this type. Type 2 is the nonprejudiced discriminator, who discriminates because of social pressure. This person will not say anything when racists or bigots speak out, but will feel guilt and shame because he/she acted against his/her beliefs. Type 3 is the prejudiced nondiscriminator who is more of a coward or a timid racist or bigot. This person harbors stereotypes of racial minorities and may feel hostile toward them, but he/she keeps quiet around others who feel differently about minorities. Type 4 is the prejudiced discriminator who is a blatant, active, out in the open racist or bigot. He/she is openly prejudiced,

discriminates as freely as he/she likes, and feels that it is his/her duty to do so.

Finally, racism is the most dangerous barrier and encompasses all of the aforementioned barriers to positive race relations. Racist individuals believe that their race is superior to others and that there is no such thing as racial equality. To them, racial equality just simply does not exist. They assume that their color, culture, mental, and physical capabilities are superior to other races. Racists have prejudiced beliefs and discriminate against other racial and ethnic groups. These beliefs are justified because of their racist perceptions of minorities (Parrillo 1985; Kitano 1985; Feagin 1989).

Racism may be overt or outwardly shown, or covert, hidden or subtle and buried within policies or practices. In a society such as the United States, racism is an expression of power based on race alone. Racists in America are only benefitted through their use of power or their dominant majority status in the society. Therefore, in the United States of America, only Whites can be racists because they are the powerful majority and have the ability to impose their will and racist culture upon minorities against their will (Parrillo 1985; Kitano 1985; Feagin 1989).

Although not all white Americans are racists, they continue to benefit from racism, particularly institutional racism, which is embedded in America's key institutions such as the educational, political, and economic systems. Therefore, racism is also a problem for Whites in America, who may not understand the total effects of racism on everyone in America. Some Whites, wanting to engage in racial equality, may simply not know how to begin because they simply do not understand racism themselves. Again, it is one thing to "know" what the problem is and another thing to "understand" what the problem is. Hence, developing a sociological imagination will greatly aid in this understanding among all Americans. All Americans need to understand racism, this too is easier said than done, but a real stride toward attempting to unravel America's worst nightmare, is worth the time and effort of all Americans to pursue.

Institutional racism entered the system during European colonization of America. It has always been a part of the American society from the very beginning. When an ill is ingrained in the foundation of a society itself, it becomes extremely hard to eradicate, could go unnoticed, and could be taken for granted by those who are unaware of it or not impacted by it. In the beginning, Europeans had paternalistic and ethnocentric attitudes toward people in other parts of the world. Hence, there has been much evidence indicating that racist attitudes preceded slavery. So, when Africans were brought to the United States in chains, they were immediate targets of racism (Parrillo 1985; Kitano 1985; Feagin 1989).

AFRICA AND AFRICANS

AFRICA!! The second largest and perhaps the most beautiful and unique continent in the world, is the birthplace and home to all of humanity. As the "Mother" of humankind, every racial and ethnic group in the world has roots in Africa (Reader 2007). "We are all Africans and we all belong to Africa" (Reader 2007, 7)!

According to anthropologists and archaeologists, humans originated and evolved in Africa more than four million years ago (Reader 2007). Our physical appearances and sensory-motor skills (the way we stand and walk), our skin itself (regardless of the actual color), and scope of our mental faculties are all traced back to the evolutionary adaptations to the African environment (Reader 2007). Humans were not found anywhere else in the world until a few of them left the motherland of Africa about 100,000 years ago. It was these African descendants who eventually colonized every inhabitable place on Earth (Reader 2007). Therefore, it was Africans who really "colonized the world."

The African continent is an amazing creation! It is rich in diamonds, gold, and other precious jewels and minerals like copper and coal. Africa has some of the most magnificent landscapes and structures in the world, such as its Great Lakes found in the center of the continent and ranks among the largest and deepest worldwide (Reader 2007). It is also home to incredible

structures such as the great pyramids and the Sphinx. Africa has some of the most fascinating animals in the world such as elephants, hippopotamus, giraffe, rhinoceros, wildebeest, zebra, lions, cheetahs, hyena, among others (Reader 2007). Nonetheless, given all of these great creations found on the continent, perhaps the greatest creation of all are her people, who are also very culturally diverse.

Although Africa is the birthplace of humanity, a lot of people are still unaware of this most significant fact. The continent continues to be misunderstood and indeed misused by the rest of the world (Reader 2007). So much so, that it is still widely known as the "dark continent." This negative connotation is burdened with several meanings and interpretations. Some think it refers to Africa's "dark" forests and jungles, while others believe it is associated with the "darkness" of African skin color. However, the most disturbing stigma associated with Africa being considered the "dark continent," is the widespread ignorance of others about Africa, which in itself, results in the "darkness of Humanity." Knowing about Africa and appreciating the greatness of the continent should be on everyone's agenda, since the roots of every human being are found in Africa (Reader 2007).

Although much of Africa's history and culture were told by others, much of it is still not revealed or revealed inaccurately. In fact, much of it is told with ethnocentric, paternalistic, and even racist overtones. Nonetheless, Africans believed that knowledge of the past was very important, and used verbal stories to share this knowledge through storytellers and the elderly. Thus gerontocracy, or rule by the elderly, became Africa's self defining social and political systems (Reader 2007). Unfortunately, Africans did not write down much of the rich African history, and therefore left the opportunity for others to interpret and/or misinterpret Africa's history.

Africans were content with their culture and way of life and many African communities stayed just the size they wanted to be, in order to fulfill their needs. Many African communities concentrated on minimizing failure rather than maximizing fortunes and were pleased with having just enough of what they needed to survive. However, outsiders around the world, especially in Europe, who developed a desire for prosperity and domination of others, became aware of Africa's social structure and began to exploit it for their own desires and greed (Reader 2007). What happened next in Africa's history is one of the most incredible and unimaginable events on the face of the Earth, human degradation of one race by another.

Once this human degradation was set into motion, the whole world changed. Africa would never be the same again, as Whites dominated, degraded, and dehumanized Blacks. As this insurmountable nightmare on the ocean began, Africa's subsequent generations of humans would then experience a voyage beyond any reasonable comprehension that would continue to haunt them throughout the African diaspora and the world. It is this human degradation and dehumanizing that has prompted the need to develop a sociological imagination in order to "understand" the "Sociology of the Black Experience" beginning with Africa.

By the end of the fifteenth century, it was estimated that approximately 47 million people populated the African continent (Reader 2007). It was also estimated that the African population would have been about 100 million by 1850, had foreigners not taken, stolen, or exploited nearly 50 million Africans (Reader 2007). In the beginning, Europeans went to the Atlantic coast of Africa in search of gold, but shortly thereafter people, more specifically slaves, became the number one commodity. It is also estimated that between 1500 and 1850, eighteen million slaves left Africa (Reader 2007); further, it is estimated that for every nine slaves that made it across the Atlantic Ocean, another twelve did not due to death (Reader 2007). Without a doubt, this exploitation of Africans during the slave trade weakened this great continent and negatively impacted the demographic, economic, and political social structure of Africa. Even today in 2011, compared with other continents, Africa is under-populated (Reader 2007).

It was not enough that Europeans stole or took Africa's people, they also took Africa itself. By the time the slave trade was abolished in the mid-1800s, European colonization of the African continent had replaced it as the main focus for Africa's destiny. The European

Library of Congress

DR. WILLIAM EDWARD BURGHARDT DU BOIS (W. E. B. DU BOIS)

W. E. B. Du Bois was born right after slavery ended in America in 1868 in Great Barrington, Massachusetts. Du Bois became the first black person to receive a Ph.D. from Harvard University in 1895. He eventually joined the sociology faculty as department head at Atlanta University in Georgia. He spent most of his career teaching and researching about African Americans, and was the first to conduct a systematic study on racism in America, through his seminal work, *The Philadelphia Negro*. Other seminal works include *The Souls of Black Folk, Black Reconstruction, The Negro, The Gift of Black Folk,* among others. He was one of the founders of the National Association for the Advancement of Colored People (NAACP) in 1909. For many years, he served as the founding editor of *The Crisis*, the organization's magazine (Shepard, Persaud, and Hughes 2009). W. E. B. Du Bois is the most well-known and prolific black sociologist to date. *(Library of Congress)* paternalists divided up the continent among themselves and like vultures, fought over Africa's valuable raw materials and rich mineral resources. Before long, Europeans and other colonial imperialists gained control and governance of the African continent itself. Fortunately, Africa regained its independence from this colonization and began to rule its own destiny. Africa is now a popular tourist's attraction, and much attention is given to its enlightenment, as well as to humanity issues such as hunger, diseases, and warfare (Reader 2007).

Globally, others are beginning to recognize and appreciate the greatness of Africa. This amazing continent is more than just great wild animals, jungles, deserts, and tribes. It also has a legacy of slavery which has linked it to the most powerful country in the world, The United States of America. Chapter 2 explores this most unique legacy and sets the stage for the remainder of the book. It focuses on slavery, which provides the foundation for understanding black Americans in the United States. Subsequent chapters examine the institution of slavery and its impact on African American culture in the United States of America.

African American Firsts

(Potter and Claytor 1994, 71–93)

- Crispus Attucks was the first person to be shot and killed in the Boston Massacre during the American Revolutionary War in 1770.

- Paul Cuffe was the first to lead a fight for Civil Rights for Blacks in the state of Massachusetts in the late 1700s.

- Prince Hall founded the first African American Masonic Lodge in 1776 in Boston, Massachusetts.

- Jean Baptist Pointe Dusable was the first settler of the City of Chicago, Illinois, in the late 1700s.

- Sojourner Truth (real name was Isabella Baumfree) was the first black woman to lecture against slavery.

- Harriet Tubman (also known as the "Black Moses") was the first black woman to be honored on a postage stamp in America. She was responsible for operating the Underground Railroad, which led many slaves to freedom.

- Allen Allensworth, an escaped slave, established the first town in California for African Americans in the early 1900s, named Allensworth, which was located between Los Angeles and San Francisco.

- Matthew Henson was the first person to reach the North Pole in 1909 and planted the American flag there.

- Ida B. Wells was the first writer to document the lynching of black Americans in March 1892, when she wrote about the lynching of three black store owners in Memphis, Tennessee.

DISCUSSION QUESTIONS

1. What is the Sociological Imagination and how does it apply to the "Sociology of the Black Experience"?

2. Why does "race matter" in America?

3. Discuss the main barriers to effective race relations in the United States. What can be done to address and potentially eliminate them?

4. Discuss the four elements of prejudice.

5. What is the difference between prejudice and discrimination?

6. Do all prejudiced people discriminate? Are all discriminators prejudiced?

7.   What is racism in America? Who can be racist in America and why?

8.   What are stereotypes? Discuss some that have existed during slavery and that are still in existence today.

9.   How did white America create black America?

10. Why are Americans uncomfortable talking about race, racism, slavery, and even Africa?

11. Describe the African Continent before colonization. Comment on the uniqueness of the great wonders of this amazing continent.

12. Why is Africa the "Motherland of all Humanity"?

13. In what unique way is Africa linked to the United States in terms of people and population?

1. **Reflections Activity:** Based on the information in the chapter, reflect upon the statement, "Who am I," and write an essay describing yourself in terms of "your" black experience. Any racial and ethnic group member can do this activity since everyone is likely to have had some experience with the African American culture, either directly or indirectly.

2. **The Sociological Imagination Forum:** Throughout your life, many sociological issues, including racial issues will be apparent. As you go through life, you will come across a racial issue that you are very, very interested in, and must know more about! Therefore, once you decide on your "burning racial issue," you will then complete the statement: "If I were a sociologist, I would use my sociological imagination to determine, examine or explore *(the selected burning racial issue)*." Next, research the "burning issue" by responding to the **"What, Why, Where, When, Who, and How"** as they relate to the issue. Finally, be prepared to "perform/role play" in a sociological forum. The forum will be a lively discussion of the "Issues," which will engage the audience in understanding the problem through social interaction.

TEN THOUGHTS ACTIVITY

1. List 10 thoughts on what comes to mind when you think of Africa.

    _____

    _____

    _____

    _____

    _____

    _____

    _____

    _____

    _____

    _____

2. List 10 thoughts on what comes to mind when you think of America.

    _____

    _____

    _____

    _____

    _____

    _____

    _____

    _____

    _____

    _____

3. List 10 thoughts on what comes to mind when you think of African Americans.

_____

_____

_____

_____

_____

_____

_____

_____

_____

_____

SUGGESTED RESOURCES

www.infoplease.com/spot/bhmfirsts.html

www.blackpast.org/?q=aah/101-african-american-firsts

www.blackamericaweb.com/

www.africanamericanhistorymonth.gov/

REFERENCES

Curran, Daniel J., and Claire M. Renzetti. 1987. *Social Problems: Society in Crisis.* Boston: Allyn and Bacon.

Daniels, Roger, and Harry Kitano. 1970. *American Racism: Exploration of the Nature of Prejudice.* Englewood Cliffs, NJ: Prentice Hall.

Farley, John E. 1995. *Majority-Minority Relations,* 3rd ed. Englewood Cliffs, NJ: Prentice Hall.

Feagin, Joe R. 1989. *Racial and Ethnic Relations,* 3rd ed. Englewood Cliffs, NJ: Prentice Hall.

Henslin, James M. 2011. *Essentials of Sociology,* 9th ed. Boston: Allyn and Bacon.

Kitano, Harry H. 1985. *Race Relations,* 3rd ed. Englewood Cliffs, NJ: Prentice Hall.

Merton, Robert K. 1949. *Social Theory and Social Structure.* New York: The Free Press.

Mills, C. Wright. 1959. *The Sociological Imagination.* New York: Oxford University Press.

Parrillo, Vincent A. 1985. *Strangers to These Shores: Race and Ethnic Relations in the United States,* 2nd ed. New York: MacMillan.

Potter, Joan, and Constance Claytor. 1994. *African American Firsts.* New York: Pinto Press.

Reader, John. 2007. *Africa.* National Geographic Society, Washington, DC.

Rose, Arnold. 1951. *The Roots of Prejudice.* Paris: UNESCO.

Schaefer, Richard T. 1979. *Racial and Ethnic Groups.* Boston, MA: Little, Brown and Company.

———. 1986. *Sociology,* 2nd ed. New York: McGraw-Hill.

Shepard, Jon M., Narayan Persaud, and Brenda Hughes. 2009. *Sociology,* 10th ed. Thomson/Wadsworth, Publisher.

Van den Berghe, Pierre L. 1967. *Race and Racism: A Comparative Perspective.* New York: Wiley.

CHAPTER 2

Slavery

Slavery in America was a state of social and moral death that has been described as the most inhumane condition ever imposed upon one race by another. Historically, in America this was the case between the dominant white race and the subordinate black race. However, slavery provides the foundation for understanding the black experience in America. Thus, it is extremely important to first understand slavery in order to better understand the subsequent and current experiences of Blacks in America. Slavery's unique legacy is briefly described in this chapter.

Although black slaves were mostly responsible for the South's wealth, the economic need of the South is only half of the explanation for the enslavement of Blacks; blatant racism is the other half of the explanation (Ebony 1971; Hraba 1979; Parrillo 1985; Kitano 1985; Feagin 1989). Much evidence revealed that racism preceded institutionalized slavery. For example, at least two aspects of racism, ethnocentrism and paternalism toward other races (Africans, Asians, Hispanics, Native Americans), have always been a part of European beliefs from the beginning of contact with these races (Hraba 1979; Parrillo 1985; Kitano 1985; Feagin 1989).

So, upon the arrival of Africans in America, they were immediately subjected to prejudice, discrimination, and blatant racism. Even worse, the degradation of Africans began before they arrived in America with the savage capturing and kidnapping of them for a horrifying life of slavery. Nonetheless, racism and slavery reinforced one another, as there were laws governing the master's rights over the slaves in America that were rigidly enforced. As well, slavery was legally protected by the United States Constitution (Hraba 1979; Parrillo 1985; Kitano 1985; Feagin 1989). However, during slavery a few Blacks had their freedom but were never as free as Whites. Unfortunately, they were still treated as inferior and as second-class citizens. Yet, by the time of the Civil War, there were close to four million African slaves in the United States, about a million or so less than Whites in the South (Ebony 1971; Curran and Renzetti 1987; Parrillo 1985).

Black history in America began a year before the Mayflower landed at Plymouth Rock, Massachusetts, with the arrival of a Dutch ship in Jamestown, Virginia, in 1619. There were twenty Blacks on board whose origin was undetermined. The captain of the ship exchanged them for food and necessities with the colonists who were already there. It is said that the first twenty blacks did well in the new world, which was later to become the United States of America. Although they became indentured servants just like some of the Whites during that time, some Blacks gained full freedom, acquired land, and had the right to vote. Amazingly, some Blacks became affluent and owned servants just like the Whites did (Stampp 1965; Ebony 1971; Sirimarco 2007). Reportedly, one black man even owned a white servant (Ebony 1971).

Fortunately, when the first twenty Blacks arrived in America, chattel (property) slavery was not yet in place. At that time, "race" was not significant in servitude in America. Being black did not yet mean that one would be a slave. In fact, the race of the work force was not yet a major concern among most of the planters. Indeed, some planters had occasionally tried to use the white indentured servants on the plantations. These white servants were mostly poor Europeans who volunteered or were under some other type of pressure to come to America. Some had contracted a set number of years of work to pay for their way to America (Ebony 1971; Hraba 1979; Parrillo 1985; Kitano 1985; Feagin 1989).

There were also many disadvantages of using white indentured servants on the plantations. These included the difficulty of obtaining large numbers of them at one time. Further, other Whites would not have allowed them to be treated too badly. Plus, their terms of servitude ended after a certain period, thereafter they were set free and given money to begin a new life (Stampp 1965; Ebony 1971; Hraba 1979; Parrillo 1985; Kitano 1985; Feagin 1989).

White planters also tried to use Native Americans as servants and slaves but were unsuccessful since they knew the land well and often escaped. Conversely, those who were unable to escape would often become sick or sometimes died from the pressures and stressors of working on the plantations. Nevertheless, as "King Cotton" began to reign in the southern economy, the need for cheap labor increased to immeasurable levels as the southern planters became desperate for the "best suitable workers." Consequently, as the continent of Africa was being exploited by Europeans and the capturing of Africans became the new commodity, it was

not long before the burden of slavery was placed upon Blacks in America (Ebony 1971; Hraba 1979; Parrillo 1985; Kitano 1985; Feagin 1989).

Unlike Native Americans who knew the land and were often able to escape slavery and go back to their tribes, Africans were strangers to the American shores. Due to their dark complexion, Africans were very easy to identify and they had nowhere to go even if they did escape. Therefore, most could not escape the horrors of what laid ahead of them in slavery (Stampp 1965; Hraba 1979; Parrillo 1985; Kitano 1985; Feagin 1989). Unfortunately, many cotton planters believed that "one Black could do the work of four Indians" (Ebony 1971, 65). So, as life in America began to expand, the exploitation of Africans was sought because of the insatiable demand for labor, and Whites' religious view of them as heathens. As a result, the degradation of Africans took place, and the onset of European exploitation of African labor began, thereby providing the foundation for racial oppression of Blacks in America. Slavery was instituted and became a part of southern culture (Parrillo 1985; Feagin 1989).

Blacks share a unique history unlike any other ethnic or racial group in America. Most did not immigrate to the United States of their own free will. Instead, they were brought to America through the triangular trade, which was one of the most dehumanizing actions in the United States' history. Through the triangular trade, Blacks entered the United States as involuntary immigrants, or more specifically as slaves. The voyage across the Atlantic Ocean from Africa to America was called the "middle passage," because it was the middle of the triangular trade (Stampp 1965; Ebony 1971; Hraba 1979; Parrillo 1985; Kitano 1985; Feagin 1989). The triangular trade involved shipping European manufactured goods to West Africa and exchanging them for human slaves; then shipping human slaves to America and exchanging them for sugar, tobacco, cotton, and rum; and then shipping these commodities back to Europe. Africans suffered horribly; today the extent of the human misery of the "middle passage" is probably unimaginable. It was not unusual for half the slaves to die en route due to disease, starvation, or suicide. The triangular trade, though outlawed by both

England and America in 1808 continued until the Civil War (Stampp 1965; Ebony 1971; Hraba 1979; Parrillo 1985; Kitano 1985; Feagin 1989).

Yet, before the horrifying "middle passage," the insurmountable, surreal nightmare for African Americans began on the continent of Africa, when the Portuguese spearheaded the way for the rest of Europe to follow in the slave trade (Stampp 1965; Ebony 1971; Hraba 1979; Parrillo 1985; Kitano 1985; Feagin 1989). At the close of the fifteenth century, other Europeans such as the Dutch, French, Swedes, Danes, Prussians, and of course, the English had joined the Portuguese in the slave trade. Soon the English became the forerunners in the slave trade and perfected it into a lucrative business. In fact, Liverpool, England, became the hot spot of the English slave trade. There were incredible profits being made from the sale of African humans, a real "Black Market," that even small businessmen pooled their funds to cash in on the profits. The profits could yield up to fifty percent on initial investments (Ebony 1971).

To initiate the slave trade, the Europeans set up a system of slave bases on the West African coast to establish the site for capturing slaves. Many Africans themselves, some at war with each other at the time, participated in this scheme by assisting the Europeans with the captures of other Africans in exchange for commodities such as mirrors, whiskey, and guns. The Europeans became good at playing African tribes against each other and even assisted one of the warring tribes by supplying ammunition to them (Stampp 1965; Ebony 1971; Hraba 1979; Parrillo 1985; Kitano 1985; Feagin 1989).

Unfortunately, there were different ways of obtaining and capturing slaves. One way was to purchase Africans who were prisoners of African tribal wars. Another way was to organize raiding parties and kidnap the slaves. Many Europeans also used trickery, bribes, and blatant violence against the Africans in order to capture them for enslavement. In the end, the Africans themselves would help the European slavers in capturing and chaining the captives (men, women, and children) together in coffles, then herding them like cattle to the coast, often naked and without shoes

(Stampp 1965; Ebony 1971; Hraba 1979; Parrillo 1985; Kitano 1985; Feagin 1989).

Most of the slaves were captured near the western coastline of Africa between the Senegal River and Angola. During the terrible march from where they were captured to the coastline of the waiting slave ships, many slaves died along the way. There were skeletons found on the path they took (Stampp 1965; Ebony 1971). Once the herded coffles of slaves reached the coastline, they were then prepared to be shipped to the Americas in the many receiving forts and factories. There they were inspected for diseases and defects and sorted based on these inspections. The slaves who were sold at the forts and factories were first branded like animals on their chests and then rowed to the slave ship to make the five- to eight-week voyage to the Americas in the horrifying "middle passage" of the triangular trade (Stampp 1965; Ebony 1971; Hraba 1979; Parrillo 1985; Kitano 1985; Feagin 1989).

Scholars estimated that between thirty and fifty percent of the slaves did not survive the long, miserable "middle passage" across the Atlantic Ocean (Stampp 1965; Ebony 1971; Hraba 1979; Parrillo 1985; Kitano 1985; Feagin 1989). The slaves were literally stacked in the bottom of the ship decks like sardines in a can. Chained to each other and bolted to the floor, many suffocated and died from the foul air on the ship. Frequently, there was little space, less than 2 feet between the floor and the ceiling where they were stacked. Most of the slaves died from diseases and unsanitary conditions, some committed suicide either by crashing their heads against a wall or ship deck floors and by cutting their wrists. Some even jumped overboard into the dark, shark-infested waters whenever they could. Many times slaves could lie beside a dead body for weeks during the voyage. Some mothers even killed their own babies and children to spare them further suffering during the dreadful "middle passage" to America (Ebony 1971).

Since no one actually knows, and is unlikely to find out the exact number of African slaves who were taken from Africa and brought to the Americas, many have estimated that during the peak of the triangular trade, which started in the 1600s and lasted until the 1800s,

economics & racism = 2 factors for the success of black slavery.

between fifty and one hundred thousand slaves left Africa each year (Stampp 1965; Ebony 1971; Hraba 1979; Parrillo 1985; Kitano 1985; Feagin 1989). It was estimated that North America received about one million African slaves. However, these estimates are of only those slaves who actually survived the "middle passage" and do not include those who died en route to the Americas, which was about thirty percent of those captured in Africa. These estimates also do not include those who died in the coffles during the forced march to the coastline to board the slave ships. Therefore, the triangular trade's "middle passage" is estimated to have robbed Africa of about one-fourth of its population (Ebony 1971).

Moreover, since Africa supplied other entire continents with cheap human labor, Africans actually aided Europeans in developing the Western Hemisphere and helped them to gain control in that part of the world. Thus, it seems that Africa stimulated the beginning of the Industrial Revolution, helped to strengthen the European economy, and began the development of capitalism, yet Africa was given little to no credit for these contributions (Ebony 1971).

Other ills of the triangular trade included a disrupted social structure that left Africa's tribes fighting against each other and not truly realizing the significance of what would later happen to the African diaspora in the racist new world of America (Ebony 1971). From the beginning of slavery, and right up to the present, racist Europeans and Americans alike have been successful at pitting Africans against Africans as well as African Americans against African Americans. Further, slavery brought into view the audacity of white racism, which is based on power and allowed the white race to dominate the black race by imposing slavery upon the Blacks against their will. Racism also encouraged the stereotypic view that the dominant white race was mentally, morally, and culturally superior to the subordinate black race. This racist mentality allowed Whites to justify their systematic exploitation and abuse of Blacks during and even beyond slavery in America (Ebony 1971; Hraba 1979; Parrillo 1985; Kitano 1985; Feagin 1989).

Hence, the Africans who survived the "middle passage" and made it to racist America, found themselves terri-

fied and confused as they stood on the auction blocks to once again be inspected and sold to plantation owners, as if they were property and/or cattle. African men, women, and children of all statuses, including royalty and other high ranking individuals while in Africa, were sold like cattle during slavery in cities like Charleston, South Carolina. There was no consideration for families let alone keeping them together, as Whites intentionally tried to separate members of the same tribes (Stampp 1965; Ebony 1971; Hraba 1979; Parrillo 1985; Kitano 1985; Feagin 1989; Sirimarco 2007).

Institutionalized slavery was primarily concentrated in the South. Its justification grew out of ethnocentric, stereotypic, and racist ideologies. Whites considered Africans as subhuman and justified slavery on that ground. Thus, slaves were treated as property and not as humans. Slave masters intentionally tried to rid Africans of their culture, thereby stripping them of their true identities. They broke up African families, forbad them to speak their own language, forced them to abandon their own religion and to adopt Christianity, and would not allow them to become educated. For the most part, the only skills Africans learned were those associated with being slaves. Virginia and Maryland were the first to solidify the slave caste system of Blacks, when in the 1660s they enacted laws which made Blacks servants for life (Stampp 1965; Ebony 1971; Hraba 1979; Parrillo 1985; Kitano 1985; Feagin 1989).

As chattel (property), a master could do with his slaves as he pleased. He could sell, rent, or mortgage them, as well as barter them, give them away, or deed them. Slaves could even be used as collateral in business transactions, or bought and sold like stocks and bonds on the fluctuating slave market, if the master so desired. Slaves were also used in raffles and lotteries as the winning prizes, and promised as gifts even before they were born (Ebony 1971).

However, perhaps one of the most dehumanizing and degrading parts of slavery was the breeding of slaves (Ebony 1971), in hopes of creating the "ideal" mammy or brute which made for a better slave. Another dehumanizing aspect was the treatment of slave families. Since slaves could not legally get married, a slave family had no legal status and could be broken up at any time by the sale of family members at the will of the slave owner. This often occurred, particularly if the slave owner died. Upon his death, slaves who were considered a part of his estate were divided among his heirs (Stampp 1965; Ebony 1971).

Although widely believed by most Americans, the average white man in the south did not own a wealthy slave plantation. In fact, most white men did not even own slaves. Only about one-quarter of white southerners owned slaves and about one-third of them owned fewer than five slaves (Ebony 1971). Not every white southerner could afford to buy and own slaves. However, many Whites accumulated more slaves by mating with African slaves and then enslaving their own offspring. From this point Blacks could be slaves or free, depending on the status of the mother (Stampp 1965; Ebony 1971).

In regard to mulattos, the child's race and status were usually determined by the mother's race and status. Therefore, if a black slave mother gave birth to a child fathered by a white man, then the child was a black slave. However, if the mother was a white woman and the father a black slave, then the child was considered a "free-born" but not a white child or a white slave. Nonetheless, unless Blacks could produce upon demand "freedom papers," they were generally considered to be a slave, regardless if they were free or not (Stampp 1965; Ebony 1971).

Slaves were further stratified on the plantations in three major categories: the foremen, house servants, and field hands. Foremen served as the "black" slave overseers, assisting the white slave overseers in making sure the field hands did their work and kept up the work pace. They sometimes used a whip when needed. Foremen were responsible for slave work assignments, giving out food to slaves, and blowing the horn in the mornings before work and in the evenings after work. Foremen were usually treated better than the other slaves and did not do the actual field work. They also received more food and clothing and could move about the plantation with ease (Stampp 1965; Ebony 1971).

House servants shared the same type of status as the foremen, and sometimes higher status depending on the plantation. They tended to be the lighter-skinned slaves who were likely the offspring of a white parent and a slave parent. They served as mammies (nursemaids), cooks, butlers, coachmen, and other domestics. Many of the house servants became like family members in the big house and were laden with heavy family secrets and burdens of their masters and mistresses, as well as other family members. They usually lived in the big house in servant quarters or in cabins next to the big house. Some of the house servants, especially the lighter complexioned ones, thought they were much better than the field hands and looked down upon the slaves who worked the fields (Ebony 1971).

Another category of slaves were those with needed skills such as carpenters and blacksmiths. They were more closely stratified with the field hands, the next major category at the bottom of the strata. Field hands and other slaves lived in small, dismal, often windowless, leaky cabins that had just the basics such as a stove and which seemed little more than a "dog" house. Often slaves slept on the cold, sometimes muddy dirt floors. These cabins were near the big house and were referred to as slave quarters or "the quarters" (Stampp 1965; Ebony 1971).

Legally, slave owners had to provide food and clothes for the slaves or they could be fined and the slaves would be sold. However, this rarely occurred since slaves had no legal rights. Slaves received poor nutritional food rations once a week such as salt pork, a few pounds of bacon and some corn. Since these small rations were hardly enough to live on for a week, slaves often raided the master's corn fields and chicken coops to get enough food to eat. They also caught rabbits, raccoons, opossums, and other small game to help supplement their small rations. Depending on the plantation, slaves received clothing and shoes at least once a year and sometimes twice. Every two or three years they received blankets (Stampp 1965; Ebony 1971).

Slaves were not allowed to become educated. They were not allowed to read or write, including reading the Bible. This was due to the fear of Whites that the slaves might get exposed to ideas that could lead to a revolution, if they realized how badly they were treated, or if they had the opportunity to communicate among themselves. This fear also extended to some of the slaves, who sometimes betrayed other slaves and told

*① Exam
* mulattos, child's race & status were usually determined by their mother's race & status.

the masters of slaves' plans to escape or start a revolt (Stampp 1965; Ebony 1971).

Slaves lived a hard life of labor and worked from sunup to sundown every day. They often prayed and sang while they worked and their songs reflected a life of great sorrow, extreme pain, and lifelong suffering. However, their religious faith helped them to survive from day to day while living a never ending nightmare. Further, during cultivating and harvesting of crops season, slaves worked up to 16 hours per day. Many did not have a rest period and got very little sleep before going right back to the fields the next day. Many slaves ate their food and put their clothes on in the field for fear of being late to work. If they were late, they would be whipped, sometimes by the black overseers. Some slave women even gave birth or miscarried their babies right in the fields. Sadly, some slaves literally worked themselves to death in those fields (Stampp 1965; Ebony 1971).

To make slavery even harder for the black slaves were the "Black Codes," which were a legal set of codes intended to "keep slaves in their place," and to make sure that they remained powerless property in America. Although slaves did not have "any" rights, not even as human beings in America, they could still be held liable for violating these codes. Violations of the codes or any other violation by Whites or slaves meant more severe punishments for slaves than for Whites for the same violation. The basic premises of the codes were that Blacks remained submissive to their masters and showed respect for all Whites at all times, no matter the status of the Whites. Even very young white children had to be addressed as "sir" and "ma'am" (Stampp 1965; Ebony 1971).

Some examples of this submission and respect under the "Black Codes" were that slaves could not point at Whites, use bad language, hit back when hit by a white person, beat drums, have guns or liquor, administer drugs to Whites, nor be a part of a group of more than five unattended slaves at any time. Slaves had to move out of a white person's way and were not allowed to roam about without a pass, which they had to have with them at all times and had to show it upon demands from Whites. Even worse, in some cases if slaves

did not stop when ordered by white men, the white men were obligated to legally shoot them. Slaves could not own property or testify against Whites, and could only be witnesses if the case involved other slaves. Some slaves could not even be on the streets after dark. Free Blacks were also subjected to some of these "Black Codes" (Stampp 1971; Ebony 1971).

To state that slaveholders were very inhumane to their slaves would be an understatement, particularly based on the punishments that were given to the slaves for any type of offense or violation of the "Black Codes." Flogging or a severe whipping in public was the most common punishment given to a slave for minor or major violations. The most common number of lashes given during a regular flogging tended to be 39 or less, but there were many cases that well exceeded that number. Sometimes floggings were given in doses and could last for several days, at which time more lashes could be given to the slave (Stampp 1965; Ebony 1971).

Slaves also endured other types of punishments such as imprisonment, branding, and mutilation. However, imprisonment was rarely used, as it meant the planter would be missing out on the slave labor on the plantations. Sometimes stubborn slaves could be branded or mutilated in places on their bodies that would not interfere with their work. Some examples of this included cutting off slaves' ears or burning their hands and faces. Although there were stiff penalties for Whites who murdered slaves, most were never convicted for doing so. Without a doubt though, the slaves' fate was the death penalty for any violent offense like murder, robbery, and of course rape or attempted rape of white women. This punishment was usually a public lynching but slaves were also publicly burned alive. However, all was not lost after a slave's death due to punishment. His master was given compensation from the state for destroying his property (slave). Nevertheless, most of the punishments of slaves were given by their masters, overseers, and foremen (Stampp 1965; Ebony 1971).

There were others involved with punishing slaves such as slave breakers, who were hired to break in new slaves by inflicting pain upon them before they even began their work. The slave catchers were also hired by slave masters to track down and capture runaway slaves with dogs that would maul the slaves when found. Other cruel acts were also inflicted upon slaves, such as making them wear heavy chains and unbearable, heavy irons around their necks, ankles, and other body parts. Slaves endured some of the worst and brutal whippings ever inflicted upon man or beast. These included being hogtied, stripped naked, and hung from ceilings or other places, and then severely beaten with a thick, rough cowhide whip until their bodies were bloody with flesh hanging and being near death (Stampp 1965; Ebony 1971; Andrews and Gates 1999).

Other unimaginable cruelty to slaves included a slave having to eat the worms he did not pick off of tobacco leaves in Maryland, and disobedient male slaves in Louisiana who had to dress in women's clothing for humiliation. Further, more cruel acts included beatings with cowhide whips where slaves were lashed over and over on their heads and faces until they were weak and bloody and their flesh was like jelly and literally torn from their bodies, and still the slave owner or overseer would not stop the beatings. Many were beaten near death or would soon die from the floggings. One incident included a pregnant slave woman being beaten so severely that she delivered a dead child. Later her body was swollen with water until one day the water literally burst out of her body and she died. The other slaves filled with sorrow for this unfortunate soul, thought that death was a good thing for the severely flogged woman (Stampp 1965; Andrews and Gates 1999; Sirimarco 2007).

Many times the floggings would cause the flesh and the skin to have open wounds that would be further doused with alcohol (rum) or salt to further torture the slave in agonizing pain. Men, women, and children were severely beaten. A small female slave child was tied to a tree for about a week and beaten severely each day until her flesh was like jelly. Abused slaves were expected to get up from a severe beating and go right back to work. There were no medical treatments for slaves. They had to come up with their own medical remedies or just suffer (Stampp 1965; Andrews and Gates 1999; Sirimarco, 2007).

Female slaves were also sexually abused and male slaves could do nothing to protect their mothers, wives, or daughters from this abuse. Slave women and girls were repeatedly raped by their masters and overseers and many produced mulatto children, which may explain the differences in African American skin tones even today. White women were powerless too, as many of the rapes took place right in the houses where they lived. Most of the white women knew exactly what was going on behind closed doors in their homes but could do nothing about it since they were also powerless. But since female slaves were considered property, masters could do as they pleased with them, where and when they so desired (Stampp 1965; Ebony 1971).

Perhaps the most cruelty though, resulted from the ripping apart of slave families right before their eyes. The heartless and ruthless masters did not care about preserving slave families. Mothers begged and cried mercilessly as their children were sold away from them, never to be seen again. Husbands also watched brokenheartedly as their wives were sold away from them. Many times this was done on the spur-of-the-moment and without any warning (Stampp 1965; Andrews and Gates 1999; Sirimarco 2007).

Given these cruelties endured by slaves it is not surprising that they would at least try by any means necessary to cope with or to escape this horrible condition. Many resorted to faking illnesses such as being paralyzed, deaf, blind, having diseases, and even insanity. Many even self-mutilated their bodies by cutting off their own limbs, and some committed suicide. Other coping mechanisms to release stress, frustration, and rage included burning down buildings and crops, or poisoning their masters and sometimes the whole family by using arsenic. Some slaves even used finely chopped glass in their masters' food and added ground up spiders to their milk. Some simply lost all sense of reality of inevitable death to them, and just beat, shot, or chopped up masters and other Whites with axes or set their houses on fire and watched them burn to death (Ebony 1971).

Slavery was so bad that many slaves just ran way on a whim with nowhere to go, just to be caught and then endured more torture. However, some came back willingly at the risk of starving to death. Luckily, some successfully escaped on their own and through the

Underground Railroad, which was a secret network of places set up by abolitionists, both black and white, to help slaves escape. Harriet Tubman, also known as the "Black Moses," was very instrumental in this network (Ebony 1971).

Fortunately, slavery was not approved by all Whites, but unfortunately, they were in the minority on the power structure scale. The Quakers were the first to speak against slavery as early as 1688 in Germantown, Pennsylvania. This sparked the antislavery movement, but it was mainly supported among the Quakers, although some white men wanted to establish Bible schools for Blacks. However, most Whites still feared that even learning how to read the Bible would be bad since Blacks might develop the desire to be free from slavery if they were educated (Ebony 1971).

However, as America moved closer to gaining its own freedom from England, some sensitivity did focus on the fate of slaves, when the Continental Congress unanimously voted against importing slaves into the American colonies in 1776, just a few months before the Declaration of Independence was signed. Former President Thomas Jefferson, the father of the Declaration of Independence, even spoke and wrote against slavery, yet he too was a slaveholder of a huge plantation (Stampp 1965; Ebony 1971). Many Whites knew and felt in their hearts that slavery was wrong, but still chose to remain quiet since many other Whites did not feel the way they did. Therefore this "groupthink" remained in place throughout and after the American Revolutionary War against England, in which America ultimately received its freedom, although only some of the country's citizens were freed. The others (Blacks) were not even considered "American citizens," and obviously did not need to be free. It would take another war on American soil before this was realized.

As time went on, it seemed that America's deep "dark" secret (slavery) was being exposed to the rest of the world, especially since the country won the war with England for "its" own freedom. Although this was successfully accomplished, it still did not dawn upon the American forefathers, who seemed to be hypocrites at the time that "freedom was still an issue" in America and that only "white Americans" were freed while "black Americans" were still slaves. Obviously, the shame on America had become too much to bear, so in 1808 both England and the United States outlawed the slave trade, but from the beginning there was little enforcement. As the unprotected West African coastline along with the persistent demand for slave labor, and the enormous profits for the slave masters all combined to keep the triangular trade intact until the bloodiest event in American history took place—the Civil War, which finally brought a temporary end to America's shame and freed the slaves as a result (Stampp 1965; Ebony 1971; Hraba 1979; Parrillo 1985; Kitano 1985; Feagin 1989). Sadly it would still take another hundred years before this freedom was actually realized due to the Black Civil Rights Movement of the 1950s and 1960s.

Library of Congress

SLAVE SHIP WITH BLACKS STACKED IN LIKE SARDINES

African Americans (Blacks) and Native Americans (Indians)

A COMMON DESTINY—A COMMON BOND

Some scholars believe that Blacks and Indians knew each other before the arrival of the Europeans (The Pilgrims or Columbus) to the Americas. Unfortunately, they became the two major victims of European racism. Nonetheless, early in American history "A Common Destiny and a Common Bond" developed between them and was strengthened during slavery. Like Blacks, some Indians were also captured and forced into slavery. Consequently, racial lines between Blacks and Indians were almost invisible. Further, Indians and Blacks lived and schemed together and helped one another escape from slavery. Virtually, to discourage Indians from assisting black slaves, Whites would add a clause in treaties with Indians which required Indians to help return slaves who had run away. Fortunately, only a few Indians complied with this clause. In fact, Indians usually spared Blacks when they attacked and killed Whites. Some Blacks even became influential and held high status positions within the Indian tribes, even the rank of Indian chief, as was the case with the Crows. This common destiny and common bond between Blacks and Indians began to make Whites fearful and uncomfortable, as more and more intense Indian uprisings that were encouraged by Blacks took place. One example was the Seminole Wars in Florida during the early 1800s in which Blacks extensively participated and held leadership roles. Although some Indian tribes also enslaved Blacks, it was nothing like slavery in the South by Whites. By the time of the Civil War, Indian tribes including the Seminoles, the Cherokees, and the Chickasaws each had roughly three thousand slaves. Indians commonly married their slaves and usually only required a portion of the slaves' crops. Many slaves and free Blacks married Indians and raised their children as Indians. Because of this intermarriage and great bond between Indians and Blacks, entire Indian tribes were absorbed into the Black race (Ebony 1971). Today, many Blacks also have a rich Indian heritage.

DISCUSSION QUESTIONS

1. Imagine the capturing of humans and herding them like cattle to a slave ship . . . what impact will this have upon an individual's psyche?

2. After enduring the slave trade where some Africans themselves sold other Africans into slavery, how do African Americans feel about Africans today?

3. What impact did slavery have on white Americans during the institutionalization of slavery? What about today?

4. How did white Americans justify slavery?

5. How could white Americans want and fight for their own freedom from England, but at the same time continued to enslave Blacks?

6. How did the stereotype, "Blacks are lazy," come about given their forced labor for Whites during slavery?

7. How can Blacks and Whites ever move beyond the inhumane institution of slavery and work toward a color–blind society?

8. Why is slavery such a sensitive topic of discussion between Blacks and Whites?

9. Why do Whites tend to avoid discussing slavery?

10. Should black Americans celebrate the 4th of July?

1. Imagine and then try to understand the institution of slavery from the time the Africans helped the Europeans capture, chain, and march other Africans to the coastline of West Africa to board the slave ships. Now describe your thoughts on this event.

2. Next, imagine being a part of the "middle passage." Close your eyes and think about that voyage, then try to understand what that was like for Africans coming to America. Now describe your thoughts on this event.

3. Finally, imagine and try to understand the impact of arriving in America, being sold like animals, treated like property, and not being considered as humans. Now describe your thoughts on this condition.

TEN THOUGHTS ACTIVITY

1. List 10 thoughts on what comes to mind when you think of slavery.

    _____

    _____

    _____

    _____

    _____

    _____

    _____

    _____

    _____

    _____

    _____

2. List 10 thoughts on what comes to mind when you think of "being white in America during slavery."

    _____

    _____

    _____

    _____

    _____

    _____

    _____

    _____

    _____

    _____

    _____

3. List 10 thoughts on what comes to mind when you think of the current state of African Americans today.

_____

_____

_____

_____

_____

_____

_____

_____

_____

_____

SUGGESTED RESOURCES

Africa and Slavery—African History on the Internet

www-sul.stanford.edu/depts/ssrg/africa/history/hislavery.html

Africans in America

www.pbs.org/wgbh/aia/home.html

The Atlantic Slave Trade and Slave Life in the Americas: A Visual Record

http://hitchcock.itc.virginia.edu/Slavery/

Born in Slavery: Slave Narratives from the Federal Writers' Project, 1936–1938

http://lcweb2.loc.gov/ammem/snhtml/snhome.html

The Gilder Lehrman Center for the Study of Slavery, Resistance, and Abolition

http://www.yale.edu/glc

Virginia Runaways

http://people.uvawise.edu/runaways

REFERENCES

Andrews, William L., and Henry Luis Gates, Jr., eds. 1999. *The Civitas Anthology of African American Slave Narratives.* Washington, DC: Civitas Counterpoint, Publisher.

Curran, Daniel J., and Claire M. Renzetti. 1987. **Social Problems: Society in Crisis.** Boston: Allyn and Bacon.

Ebony Pictorial History of Black America, Volume 1. 1971. Nashville, TN: The Southwestern Company.

Feagin, Joe R. 1989. *Racial and Ethnic Relations,* 3rd ed. Englewood Cliffs, NJ: Prentice Hall.

Hraba, Joseph. 1979. *American Ethnicity.* Itasca, IL: F. E. Peacock.

Kitano, Harry H. 1985. *Race Relations,* 3rd ed. Englewood Cliffs, NJ: Prentice Hall.

Parrillo, Vincent A. 1985. *Strangers to These Shores: Race and Ethnic Relations in the United States,* 2nd ed. New York: MacMillan.

Sirimarco, Elizabeth. 2007. *American Voices from the Time of Slavery.* New York: Marshall Cavendish Benchmark, Publisher.

Stampp, Kenneth. 1965. *The Peculiar Institution.* New York: Alfred A. Knopf, Publisher.

CHAPTER 3

From Civil War to Civil Rights

The legacy of slavery in America is interwoven throughout African American experiences in the United States. Still, the profound impact of the devastation of slavery can be seen in many aspects of black life and culture. Although some have argued that the period right after slavery and the Civil War was worse for Blacks than slavery itself (Hraba 1979), others believe that nothing in this world could compare to the institution of slavery in America (Franklin 1965). Therefore, this chapter briefly describes the significance of the Civil War, and the period in American society known as Reconstruction, or the post slavery era. It concludes with a discussion of the great migration when thousands of Blacks left the South in search of better opportunities and to escape the Jim Crow oppression.

The Civil War, also known as the War Between the States was a blessing in disguise for African Americans in the United States. Although it is considered the bloodiest and saddest war ever fought in America, which literally pitted the country against itself, and brother against brother, it was a saving grace for African Americans. By the end of the war, all slaves were freed and America would never be the same again. Instead, it would later become the greatest country in the world, yet it still had a problem—the newly freed African Americans, the "Negro Problem."

After America won its freedom from England in 1776, it would be nearly a hundred years later before "freedom" became an American way of life for all of its citizens. As America began to shape its own destiny, it could no longer ignore the issue of slavery which was becoming more and more of an issue in society, especially since England had already ended its slavery. Amazingly, the slave trade and slavery were still in full force in America right up to the dawning of the Civil War, when the last slave ship delivered the last batch of slaves at Mobile Bay, Alabama, in 1859 (Bennett 1969).

Still, abolitionists (Blacks, Whites, males, and females) such as Frederick Douglass, Sojourner Truth, Harriett Tubman, and John Brown in addition to the Quakers were rampant and constantly fighting against slavery. Slavery became so distasteful to mostly northerners and abolitionists that it was becoming a major issue on moral and ethical grounds. Many antislavery societies came into existence mostly in the North and other non slaveholding states. At the same time, slavery was so lucrative in the South that southerners could not see

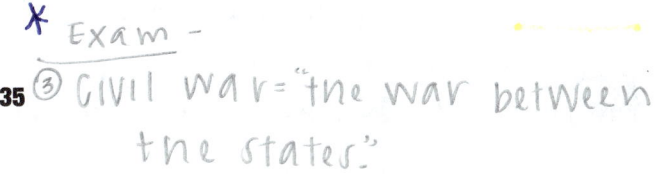

emselves without it and were willing to defend it at ll cost. Those southerners wanting to keep Blacks enslaved began to perpetuate violence on them and on those who supported freedom for slaves (Franklin 1965; Bennett 1969; *Ebony* 1971; Pinkney 2000). After all, it was the southern way of life.

Slavery became so intolerable that John Brown, a white abolitionist, met with and tried to recruit Frederick Douglass, a black abolitionist to plan and execute a raid on Harpers Ferry, Virginia. Douglass told Brown that the raid would likely be unsuccessful. Nonetheless, Brown, 13 Whites, and 5 Blacks attacked Harpers Ferry on October 16–17, 1859. It was a mistake as most of the Blacks in Harpers Ferry did not turn out to support him. Of the five that did, one of the Blacks escaped, two of them were captured, and two of them were hanged in Charlestown, Virginia, on December 16, 1859. John Brown was also hanged in Charlestown, Virginia, on December 2, 1859 (Bennett 1969).

As Americans reasoned with reality, slavery and all of the ill imposed atrocities associated with it, could no longer be ignored. A variety of proposals for dealing with slavery were discussed on a federal level but no alternative seemed suitable. The country became divided on the issue and was on a collision course with itself as the tensions and stubbornness on both sides (North and the South) had reached a point of no return. A bloody confrontation seemed inevitable and right around the corner (Franklin 1965; Bennett 1969; *Ebony* 1971; Pinkney 2000).

Politically, Abraham Lincoln during his platform had said that he was opposed to slavery and would put an end to it. Yet, he did not feel that Blacks were equal to Whites and therefore expressed segregationist's views as well. It was unclear as to how he really viewed slavery, but the South had made plans if he became president. On November 6, 1860, Abraham Lincoln was elected president of the "United States of America." On December 18, 1860, South Carolina seceded from the Union (Franklin 1965; Bennett 1969; *Ebony* 1971; Pinkney 2000).

Other southern states followed South Carolina's lead and together they decided to form the eleven confederate states, and began to impose self-rule including electing their own president, Jefferson Davis. The South, without a doubt, was the wealthiest region of the country due to the slaves providing free labor which yielded huge profits with a low overhead. Cotton was still king and still a major commodity needed all over America. Therefore, they believed that they could survive without the assistance of the North, which obviously needed the southern economy to stimulate the northern industrial growth (Franklin 1965; Bennett 1969; *Ebony* 1971; Pinkney 2000).

When Abraham Lincoln, a Republican, assumed the presidency in 1861, the nation was literally on the brink of falling apart as a Union. The Civil War was imminent if the United States of America was to remain. President Lincoln had no other choice but to commence a war between the states and on April 12, 1861, the South fired the first shot at Fort Sumter, South Carolina (Franklin 1965; Bennett 1969; *Ebony* 1971; Pinkney 2000). From this point on, America would never be the same, and by the end of the war, Blacks could finally call themselves African "Americans" instead of "African slaves in America." Ironically, the South unknowingly began the battle to free the slaves when it fired the first shot of the Civil War. To be sure, many issues caused the Civil War, but without a doubt slavery was at the center of the effort in ending it. Throughout the entire war, slavery was a political and moral factor. Unfortunately, President Lincoln made it very clear that the war was to preserve the Union and not to free the slaves (Franklin 1965; Bennett 1969; *Ebony* 1971; Pinkney 2000).

As the Civil War continued, the president and the North expected the dispute to be a quick war, but the South had other plans to rule itself and to keep slavery institutionalized. They also had slave power and took some of the slaves to war with them, but still kept them off of the battlefields. The slaves fed, assisted, and energized the confederate soldiers and helped to keep the South in the battle, while at the same time, those who stayed at home kept the plantations running. This was apparent to northerners and they realized that in order to attain economic and political superiority over the South, they had to either stop slavery from spreading or abolish it all together. Although northerners did not agree with slavery and felt that it was morally wrong, they still felt that Blacks were inferior to Whites (Franklin 1965; Bennett 1969; *Ebony* 1971; Pinkney 2000).

President Lincoln, the great thinker, kept toying back and forth in his head with the "slavery issue." He was often confused on what to do; on the one hand he thought slavery was wrong but on the other hand, he did not think Blacks were equal to Whites. Thus, he seemed to be opposed to both institutionalized slavery and racial equality. Early in the war, by 1862, it was clear that the war was going to be a long, bloody, dreadful event and that the Union forces were going to need all the help they could muster (Franklin 1965; Bennett 1969; *Ebony* 1971; Pinkney 2000).

Blacks also felt that if the North won the war, that would eventually end slavery and give them better life chances, so Blacks were eager to fight in the war. Unfortunately, Blacks were rejected and told it was a white man's war. Nonetheless, Blacks were not about to let the South or the North decide their fate in the aftermath of the war, so they took matters into their own hands by preparing themselves for battle. Whenever the Union forces were close enough, slaves ran away and joined the Union forces whenever the opportunity presented itself. Initially, the Union forces returned them to their masters, but later decided to keep them as "contraband" when caught and captured by Union soldiers. Eventually the North allowed Blacks to participate in the war, but the South was still afraid that Blacks would have turned on them for keeping them enslaved and did not allow them to fight, a decision that would come back to haunt them in the later years of the war (Franklin 1965; Bennett 1969; *Ebony* 1971; Pinkney 2000).

As the war dreadfully continued, with no finish line in sight, the conditions of the Civil War were gradually leading to the emancipation of slaves. Abolitionists such as Frederick Douglass, who was the black leading figure of the Civil War period, continued to personally recruit other Blacks to fight in the Union forces. He and others continuously pressured President Lincoln, both politically and militarily, to issue the Emancipation Proclamation. The president, the great thinker, knew that it would greatly surprise and weaken the South's military strength by freeing all at once, turning loose about four million slaves. Strategically, at the same time, it would strengthen the Union forces, which would gain additional manpower, as Blacks would surely rush to the battlefields and fight under the Union banner, rather than just cook on the Union stoves (Franklin 1965; Bennett 1969; *Ebony* 1971; Pinkney 2000).

As President Lincoln's great thoughts began to materialize, he would later move away from just being the "Great Thinker," and would later become the "Great Emancipator." He had been constantly thinking about how to handle the delicate slave issue which had become center stage at this point in the war. From the beginning of the war, he made strides in the direction of freeing slaves. On August 6, 1861, the first Confiscation Act allowed all slaves who were captured by Union forces to be kept as prizes by the Union forces, if their masters used them in rebelling against the Union. In the spring of 1862, Congress passed anti-slavery legislation that prohibited slavery in the United States territories; abolished slavery in Washington, DC; forbade Union soldiers to return runaway slaves to their masters; and provided for the eventual end of the slave trade (Franklin 1965; Bennett 1969; *Ebony* 1971; Pinkney 2000).

On July 17, 1862, the second Confiscation Act made all slaves of rebel masters "forever free." On September 22, 1862, President Lincoln issued a preliminary Emancipation Proclamation which declared free, as of January 1, 1863, all slaves in most areas of the rebellious states. The Emancipation Proclamation was a pivotal and grand decision in the Civil War. It changed the tone and the direction of the war and the North received the added "Black" power and strength it needed to further crush and defeat the South (Franklin 1965; Bennett 1969; *Ebony* 1971; Pinkney 2000).

At the same time the South was faced with its toughest decision yet, when it had to choose between either keeping slavery or losing the war. Reluctantly, with their backs against the wall, Confederate General Robert E. Lee finally agreed to use black soldiers. However, this decision was too late, as it was nearly the end of the war, and too late for the South to win the war. On April 9, 1865, General Robert E. Lee surrendered to Union General Ulysses S. Grant and the North won the war. In the end, the South lost both the war and its most prized possessions—the slaves, as all slaves were set free at the end of the war. Nonetheless, it has been reported that without the Blacks, the North may not have won as quickly as they did and may not have won at all. Without a doubt, Blacks were crucial to the overall Union war success and contributed tremendously and bravely to securing their own freedom (Franklin 1965; Bennett 1969; *Ebony* 1971; Pinkney 2000) in the "land of the free and home of the brave."

However, the biggest stride toward freeing the slaves was the 13th Amendment to the United States Constitution, which was passed by Congress on December 18, 1865, after the war had ended and President Lincoln was assassinated. This great Amendment both legalized and fortified the Emancipation Proclamation of the slaves. In addition, it prohibited slavery in all parts of the United States of America, including the South (Franklin 1965; Bennett 1969; *Ebony* 1971; Pinkney 2000). President Lincoln went from being the "Great Thinker" to the "Great Emancipator" posthumously.

THE POST CIVIL WAR PERIOD (RECONSTRUCTION): 1865–1877

After the Civil War, the U.S. Constitution was amended. Several amendments supposedly gave rights to Blacks. The 13th Amendment abolished slavery, the 14th made Blacks citizens and gave equal protection under the law, and the 15th gave Blacks the right to vote (Franklin 1965; Bennett 1969; *Ebony* 1971; Pinkney 2000). Yet, the reality of freedom was so overwhelming, unexpected, and incredible that unfortunately many Blacks did not even know or did not believe they had been freed, and therefore, some remained in slave-like positions. Many Whites obviously did not tell them, or lied to them because they knew that many Blacks were illiterate and would not know any better. Sadly, some Blacks were afraid and did not want to be free. However, for those who knew and

wanted to be free, most immediately walked off of the plantations and wandered directionless into the bliss of freedom. Many had no place to go but into the thin air, yet they did just that, while others quickly tried to flee north to find family members and other loved ones. Unfortunately, many had to return to the ex-masters for mere survival. The major handicap though, was that most were illiterate and could not read or comprehend written materials, since they were forbidden to become educated during slavery (Franklin 1965; Bennett 1969; *Ebony* 1971; Pinkney 2000). Whites knew this and certainly took advantage of their precarious situation and condition.

Nonetheless, since the Civil War was mainly fought in the South, this region was nearly destroyed. At the end of the war, the South was badly beaten and the war-torn area was in major disarray, it was unorganized, burned, and Whites were left picking up the pieces. The South was defeated in its attempt to secede from the Union and form the Confederate states, thus forced to remain in the country. Their economy as they knew it was no more, they had lost the war and their labor force, the slaves. Blacks were freed! Southerners now had to adjust to not having free labor and they were not accustomed to that. Their whole economy was ruined as masters and overseers now had to do their own work and labor in their own fields, as Blacks simply left the fields as soon as they were freed and convinced of this freedom (Franklin 1965; Bennett 1969; *Ebony* 1971; Pinkney 2000).

White southerners were shocked as they witnessed helplessly the "inferior" Blacks experiencing life as only Whites once did. Plus, northerners were still controlling the South which was divided into military districts and run by military commanders. As well, Blacks were protected by and became wards of the government, as stipulated by Congress (Franklin 1965; Bennett 1969; *Ebony* 1971; Pinkney 2000). White southerners could not deal with this reality and as they began to rebuild the South, resentment, meanness, and pure hatred developed within them against Blacks. They could not wait to put these "inferior" Blacks "back in their place."

At the same time, white southerners also developed a pure hatred for the northern whites who had just defeated them, crushed their southern pride, and encouraged the "inferior" Blacks to assume they were more than chattel (property). This hatred often took the form of violence against Blacks. Whites began to riot, beat, and murder Blacks every chance they got, which seemed to be daily, and President Andrew Johnson, a racist, who had succeeded President Abraham Lincoln, was indifferent to Blacks, and condoned this violence against them. Southerners even began to literally re-enslave Blacks by passing and trying to reinstate the black codes against them. Like in slavery, these codes were intended to take the advantage of Blacks while they were in a precarious, weak position (Franklin 1965; Bennett 1969; *Ebony* 1971; Pinkney 2000).

Nonetheless, the period immediately after slavery was a very interesting one for Blacks in America, particularly in the South. This is the period when Blacks "almost" got on an equal footing with Whites. It was both a glorious time and a difficult time for Blacks as positives and negatives compelled each other. For the first time in American history, though, Blacks were finally treated as humans and accorded citizenship. They experienced brief power in the political arena, and since President Lincoln was a Republican and the Republican Party was the party that had emancipated them, Blacks remained loyal to the Republicans (Franklin 1965; Bennett 1969; *Ebony* 1971; Pinkney 2000).

Further, Blacks enjoyed the same public accommodations as Whites, the Freedman's Bureau was set up to help them, northern troops remained in the South to protect them, and since most of them were illiterate, they all flocked to schools and were assisted by northerners who came down to help educate them. It appeared that Reconstruction was going great and Blacks were succeeding as citizens in America (Franklin 1965; Bennett 1969; *Ebony* 1971; Pinkney 2000). However, being bitter and ever resentful, this was too much for southern Whites to take. So as northerners and newly freed Blacks continued to bask in the sunny days of the South, southern Whites visualized, planned, and plotted on how to "take the South back and how to get Blacks back in their place." Unfortunately, one major political mistake, the Compromise of 1877, allowed white southerners to realize their vision and to regain full control of the South, which nearly threw Blacks

right back into slavery (Franklin 1965; Bennett 1969; *Ebony* 1971; Pinkney 2000).

The Compromise of 1877 came about as the result of the disputed election of Republican President Rutherford B. Hayes in 1876 by Congress. This was the worst political stance that came about during Reconstruction that would literally nearly overturn everything that had been accomplished for Blacks within the very short period after the Civil War. In fact, during the compromise, the Republican Party abandoned Blacks and threw them "under the bus," to their former masters in the South. However, the Republican leaders thought that the Compromise of 1877 was the only way to avoid another civil war. Nevertheless, this compromise gave White southerners the muster they needed to "get Blacks back in their place." Hence the onset of white supremacy was back (Franklin 1965; Bennett 1969; *Ebony* 1971; Pinkney 2000).

The reality of the Compromise of 1877 removed the remaining troops from the South, giving the South absolute home rule and other negotiated favors. Perhaps the most dreadful favors promised the South was political autonomy, and that there would be no intervention in southern matters pertaining to race and policy. In exchange for these favors, the southern leaders promised that the constitutional rights of Blacks would be adhered to and that Blacks would be protected. Federal politicians were well aware of southerners' intentions of how they wanted to restructure the South, but still appeared to be more interested in politics than in the rights of Blacks. Thus, within a short span of time, almost all of the accomplishments for Blacks during Reconstruction had been overturned and southern Whites were determined to disfranchise them. For Blacks, all of their hopes and dreams went up in smoke as the South quickly went back to the status quo and headed back toward slavery. White supremacy was back (Franklin 1965; Bennett 1969; *Ebony* 1971; Pinkney 2000).

Further, white Southerners were thought to constitute a distinct regional group that emphasized "whiteness" above all else. For southerners, the important fact was whether they were white or black; everything else was secondary (Feagin 1989). Being white was the primary indicator of self-worth and status; their race, it was thought, entitled them to powers and rights beyond those of other racial groups. Therefore, during Reconstruction (approximately from 1865–1877), southern Whites were especially bitter, because not only did they lose the war, but also lost their slaves, thus, their economy and self-pride were devastated. Slaves had become one of the prized possessions by which white southerners were stratified along class lines (Feagin 1989). Many white southerners truly believed that the South would rise again.

Hence, throughout Reconstruction, southern Whites quickly restored a dismantled, war-torn, slave plantation society, and intentionally structured the "New South" to keep Blacks "in their place." Keeping Blacks in their place referred to sub-par education, blocked economic and political opportunities, and public humiliation. To make matters worse, the Ku Klux Klan further exploited, terrorized, and murdered Blacks (Franklin 1965; Bennett 1969; *Ebony* 1971; Curran and Renzetti 1987; Hraba 1979; Kitano 1985; Parrillo 1985; Feagin 1989; Pinkney 2000).

At the same time, Blacks were still experiencing some freedom as American citizens. Nevertheless, Blacks quickly realized that any rights that had been given them were only on paper and nothing more (Curran and Renzetti 1987). And, after a very brief period of political participation, Blacks in the South were faced with policies and practices designed to preserve white supremacy. These included poll taxes, literacy tests in order to vote, white primary elections which excluded Blacks, and grandfather clauses which only allowed voting to those and their descendants who had been eligible voters before the Civil War (Franklin 1965; Bennett 1969; *Ebony* 1971; Curran and Renzetti 1987; Hraba 1979; Kitano 1985; Parrillo 1985; Feagin 1989; Pinkney, 2000).

Additionally, a new form of slavery, "the Jim Crow laws" was instituted in the South. This apartheid caste system insured the segregation of Whites and Blacks in all aspects of life (i.e., education, occupations, public accommodations and transportation, restaurants, recreational facilities, and cemeteries). To legalize this system, the United States Supreme Court in 1896 ruled in the case of *Plessy v. Ferguson,* that the principle of "sep-

arate but equal" was not unconstitutional. One important point though, which they obviously forgot, was that facilities for Blacks were never equal to those for Whites (Franklin 1965; Bennett 1969; *Ebony* 1971; Curran and Renzetti 1987; Hraba 1979; Kitano 1985; Parrillo 1985; Feagin 1989; Pinkney 2000).

As Reconstruction dreadfully wore on, Whites continued to disfranchise, coerce, and exploit the already oppressed Blacks. Though barely out of institutionalized slavery, the majority of Blacks were impoverished. This poverty would haunt them for many years to come. Plus, land reform plans (i.e., 40 acres and a mule) were never carried out, and most former field laborers became sharecroppers (Franklin 1965; Bennett 1969; *Ebony* 1971; Curran and Renzetti 1987; Hraba 1979; Kitano 1985; Parrillo 1985; Feagin 1989; Pinkney 2000), which was merely advanced slavery.

Also during Reconstruction, the concept of sharecropping was popularized. Sharecropping, for the most part, was a subtle system of forced dependency. Sharecroppers farmed tracts of land owned by Whites. The plantation owners also supplied seeds, tools, animals, and shacks (homes), in return for sharecroppers' labor. Supposedly, sharecroppers would receive half the profits from the sale of crops. Since Whites controlled the books, most Blacks did not stand a chance of profiting from sharecropping. When sharecroppers were too old to work, plantation owners no longer cared or took responsibility for them (Franklin 1965; Bennett 1969; *Ebony* 1971; Curran and Renzetti 1987; Hraba 1979; Kitano 1985; Parrillo 1985; Feagin 1989; Pinkney 2000).

Thus, it would appear that Blacks were not much better off during Reconstruction than they were during slavery. The Ku Klux Klan regularly terrorized and tortured Blacks. Thus, violence continued to be widespread against Blacks and, by the turn of the century, there were 214 reported cases of lynching of Blacks, mostly in the South. Never before was it clearer that the South was determined to maintain white supremacy over Blacks at any cost (Bennett 1969).

As the South regained and maintained its paternalistic and racist structure from 1877 until about 1954, and the rest of society began to embrace it as the "American Way," virtually every aspect of society negatively impacted African Americans. The status of Blacks was relegated into a caste system, and although society experienced many changes and the country went to other wars, including two world wars, some Blacks experienced better life chances in the North. Nonetheless, nowhere in the country could any black be expected to be treated as Whites regardless of their social status or achievement. As a result, black leaders like Booker T. Washington encouraged Blacks to accept their subordinate positions while others like William Edward Burghardt Du Bois encouraged them to continue to fight for equality (Franklin 1965; Bennett 1969; *Ebony* 1971; Pinkney 2000).

Changes in society also meant that northerners had lost interest in the welfare of black people and many began to form their own opinion of Blacks as inferiors. Meanwhile, disfranchisement of Blacks advanced very quickly and by the 1900s all black people in the South were disfranchised. Every political and social institution in the South catered to white southerners. This, without a doubt, was the doctrine of white supremacy. For some Blacks, the only way out of this oppression was to leave the South (Franklin 1965).

Moreover, ever since the Civil War, Blacks began leaving the South as fast as they could, often not realizing or knowing where they would end up. Blacks in rural areas moved to cities, Blacks in the South moved to the North, and many Blacks even moved to countries in Africa. In the 1870s, some went to the Southwest and others went on to the West. For instance, Oklahoma was a place in the Southwest where Blacks wanted to establish a nationalist, separate state and in 1891, the all-black town of Langston, Oklahoma, was established (*Ebony* 1971). Further, the Midwest, despite its cold climate became very attractive to Blacks. For example, about 50,000 Blacks left the South and settled in Kansas. As well, some went on to Iowa, where a black utopia, Buxton, existed (Gray 1984). Moreover, in 1895, about 197 Blacks boarded a ship in Savannah, Georgia, and went to the African country of Liberia. Unfortunately, this was not a good time for Blacks to go to Liberia because of the economic difficulties the country was having, and many of the natives were depressed. The new arrivals were met with many hardships upon arrival there (*Ebony* 1971).

By the early 1900s, approximately 90% of all Blacks still resided in the South. About 75% were living in rural areas under extreme oppressive and impoverished conditions. However, between 1916 and 1918, it is estimated that between a half million to 2 million Blacks left the South in what is commonly called the "Great Migration." Most of them migrated from Mississippi, Alabama, Georgia, and the Carolinas, and settled mostly in Michigan, New York, Pennsylvania, Ohio, and Illinois (Franklin 1965; Bennett 1969; *Ebony* 1971; Turner, Singleton, and Musick 1984; Hraba 1979; Kitano 1985; Parrillo 1985; Feagin 1989; Pinkney 2000).

These migrations escalated in response to better economic opportunities in the North and legally enforced racial discrimination in the South. In the North, Blacks were allowed to participate in nonagricultural economic positions. In the Deep South, in 1950, Blacks constituted about 43% of the population, but only 21% held nonagricultural positions. Those who did were mostly in custodial services, requiring little or no marketable skills (Turner et al. 1984; Karnig and McClain 1985).

Unfortunately, some Blacks who migrated to the North were not much better off than those who remained in the South. Some employers simply would not hire Blacks, and those who did find jobs were given the most menial tasks—those jobs not wanted by Whites. Further, Blacks were used as strikebreakers when white workers walked off their jobs. This proved to be a horrible predicament for Blacks, as this common practice by northern employers often added more fuel to the fires and stirred up more racial antagonism, lynchings, and race riots, usually with Blacks being the victims (Franklin 1965; Bennett 1969; *Ebony* 1971; Pinkney 2000).

Nonetheless, black history is filled with back to Africa movements. Some were even supported by President Lincoln in trying to deal with the "Negro Problem." However, Marcus Garvey's back to Africa movement was one of the most popular, mainly because it was apparent that white America was not willing to accept black America, and Garvey advocated for Black Nationalism. Garvey, a Jamaican Black, formed the Universal Negro Improvement Association (UNIA) in 1916. By the 1920s, his following was estimated to range between 2 and 6 million. However, some middle-class Blacks, who did not want Blacks to leave the United States fought against his movement and it collapsed in 1925. Still Garvey's movement was successful in uniting a large number of Blacks in self-pride. His work even paved the way for other forms of nationalist groups such as the present Black Muslim Organization in America today (Franklin 1965; Bennett 1969; *Ebony* 1971; Pinkney 2000).

Unfortunately, The Great Depression of the 1930s put a halt to the great migration of Blacks from the South. Yet, for every black who left the South, about ten thousand more stayed there and endured Jim Crow and blatant racism (*Ebony* 1971). Still, no matter how painful life continued to be for African Americans, they continued to keep their eyes on the prize. Hence, the one thing they did do right was the day they really started to fight, all the way to The Civil Rights Movement, which was followed by The Black Power Movement.

BUXTON, IOWA: A BLACK UTOPIA IN THE MIDWEST

In the early 1900s, life chances for black Americans were restricted. They experienced economic dependency, deprivation, and systematic legal barriers to their participation in the larger American society. In contrast, Blacks in Buxton, Iowa, had equal access to the town's opportunities, and there was no enforced segregation. Blacks had access to all public accommodations in Buxton. They were not segregated in the movies, restaurants, or in stores. There was no Jim Crow law and no race-etiquette. Although groups such as the Ku Klux Klan existed right outside of Buxton, no violence or intimidation took place within Buxton. Blacks in Buxton could also vote, and often exercised this right in elections. Blacks were experiencing the same life chances as Whites in Buxton. Although most of the black workers were miners, they were well paid and experienced middle-class lifestyles. There were also black professional and business people, such as attorneys, physicians, pharmacists, school teachers, and businessmen. Hobert A. Armstrong, a black businessman, was the wealthiest man in Buxton. Ben Buxton, The Consolidated Coal Company's manager in Buxton, in alliance with Armstrong also made certain that black employees experienced life chances equal to that of Whites. It was a mutual beneficial relationship involving the company, Armstrong, and black residents. The Company hired Armstrong to recruit Blacks from the South to break a strike and Blacks worked the mines. With their wages, black miners and their families consumed goods from the Company Store and from Armstrong's meat market. Moreover, the Company provided Blacks with good housing and Blacks paid them rent. Therefore, the more Blacks recruited the more goods they consumed, and the more money the Company and Armstrong made. Blacks in Buxton, in turn, had the protection of the Company in a controlled environment. Because of the local alliance between Hobe Armstrong and Ben Buxton, a white man, no caste system developed in Buxton and even black miners experienced a middle-class lifestyle. In addition, a black professional and business class developed, serving Blacks and Whites. Around 1914, however, a change in the power structure of Buxton took place. Buxton got a new superintendent and the Buxton/Armstrong alliance deteriorated. Also, the mines were being worked out, and Whites were displacing Blacks in the mines. At first, black professionals increased while the numbers of white professionals declined, but ultimately Buxton was abandoned. By 1920, Buxton had become almost a ghost town. After leaving Buxton, former black residents were to experience the racial caste system in the larger society, including the racial exclusion that was developing in northern cities (Gray 1984; Schwieder, Schwieder, and Hraba 1987).

Hence, the next chapter focuses on one of the most significant events in the history of Blacks as they struggled for basic human rights in America. Blacks' long, hard road to humanity in America would once again resemble the Civil War as they continued to fight mainly in the South, for their civil rights. However, after several long, war-like years of collective behavior among Blacks "to end slavery for once and for all," America was finally deserving of its slogan, "the land of the free and the home of the brave."

African American Facts

William Edward Burghardt Du Bois (W. E. B. Du Bois, 1868–1963) was the first sociologist to systematically study racism and the black community in America. His two most popular books are *The Philadelphia Negro* (1896) and *The Souls of Black Folk* (1903). He was a founder of the National Association for the Advancement of Colored People (NAACP) in 1909, which is the oldest civil rights organization in America (Shepard, Persaud, and Hughes 2009).

Annie J. Cooper (1858–1964), a sociologist, published a book titled, *A Voice from the South: By a Black Woman from the South*. She was a feminist and prominent educator who wrote against racism and oppression of Blacks. In 1925, she was the fourth black woman to earn a doctoral degree (Shepard, Persaud, and Hughes 2009).

Ida B. Wells (1862–1931), a journalist and social activist, wrote extensively about the lynching of Blacks in America. In 1892, she published her work on lynching in a pamphlet titled "Southern Horrors: Lynch Law in All Its Phases." She also assisted W. E. B. Du Bois, Mary Church Terrell, and others in the founding of the NAACP, and with the launching of *The Crisis* newspaper (Shepard, Persaud, and Hughes 2009).

Mary Church Terrell (1863–1954) wrote her autobiography titled *A Colored Woman in a White World*, which focused on the difficulties of females growing up black in white America. She was a co-founder of the NAACP and the President of the National Association of Colored Women in 1896 (Shepard, Persaud, and Hughes 2009).

Juneteenth is an African American holiday celebrated on June 19th in at least 36 states. It is a celebration of the Emancipation Proclamation by President Lincoln, which freed the slaves during the Civil War. Unfortunately, slaves in Texas did not know about it until after the war ended in 1865. Therefore, once they were told, they rejoiced and celebrated on June 19, 1865. On January 1, 1980, Texas declared Juneteenth a state holiday (http://afroamhistory.about.com/od/africanamericanculture/a/Juneteenth.htm).

DISCUSSION QUESTIONS

1. What was the mentality of Whites in the South during Reconstruction?

2. What, according to President Abraham Lincoln, was the real reason for the Civil War? What other significant event occurred as a result of the Civil War?

3. What was the Emancipation Proclamation? Should African Americans celebrate this instead of the 4th of July?

4. How did the end of Reconstruction affect African Americans in the South?

5. What was the "Great Migration" and how did it impact Blacks in the North and in the South?

6. Why is the Confederate flag offensive to most Blacks but not to southern Whites?

7. What was the social, economic, and political impact of Reconstruction?

8. Why were white southerners so angry after the Civil War?

9. Explain the Compromise of 1877 and how it was a devastating blow to the progress of African Americans.

10. Describe the violence that occurred to Blacks during Reconstruction. Why do you think Blacks were targets?

11. Describe the Jim Crow laws in the South.

1. If President Johnson had not been a racist and had supported Blacks during Reconstruction, what may have been the outcome for Blacks today?

2. Research, compare, and contrast the ideas of Booker T. Washington and W. E. B. Du Bois in terms of their leadership and ideas for black Americans.

3. Imagine being a slave and then finally set free during a bloody civil war; what do you think that would have felt like?

TEN THOUGHTS ACTIVITY

1. List 10 thoughts on what comes to mind when you think of the Civil War.

_____

_____

_____

_____

_____

_____

_____

_____

_____

_____

2. List 10 thoughts on what comes to mind when you think of Reconstruction in the South.

_____

_____

_____

_____

_____

_____

_____

_____

_____

_____

3. List 10 thoughts on what comes to mind when you think of the "Great Migration."

_____

_____

_____

_____

_____

_____

_____

_____

_____

_____

SUGGESTED RESOURCES

Abbott, Martin. 1967. *The Freedmen's Bureau in South Carolina 1865–1872*. Chapel Hill: University of North Carolina Press.

Boyd, Candy Dawson, Rita Geiger, James B. Kracht, Valerie Ooka Pang. 2006. *Growth of a Nation*. Glenview: Scott Foresman.

Civil War & Reconstruction

http://afroamhistory.about.com/od/civilwar/The_Civil_War_Reconstruction_Period.htm

Foner, Eric. 1988. *Reconstruction, America's Unfinished Revolution 1863–1877*. New York: Harper & Row Publishers.

Hansen, Joyce. 2000. *Bury Me Not in a Land of Slaves: African-Americans in the Time of Reconstruction*. New York: Grolier Publishing.

The Reconstruction Era

http://afroamhistory.about.com/od/reconstruction/The_Reconstruction_Era.htm

Sterling, Dorothy. 1976. *The Trouble They Seen: Black People Tell the Story of Reconstruction*. New York: Doubleday & Company, Inc.

"American History in Black and White" by David Barton - Reader ...

http://afroamhistory.about.com/u/reviews/africanamericanculture/Best-African-American-History/American-History-in-Black-and-White-by-David-Barton.htm

African-American History - By Category

http://afroamhistory.about.com/od/

African-American History

http://afroamhistory.about.com/

http://afroamhistory.about.com/b/2010/08/04/wordless-wednesday-7.htm

REFERENCES

Bennett, Lerone, Jr. 1969. *Before the Mayflower: A History of Black America*. Chicago: Johnson Publishing Company, Inc.

Curran, Daniel J., and Claire M. Renzetti. 1987. *Social Problems: Society in Crisis*. Boston: Allyn and Bacon.

Ebony Pictorial History of Black America, Volume 1. 1971. Nashville, TN: The Southwestern Company.

Feagin, Joe R. 1989. *Racial and Ethnic Relations*, 3rd ed. Englewood Cliffs, NJ: Prentice Hall.

Franklin, John Hope. 1965. *From Slavery to Freedom*, 2nd ed. New York: Alfred A. Knopf.

Gray, Phyllis. 1984. *Buxton, Iowa: A Black Utopia in the Midwest.* Unpublished Masters Thesis. Iowa State University, Ames, Iowa.

Hraba, Joseph. 1979. *American Ethnicity.* Itasca, IL: F. E. Peacook.

http://afroamhistory.about.com/od/africanamericanculture/a/Juneteenth.htm.

Karnig, Albert K., and Paula D. McClain. 1985. "The New South and Black Economic Development: Changes from 1970 to 1980." Western Political Quarterly 38:538–550.

Kitano, Harry H. 1985. *Race Relations,* 3rd ed. Englewood Cliffs, NJ: Prentice Hall.

Parrillo, Vincent A. 1985. *Strangers to These Shores: Race and Ethnic Relations in the United States,* 2nd ed. New York: MacMillan.

Pinkney, Alphonso. 2000. *Black Americans,* 5th ed., New Jersey: Prentice Hall Publisher.

Schwieder, Dorothy, Elmer Schwieder, and Joseph Hraba. 1987. *Buxton: Work and Racial Equality in a Coal Mining Community.* Ames: Iowa State University Press.

Shepard, Jon M., Narayan Persaud, and Brenda Hughes. 2009. *Sociology,* 10th ed. Thomson/Wadsworth, Publisher.

Turner, Jonathan H., Joyce Singleton, Jr., and David Musick. 1984. *Oppression.* Chicago: Nelson-Hall.

CHAPTER 4

Social Movements: Civil Rights and Black Power

Collective behavior leading to social movements can be powerful tools for social change, especially if headed by visionary leaders. This chapter examines two major social movements which challenged the racist fabric of the United States of America: The Civil Rights Movement and The Black Power Movement. These movements pushed America to a collision with humanity and reality. Together they further served as a turning point in black history and culture in America, which as a result, became the most significant event for African Americans since the Civil War. As well, this chapter examines the impact of racial conflicts upon economic development in the South, especially during the civil rights era. In fact, it was mostly during this time period that the South got further behind, as its racial problems intensified and stunted its economic growth.

From the early 1900s and right up to the beginning of the Civil Rights Movement, Blacks continuously struggled for their basic human rights that were given to them on paper, at the end of the country's Civil War in 1865, when slavery was abolished. Yet, when "physical" slavery was officially over, "mental" slavery took its place, as Blacks were constantly fighting the bondage of racism, and still treated as second class citizens. Although Blacks learned to survive, and kept their eyes on the prize, they had to endure another "civil war," in the

form of two back-to-back social movements, just to get what was already given to them with the ending of the American Civil War—basic human rights.

Although during the early 1900s some Blacks achieved against the odds of racism, most did so within their own segregated, "colored only" communities. However, most were still left out of mainstream society and still treated as if they were "strangers to the American shores." Whites continued to resist Blacks' assimilation in most parts of the country, and were determined to keep them in their place. No matter how hard Blacks tried to advance in the United States of America, racism was always the elephant in the room. Thus, both Blacks and Whites suffered from "mental" slavery; Whites were still bitter with prejudicial stereotypes of Blacks, and Blacks were still bitter about the inferior treatment from Whites based on those stereotypes.

Although many Blacks left the South during the Great Migration, many remained. For those who were trapped there, left directionless and unprotected, life continued to worsen (Hraba 1979). Nonetheless, by the 1950s many Blacks had about as much of the apartheid racial caste system as could be tolerated. In response, The Civil Rights Movement began when Blacks literally took to the streets and openly protested white racism, domination, and exploitation during the 1950s

53

and 1960s (Morris 1984). At the same time, the South was desperately trying to develop economically (Wright 1986).

THE CIVIL RIGHTS MOVEMENT

Blacks have always fought for their civil rights since the beginning of their arrival in the United States of America. Yet, until they took collective action in the form of two major social movements, social change did not come quick enough and still may not have come, even at this point in history. However, some social change did come for Blacks, but not before the long, hard struggle for human rights took place, beginning in the 1950s and 1960s with the onset of The Civil Rights Movement. This movement advanced under the leadership of the honorable Rev. Dr. Martin Luther King, Jr., a fearless, charismatic, visionary leader who literally put his life on the line seeking social justice for black Americans, and indeed all Americans.

Dr. King led The Civil Rights Movement in non-violent protests which consisted of marches and demonstrations in which the black church was the center of the effort (Morris 1984). He made many awesome and inspirational speeches during the movement including his most acclaimed "I Have a Dream" speech where he talked about social and economic conditions of Blacks, and shared his dream of freedom and acceptance for Blacks in America one day. As well, his final speech, "I've Been to the Mountaintop" was delivered the night before he was assassinated. In it, he talked about how he may not get to the "promised land" with the masses of Blacks, but that he felt one day Blacks would be accepted in America as human beings (King 1987).

The main focus of The Civil Rights Movement challenged the Jim Crow Laws and etiquette in social and public accommodations such as transportation, hotels, parks, bathrooms, and restaurants. It also challenged human social and political rights such as voting, school integration, housing, and employment. In fact, The Civil Rights Movement laid the foundation for The Black Power Movement to go further and demand that these rights be granted to Blacks on more than just paper, but through recognition and acceptance of black culture and contributions to America. Moreover, The Black Power Movement further sought to free Blacks from total dependence on Whites for its mere existence (Pinkney 2000).

In the early part of The Civil Rights Movement, the National Association for the Advancement of Colored People (NAACP) dominated the movement and was joined by the Southern Christian Leadership Conference, which was founded by Dr. King and others, and headed by him during this time. Both groups had white members and together they worked for desegregation and the elimination of racial discrimination in America. Without a doubt, countless numbers of white Americans sought and fought for civil rights for black Americans, and many gave their lives in the pursuit of social justice in America (Morris 1984).

As The Civil Rights Movement began to pick up momentum, economic development was also picking up momentum all over the country. But by the time the South realized the importance of attracting industry, its racial conflicts were omnipresent. Obviously, within the South's industrial recruitment plan, it appeared that improving race relations was never a part of their strategy (Wright 1986). Conversely, The Civil Rights Movement sought to challenge racism. Hence, as these two events occurred together, many of the economic development strategies of the South were compromised by its racial conflicts which negatively impacted its social and economic development.

Nevertheless, the first major event of The Civil Rights Movement occurred in Baton Rouge, Louisiana. In 1953, Blacks successfully pulled off the first major bus boycott against the segregated system. Two years later, in 1955, the arrest of Rosa Parks, who refused to give up her bus seat to a white man in Montgomery, Alabama, sparked the real beginning of The Civil Rights Movement. The Montgomery Bus Boycott, organized by E. D. Nixon, head of the local chapter of the NAACP, but carried out through non-violent protests under Martin Luther King, Jr., lasted for more than a year (Morris 1984; *Life* 1988).

Earlier in 1955, about 4 months before Mrs. Parks, refusal to give up her bus seat, the brutal murder of a 14-year-old black American, Emmett Till, in Money,

Mississippi, located in the Delta region, received national and worldwide attention, when two white men admitted to murdering him were acquitted of all charges by an all-white jury, in what appeared to be a mock trial. Till was accused of "wolf-whistling" at a white woman, which allegedly violated her honor. He was kidnapped from his uncle's house by Roy Bryant and J. W. Milam, who then murdered him (*Ebony* 1986).

Emmett Till's body was found by Floyd Hodges in the Tallahatchie River, 25 miles north of Greenwood, Mississippi. His corpse was floating upside down among driftwood with his feet protruding from the water. Till's face was badly mutilated. He was shot above the right ear, and the rest of his face was either cut up or beaten. The murderers wired a cotton gin fan to his neck, to keep the body submerged in the river (*Ebony* 1986).

This unfortunate incident in the Mississippi Delta is one that Blacks and Whites will never forget, as justice was truly never served. It was a clear indication that Blacks had no protection under the law, and that their mere existence as a human race meant nothing to some Whites in the Delta, or in other parts of Mississippi and the South. For Whites, Till's murder was probably an embarrassment at the most. What normally would have been a quiet lynching in the Delta had received worldwide attention (*Ebony* 1986). For Blacks, it was an eye-opener for what would come within the next decade, as they struggled for civil rights as human beings in the apartheid, "American-style" South.

The death of young Emmett Till did nothing to improve Mississippi's external image. It brought negative attention to the Delta. The conditions surrounding the Till case were perceived as high risk factors by industries that were considering to build or to relocate in the state. However, Mississippi was not the only southern state to experience the negative impact of racial conflicts on economic development. As civil rights tensions mounted, industry began to shy away from the South (Cobb 1982).

In 1955, after the second *Brown v. Board of Education* decision, which dealt with school desegregation, industrialists seriously considered not relocating in the South. For example, a large manufacturing electrical equipment facility refused to build in Georgia after personnel were concerned about moving to the South with all the racial tensions about school desegregation. Another business machines firm decided to relocate in New York instead of Kentucky because of racial concerns (Cobb 1982). In May 1956, the Fantus Factory Locating Service reported that "at least twenty major factory moving projects were being seriously reconsidered in light of the situation in the South" (Cobb 1982, 123).

Little Rock, Arkansas, the state's capital, had a pretty good reputation in terms of race relations, and appeared to be a favorable site for industrial growth. Between 1950 and 1957, Little Rock had attracted about five new plants a year. In fact, in the early part of 1957, before the violence erupted over school desegregation, eight new plants were opened (Cobb 1982; *The Wall Street Journal* 1961). Later that year Winthrop Rockefeller, chairman of Arkansas' Industrial Development Commission, warned "That if a state or a community developed an 'unhealthy reputation' in regard to race relations, industry would be scared away" (Cobb 1982, 123).

Rockefeller's warning was not taken seriously, and in that same year, nine black students had to be escorted by National Guardsmen as they integrated Central High School. Angry mobs of Whites resisted and attacked the students, but they were finally admitted. From that point on, Little Rock's image was damaged and its economic future came to a blistering halt (Cobb 1982; *The Wall Street Journal* 1961). Everett Tucker, director of Little Rock's Industrial Development Commission, when describing the impact of racial violence on economic development stated that, "In the early four years since the start of the school troubles there has not been a single major industrial expansion," in Little Rock (*The Wall Street Journal* 1961, 21).

At the onset of the 1960s, race relations had not improved but seemed to have worsened, and industrialization was nearly at a standstill in most of the South. Cities in Georgia like Atlanta and Augusta had managed to keep racial tensions at a minimum, and prospered. Consequently, Atlanta was, and still is considered the city too busy to hate (Cobb 1982; Bullard 1989).

Georgia, "to busy to hate" "Hotlanta"

Unlike Georgia, cities in Alabama experienced much racial tensions, as The Civil Rights Movement gained momentum. In May 1961, the Freedom Riders, which consisted of Blacks and Whites and headed by James Farmer, who was the director of the Congress of Racial Equality (CORE), left Washington, DC, in two buses attempting to challenge the Jim Crow system of segregation on their way to New Orleans (Bullard 1989; *Life* 1988; Cobb 1982; *The Wall Street Journal* 1961). When they arrived in Anniston, Alabama, they were attacked. One of the buses was firebombed, and people were brutally beaten. This prompted Robert Kennedy, head of the United States Justice Department, to provide protection for the riders. In the meanwhile, a third bus left for Montgomery, Alabama. It encountered some violence, but was protected by the National Guard until it reached Jackson, Mississippi, where many of the Freedom Riders were thrown in the state penitentiary at Parchman for breaking segregation laws (Bullard 1989; *Life* 1988; Cobb 1982; *The Wall Street Journal* 1961).

During the Freedom Riders incident, Birmingham was negotiating a major steel products plant. The attention and violence associated with Alabama and the Freedom Riders caused the company to quickly withdraw from the negotiations. The company relocated in Tennessee (Cobb 1982).

Alabama, like other southern states, had its share of racial violence during the industrialization of the South. In 1962, Blacks, including men, women, and children were jailed, chased, and attacked by dogs, water hosed, beaten, and even killed as they nonviolently struggled for their civil rights. In Birmingham, a black church was bombed and four little girls were killed because of white resentment over the court-ordered desegregation of the University of Alabama. As a result, Birmingham lost out to New England on a big Ohio company that considered locating a pilot plant there. Businessmen were astonished by companies' refusal to locate in Alabama because of the racial unrest. It is likely that Blacks were used as scapegoats to account for the loss of economic development in Alabama (*The Wall Street Journal* 1961).

Selma, Alabama, would forever be remembered for its "Bloody Sunday" image when on March 7, 1965, civil rights marchers were severely injured and at least one killed, as they began to march from Selma to Montgomery. They were confronted and brutally beaten back by a massive police blockade as they marched across the Edmund Pettus Bridge. This incident began the Selma Voting Rights Movement that was organized by James Bevel. About a week later on March 15, President Lyndon B. Johnson used the phrase, "We shall overcome," while addressing Congress on the voting rights bill (Bennett 1969; Hraba 1979; Morris 1984). The phrase later became associated with The Civil Rights Movement as its signature song.

In 1962, the state of Mississippi apparently stood ready to go to war with the United States Federal Government over the admission of a black American, James Meredith, to the University of Mississippi (Ole Miss). Ross Barnett, Governor of Mississippi at that time, urged Whites to "stand up like men and tell them never" (*Life* 1988, 18). The violence which resulted at Ole Miss, "reinforced popular images of Mississippi as the most savage and backward of the southern states and seemed certain to undermine the state's efforts to attract industry" (Cobb 1982, 134).

By 1964, in the heat of the civil rights struggle, Mississippi was still burning when the bodies of three black and white civil rights workers, Michael Schwerner, Andrew Goodman, and James Chaney (black) were found buried in Philadelphia. Consequently, Mississippi experienced a loss of at least twelve firms that decided to go elsewhere. An executive for a Cleveland, Ohio, firm expressed to a Mississippi developer that, "We won't consider expanding in Mississippi again until the state and its people join the Union again" (Cobb 1982, 135). Likewise, to avoid having a Mississippi address, a small factory moved across the state line into Louisiana (Cobb 1982).

With regard to economic development, the entire southern region suffered from racial conflicts and violence during The Civil Rights Movement. Several states lost out on prospective industries because of their strong resistance to social change. As a result, the South, particularly the rural areas, continued to lag behind the rest of the nation, both socially, especially in terms of race relations, and economically (Cobb 1982).

Exam:

Charlotte = Queen City

THE BLACK POWER MOVEMENT

The Black Power Movement grew out of, overlapped with, and extended beyond The Civil Rights Movement. In fact, it actually picked up the struggle where The Civil Rights Movement left off with it. The name of the movement was derived from a speech delivered by Stokely Carmichael in Greenwood, Mississippi, in 1965, where he exclaimed the slogan, "Black Power!" which at the time referred to solidarity among people within The Civil Rights Movement to help fight racism. To Carmichael, it meant Blacks coming together politically to speak on their collective needs. From that point on, it was used by other organizations in their quest for black power and later took on a whole different meaning (Carmichael and Hamilton 1967).

The term "Black Power" later became synonymous with militant nationalists who advocated self-reliance and self-dependence. Organizations such as the Student Nonviolent Coordinating Committee (SNCC) and the Black Panther Party for Self Defense (The Black Panther Party) also used the slogan in their quest for black justice. Both of these organizations did not believe in the white power structure and thought that Blacks needed to help and protect themselves against it (Bennett 1969; Jenkins and Tryman 2002).

The Black Power Movement was not as organized as The Civil Rights Movement because there were several factions involved from different areas of the country, and no real identifiable leadership took over like in the South with Martin Luther King. However, in the beginning, Malcolm X was often seen as the leader as he was just as outspoken as Martin Luther King, but with a different orientation to social justice for Blacks. They both had the same message but spoke a different language. Nonetheless, the results of The Black Power Movement were significant in advocating and attaining social change in the American Society for Blacks. Moreover, this movement took place at a time in United States history when lots of transformations and social changes were taking place, including the country being at war with Vietnam (Bennett 1969; Altman 1997).

The seemingly never-ending indifference and persistent inferior treatment (mental slavery) of Blacks by Whites were making Blacks, especially the younger ones, very bitter, defiant, and full of rage and frustrations. The spirit of the movement then culminated in the frustrations that many young Blacks were experiencing. To some of them, The Civil Rights Movement was taking too long to accomplish its goals of equality and integration for Blacks. They grew restlessly impatient with Dr. King's nonviolent tactics and his followers in the South, which continued to result in countless Blacks being beaten every day, including men, women and even children (Carmichael and Hamilton 1967).

At the same time, these younger Blacks witnessed Blacks in the North being subjected to severe poverty in the cities' ghettos with no hope of ever getting out of this despair. To them, all of this was happening in America as Whites went along their merry way, turning their heads away from the massive "Negro" problem that Whites created from years of slavery, racism, and just not caring. Thus, The Black Power Movement exploded with the determination that enough was enough and that it was really time to fight fire with fire, and by any means necessary (Carmichael and Hamilton 1967; Shabazz 1970). These emotions soon reached a boiling point and led to subsequent violence in the North and other parts of the country.

There were several militants and militant groups during The Black Power Movement, including but not limited to the Nation of Islam (NOI), also known as the Black Muslims, the Student Nonviolent Coordinating Committee (SNCC), and the Black Panther Party for Self Defense (BPP). In fact, Marcus Garvey's ideas were very instrumental in the formation of the Nation of Islam, which was founded in 1930 in Detroit, Michigan, and later spread to the East and other parts of the country. It sought black separatism and nationalism, which became extremely imminent during The Civil Rights Movement and The Black Power Movement. Under the leadership of Elijah Muhammad, the Nation of Islam worked to uplift the black race in the urban slums and ghettos and to foster black pride. It also operated its own businesses to promote economic independence. However, Muhammad viewed all Whites as enemies and blue-eyed devils, and thus rejected integration (Jenkins and Tryman 2002).

Yet, Malcolm X was perhaps the most popular, and perhaps the most misunderstood, but brilliant leader of the Nation of Islam and The Black Power Movement. Born Malcolm Little in Omaha, Nebraska, as a child, the Ku Klux Klan bombed his home due to his father's support for Marcus Garvey and his teachings of black equality and black nationalism. Later, he changed his name to Malcolm X when he joined the Nation of Islam while in prison. Upon release from prison, he became the Nation of Islam's most famous minister and controversial leader. Malcolm was best known for such sayings as the "ballot or the bullet" and encouraging Blacks to defend themselves "by any means necessary," even with violence if they had too, against white domination (Shabazz 1970; Jenkins and Tryman 2002).

While with the Nation of Islam, Malcolm used militant tactics rather than King's nonviolent strategies. In a short period of time, Malcolm became more popular within The Black Power Movement and at times even more popular than Elijah Muhammad. As a result, jealousy and resentment of him within the Nation of Islam, as well as his loss of respect for Elijah Muhammad due to Muhammad's sexual scandals, caused Malcolm to leave the Nation. Malcolm then travelled to Mecca and learned more about his religious faith. Upon his return to America, he changed his name to El-Hajj Malik El-Shabazz, changed his militant perspective, worked with nonviolent groups, and formed his own: the Organization of Afro American Unity. A year after he left the Nation of Islam, he was assassinated by three of its members on February 21, 1965 (Jenkins and Tryman 2002).

The Student Non-violent Coordinating Committee (SNCC) was founded in 1960, in Raleigh, North Carolina, mainly by Ella Baker as a civil rights organization. Its main purpose at that time was to coordinate the student sit-in movement and to develop and enhance local black leadership. SNCC members also participated in the Freedom Rides that were started by the Congress of Racial Equality (CORE).

With the Council of Federated Organizations (COFO), SNCC participated in the Mississippi Freedom Summer Project in 1964. During this summer, over 1000 mostly white college students volunteered to help get Blacks registered to vote in Mississippi. Unfortunately, SNCC's work in Mississippi caused them to endure severe beatings and jailing. Yet, this was a turning point in both The Civil Rights Movement and The Black Power Movement when three members (two whites and one black) were murdered in Philadelphia, Mississippi. The federal government was forced to intervene and to investigate the Ku Klux Klan. Still, as The Civil Rights Movement dragged on with its non-violent protests, and the realization that significant results were taking too long to come, some members of the SNCC were becoming frustrated and restless and many became more radical (Bennett 1969; Altman 1997).

As a result, the SNCC eventually became another faction of the militant groups which had grown tired of The Civil Rights Movement's tactics. Most notably among them was Stokely Carmichael who, as the SNCC leader, began to use Malcolm X's philosophy and incorporated black nationalism into his own strategies. Indeed, by the mid-1960s, Carmichael had convinced other members to put Whites out of the SNCC, making it an all-black organization. Although, without a doubt, many Whites had fought hard, long, tirelessly, and gave their lives during The Civil Rights and The Black Power Movements, many Blacks still did not trust them (Carmichael and Hamilton 1967).

About a year later, Carmichael and some other members of the SNCC left the organization and wrote a book titled *Black Power*, which promoted Malcolm X's philosophy. They went even further than Malcolm, though, and promoted separatism as well as advocated breaking the country into separate nations, one for Blacks and one for Whites. The term "Black Power" then became synonymous with militant nationalists who advocated self-reliance and self-dependence (Carmichael and Hamilton 1967; Altman 1997).

The third militant faction, and perhaps the most radical of the militant groups to advocate for black power, was the Black Panther Party for Self Defense. In 1966, in Oakland, California, two young men, Huey Newton and Bobby Seale, formed the Black Panther Party for Self Defense (Black Panther Party). The main purpose of the Black Panther Party was to hit the streets and monitor the activities of police officers and their treatment of Blacks, particularly the misconduct shown to Blacks. Panthers were not to use drugs and alcohol while on monitoring duty. They also had a 10-point political program which included demands for full employment, exemption from military service for Blacks, and an end to police brutality, as well as the release of all black men from prison, among others. As well, they also set up programs in black communities, mainly in the West and North, and provided a free breakfast program for inner city children and a free health clinic in Berkeley, California (Altman 1997).

Exam 2:

Further, The Black Panther Party was the center of the Black Power Movement. However, they were not interested in nationalism, instead they often used violence in protecting the black community. Unfortunately, the Black Panther Party had volatile relations with law enforcement officials and developed an antagonistic, hostile relationship with them. Often shoot-outs and gun wars between police and Panthers ensued across the country. Whereas black nationalists such as Malcolm X spoke about revolting against white racism and domination, the Panthers were actually ready to declare war on the white power structure. They armed themselves with guns and dressed in all black and went up and down the streets looking for racist acts against Blacks. Without a doubt this type of behavior threatened and frightened Whites; therefore, the federal government also saw them as a threat and began to crack down on them in the late 1960s, thereby effectively aiding in dissolving them by the early 1970s. Although the Black Panther Party had great programs to assist the black community, corruption within the organization, crime, and continuous battles with the police led to the demise of the party in the early 1970s (Jenkins and Tryman 2002).

Nevertheless, other Blacks not belonging to any of the militant groups had enough of the white racist treatment as could be tolerated, and they aggregated and

began to riot in the streets. This was esp___ in the West and the North. The overwh___ lack of jobs and education, and no real ___ came too much to bear. So inner city Bl___ with rage and frustrations throughout the country. For example, the Watts Riots of 1965 in Los Angeles, California, was perhaps one of the worst riots on record. For nearly a week, almost 50,000 outraged Blacks looted and burned Los Angeles, attacking anyone they felt like, including Whites and other minorities. More than 30 people lost their lives and about 20,000 national guardsmen were needed to restore order to the area. As well, toward the end of The Civil Rights Movement and during the peak of The Black Power Movement, the assassination of Dr. Martin Luther King, Jr. in 1968 continued to pour more fuel on the fire and Blacks rioted again, this time throughout the entire country. When the violence finally ended, more than 30,000 people had been arrested (Bennett 1969; Hraba 1979; Altman 1997).

BOTH MOVEMENTS

With the assassination of Dr. Martin Luther King, Jr., The Civil Rights Movement lost its greatest visionary leader and its momentum. Antagonisms between and among the main civil rights organizations such as the NAACP, SCLC, SNCC, and CORE grew deeper, as well as the constant violence of the Black Panther Party and others, all led to the collapse of the movement in 1968 and 1969. By the 1970s, these groups had all but virtually disappeared. Despite this misfortune, both The Civil Rights Movement and The Black Power Movement were successful in making their marks and gains for Blacks in America. Plus, the federal government appeared sympathetic to Blacks, and passed effective legislation such as the Civil Rights Acts of 1964 which was intended to dismantle Jim Crow Laws and the Voting Rights Act of 1965 (Hraba 1979; Altman 1997).

There were different opinions on the effectiveness of both movements. Some viewed The Civil Rights Movement as a better way to get Blacks fair treatment and justice through its non-violent demonstrations,

..ich then allowed the atrocities of white racism to be shown to the rest of the world. Others thought this movement was "uncivil" because it pushed women and children to the forefront of imminent danger, allowing their lives to be on the line against real hatred in the forms of police brutalities and the Ku Klux Klan. To some, it just did not make sense to march all the time and not fight back if attacked.

As well, The Black Power Movement was viewed by some as a way to help Blacks gain full equality with Whites, but others viewed it as a militant, violent, separatist movement. The younger crowd in this movement grew impatient with the non-violent protests and believed that real social change could only come from a real revolution and not just through integrating with Whites and marching in non-violent protests. Nonetheless, by the end of The Civil Rights Movement, the ideas of The Black Power Movement had dominated both causes, especially after the death of Dr. King (Bennett 1969). As a result, Blacks viewed The Black Power Movement as a way to get Blacks recognized and respected, pro-black, while Whites viewed it as an anti-white, violent, and destined to destroy black-white race relations that had been gained during The Civil Rights Movement (Hraba 1979; Pinkney 2000).

Although The Black Power Movement was never as formalized as The Civil Rights Movement, it was very successful in helping Blacks to develop a healthy psyche about themselves and their race. It gave Blacks self-hope and black pride and made them believe in themselves, which also set the springboard for the new slogan, "Yes we can!!!" which was made popular in 2008 with the election of the first black president of the United States of America, President Barack Obama. The Movement was also instrumental in shaping and changing a new identity for the race by having Blacks go from being "Negros" to being "Black." In the late twentieth century, even with the adoption of a new identity, "African American," many Blacks still prefer the "Black" identity.

Further, The Black Power Movement insisted that black culture be recognized in American society. During this movement Blacks took pride in their culture and history, and became aware of what it meant to be

PICTURES OF MALCOLM X AND MARTIN LUTHER KING, JR.

Library of Congress

Library of Congress

Image © 360b, 2012. Used under licence from Shutterstock, Inc.

Image © Mesut Dogan, 2012. Used under licence from Shutterstock, Inc.

Library of Congress

"black" and to be "black in America." This black pride and solidarity in the black community was manifested in the fact that for the first time, Blacks were taught and thought that "Black is Beautiful." They felt "Black and Proud" as was shown in the unique black hand-shakes and black salutes with the raised fist. Blacks also wore afros and other natural hairstyles, fashions included dashikis, and many symbols displayed the colors red, black, and green which symbolically meant red for the bloodshed, black for black people, and green for Africa's land.

Moreover, educational institutions at different levels began to incorporate black history and culture into their curricula, and some major universities have departments focusing on Africana Studies and African American History. They also began recruiting black faculty, staff, and students. The white media began to add black television shows, commercials, and movies, and advertised in black outlets (Hraba 1979) such as *Ebony* magazine.

Although The Black Power Movement failed to get a nationalist state for Blacks, and was unable to end racism in America, it did provide a new perspective for Blacks and Whites to further understand one another. It also provided a foundation for other groups to use in fighting for their rights, including feminist movements, environmentalist movements, gay and lesbian movements, and other social justice movements among other races. In the end, Blacks fought day and night, from sunup to sundown, men, women, and children until finally a solid foundation for protecting the rights of Blacks as citizens of the United States of America was laid (Hraba 1979).

Significant Facts Impacting African Americans (Bennett 1969)

- Dr. Carter G. Woodson first proposed Negro History Week in 1926.

- The Tallahassee, Florida, Bus Boycott began on May 28, 1956.

- In February 1960, the student sit-ins begin with four black students in Greensboro, North Carolina.

- Elijah Muhammad, head of the Nation of Islam, calls for an all black state, July 31, 1960.

- John F. Kennedy defeats Richard Nixon in the 1960 presidential election, November 8, 1960.

- President John F. Kennedy in his historic address to Congress on June 11, 1963, states that in regard to civil rights for Blacks, that they should be given the same equal treatment as Whites.

- On June 12, 1963, NAACP field worker Medgar Evers was assassinated at his front door in Jackson, Mississippi.

- On August 28, 1963, Dr. Martin Luther King, Jr. delivers his famous, "I Have a Dream," speech at the March on Washington.

- On November 22, 1963, President John F. Kennedy was assassinated in Dallas, Texas; President Lyndon B. Johnson continues his legislative agenda and pursues justice and fairness for Blacks.

- On June 6, 1968, President Kennedy's brother, Robert Kennedy, is assassinated after his win in the California presidential primary.

- On November 2, 1983, President Ronald Reagan signs a bill to create a federal holiday for Dr. Martin Luther King, Jr.; on January 20, 1986, the first celebration of the King holiday was celebrated in America (Altman 1997).

DISCUSSION QUESTIONS

1. What was the mentality of Whites in the South during both social movements?

2. What was the last straw that made Blacks finally begin to massively fight for social change in America? What other significant event occurred as a result of The Civil Rights Movement?

3. Compare and contrast both social movements.

4. How did the end of The Black Power Movement affect African Americans in America?

5. What was meant by the slogan, "Black Power"?

6   Describe the role and mentality of college students during both social movements. Are they different today?

7. What was the social, economic, and political impact of both social movements?

8. Should African American history and culture be a required course for all students in America's universities? Why?

9. What role did children play in the movements?

10. Why did the riots take place during the movements?

11. Describe current social and economic conditions of Blacks as a result of the movements.

ACTIVITIES/FIELD EXPERIENCES

1. If President Kennedy and President Johnson had not been sympathetic to and supportive of Blacks during The Civil Rights Movement, what may have been the outcome for Blacks today?

2. Research, compare, and contrast the ideas of Malcolm X and Martin Luther King, Jr. regarding their leadership and ideas for Black Americans.

3. Imagine having a choice of being a part of both social movements; which would you prefer and why?

4. Use the link below to access and read Dr. King's "I Have a Dream" speech, then write an analysis of the social and economic conditions of Blacks based on his words.

    Link to Dr. King's speech:
    http://teachingamericanhistory.org/library/index.asp?documentprint=40

TEN THOUGHTS ACTIVITY

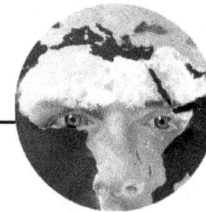

1. List 10 thoughts on what comes to mind when you think of The Civil Rights Movement.

_____

_____

_____

_____

_____

_____

_____

_____

_____

_____

2. List 10 thoughts on what comes to mind when you think of The Black Power Movement.

_____

_____

_____

_____

_____

_____

_____

_____

_____

_____

3. List 10 thoughts on what comes to mind when you think of African Americans today.

_____

_____

_____

_____

_____

_____

_____

_____

_____

_____

SUGGESTED RESOURCES

Baldwin, James. 1963. *The Fire Next Time.*

Carmichael, Stokely, and Charles V. Hamilton. 1967. *Black Power: The Politics of Liberation in America.*

Cleaver, Eldridge. 1968. *Soul on Ice.*

Cross, Theorore. 1984. *The Black Power Imperative.*

Gregory, Dick. 1964. *Nigger.*

Lester, Julius. 1968. *Look Out Whitey! Black Power's Gon' Get Your Mama!* New York: Grove Press, Inc.

Van Deburg, William, L. 1992. *New Day in Babylon: The Black Power Movement and American Culture.*

http://www.hoover.archives.gov/exhibits/africanamerican/blackpower/index.html

http://legal-dictionary.thefreedictionary.com/Black+Power+Movement

http://www.sparknotes.com/history/american/civilrights/section6.rhtml

Link to Dr. King's speech:

http://teachingamericanhistory.org/library/index.asp?documentprint=40

REFERENCES

Altman, Susan. 1997. *The Encyclopedia of African American Heritage.* New York: Facts on File, Inc.

Bennett, Lerone, Jr. 1969. *Before the Mayflower: A History of Black America.* Chicago: Johnson Publishing Company, Inc.

Bullard, Robert, ed. 1989. *In Search of the New South: The Black Urban Experience in the 1970s and 1980s.* Tuscaloosa, AL: University of Alabama Press.

Carmichael, Stokely, and Charles V. Hamilton. 1967. *Black Power.* New York: Vintage Books.

Cobb, James C. 1982. *The Selling of the South: The Southern Crusade for Industrial Development 1936–1980.* Baton Rouge: Louisiana State University Press.

Ebony magazine. 1986. "Land of the Till Murder Revisited." (March):53–58.

Hraba, Joseph. 1979. *American Ethnicity.* Itasca, IL: F. E. Peacook.

Jenkins, Robert, and Mfanya Tryman. 2002. *The Malcolm X Encyclopedia.* Westport, CT: Greenwood Press.

King, Coretta Scott. 1987. *The Words of Martin Luther King, Jr.* New York: New Market Press.

Life magazine. Special Edition. Spring, 1988. 11(5):8–66.

Morris, Aldon D. 1984. *The Origins of the Civil Rights Movement.* New York: The Free Press.

Pinkney, Alphonso. 2000. *Black Americans*, 5th ed., New Jersey: Prentice Hall Publisher.

Shabazz, Betty. 1970. *Malcolm X By Any Means Necessary.* New York: Pathfinder.

Wall Street Journal, The. 1961. Pg. 1, col. 6, and p. 21, col. 3.

Wright, Gavin. 1986. *Old South New South*. New York: Basic Books.

CHAPTER 5

Culture and Religion

This chapter and subsequent chapters will begin to examine the American society and its social structure, social institutions, and cultural aspects as they relate to African Americans' assimilation into a "different" America, which developed after the social movements discussed in the previous chapter. As a result of The Civil Rights and The Black Power Movements, the American culture embraced significant changes. Indeed, sociologists define culture as a society's way of life, which is all encompassing and includes traditions, ideas, and customs that provide guidelines for how people live in that society. Because human behavior is learned, and culture shapes this learned behavior, it too must be learned. In fact, culture is learned during the beginning stages of the socialization process (Shepard, Persaud, and Hughes 2009).

Within cultures are norms, which are rules or expectations of appropriate behavior that are shared among people within a society or its social institutions. Norms are often taken for granted, but they explain why individuals in a certain society act or behave in similar ways. Within the same society, different groups may express the norms differently, although they may relate to the same set of shared values. Values are notions of right and wrong that shape ideas in society. Values also help

shape beliefs within the culture of a society. Beliefs are ideas that focus on reality. While some beliefs may be supported by evidence, not all beliefs have to be true to have a strong impact on culture. Some individuals are strongly attached to some beliefs that appear to be unreasonable or illogical to others (Shepard et al. 2009).

It is natural in a multicultural society such as the United States to have many diverse subcultures. Within the American society, cultural diversity is widespread. Like societies, subcultures within them also have their own norms, values, and beliefs, and many groups prefer their unique subcultures to the mainstream culture of the society. Those who prefer their own subculture may also have different norms, values, beliefs, and practices that are relative to their own subculture. This means that different practices are not necessarily correct or incorrect but that they must be understood within the larger society. When individuals are aware of this relativity, then perhaps they could adjust to and accept cultural diversity with greater appreciation, though not having to engage in the subculture's activities. As a result, cultural barriers may be reduced in a multicultural society (Shepard et al. 2009), with or without social movements, as was the case of the African American subculture which developed during slavery, was sustained during social movements, and is still vibrant today in the black community.

Beyond The Civil Rights Movement and The Black Power Movement, the American culture began to change for African Americans during the 1970s and 1980s and, overall, has continued to change in a more inclusive manner. Social and cultural changes were made in the nation's public accommodations, schools, employment, and other social institutions including politics and the military. However, the church remained relatively unchanged and segregated, but more on a voluntary basis than on Jim Crow Laws or other legalities. Hence, religion seems to be the sacred untouchable, and apparently the church is the only social institution where separation of the races is acceptable by most (Blackwell 1991).

Therefore, this chapter examines the social institution of religion and its impact on African Americans. However, despite the fight for integration, equality, and inclusion, Blacks still developed a subculture within the dominant culture of the American society, with religion at the core of it. Thus, religion within the black subculture will be examined historically and culturally. Without a doubt, the black church is perhaps the most important social institution in the black community.

RELIGION

As the incredible countdown to end the biggest nightmare ever to face Blacks in America—slavery—got underway, many slaves and free Blacks were in churches counting down to the last hours, minutes, and seconds on December 31, 1862. This historic subcultural tradition by many African Americans would later be known as "Watch Night." For as the clock struck one minute past twelve midnight, and entered the dawn of the new year, it also brought in the greatest event in the lives of slaves, as they "watched" the clock end the last second of slavery and began the next second of freedom. The moment was filled with joy and jubilation as the newly freed slaves and free Blacks celebrated their newly found status in America. . . . They were finally "free at last!" In the midst of all the excitement was the church that stood at the forefront of this black libera-

tion and, to this day, it still stands as the center of the black community (*Ebony* 1971).

Today, in 2012, as in slavery, the pains of chains continue to influence race relations between Blacks and Whites in America, in nearly every social institution. Still, remnants of slavery are embedded in the cultural fabric of the United States of America. Many Blacks are still regarded as second class citizens and the prejudicial attitudes and discriminatory behaviors still exist, even in religion. Further, many scholars have claimed that the institution of slavery was so devastating and horrific that no cultural elements of Africa could have been retained, while others claimed that some African heritage and culture were sustained, especially with some religious practices (Blackwell 1991).

Scholars argued that the black subculture in society today is a product of racism, white domination, and rejection of Blacks rather than a reflection of Blacks' rich, African heritage. As well, there is probably no "pure" race in America today due to slave masters' illegitimate children. Plus, the fact that more slaves were born in the United States than in Africa would cast doubt that black Americans would have any real cultural ties to Africa. On the other hand, scholars argued that many new cultures developed as slaves fell back upon the older cultures of Africa, as they tried to adapt to the United States. Further, a strong religious faith was the one thing that did survive among African Americans, which helped them to survive the atrocity of slavery on a daily basis (Blackwell 1991).

Moreover, among the slaves were those who were high priests, priestesses, diviners, and root doctors back in Africa before coming to the United States. These slaves set the foundation for a folk religion that is still present today among Blacks. However, Whites regarded these practices (voodoo rites, medicine men) as primitive and "heathen," and thought they went against Christianity. As a result, white slave masters encouraged the slave church but forbade Blacks to practice Africa's religions, and instead forced Blacks to become Christians (Blackwell 1991).

However, the twisted view of Christianity to which the slaves were taught meant that they should always obey their masters. This obedience would then ensure them salvation and a place in God's Heaven. Slaves were taught to not question God's will by fighting slavery, because it was God's intentions that they be slaves. This brainwashing was obviously intended to keep Blacks believing that slavery was their destiny on earth in return for a place in God's Kingdom after death (Blackwell 1991; Pinkney 2000).

Nonetheless, religion was the one thing that slaves relied on to push for and pray for freedom. Fortunately, not all slaves were fooled by the lies of the white masters. Many held secret services and "hush harbors" at night in their cabins, in swamps, and deep into the woods. At night, prayer meetings and old Negro Spirituals provided some comfort for the struggle against slavery. Undoubtedly, religion helped to make slavery more tolerable. In fact, in addition to Whites encouraging the slave church, they also encouraged the slave preacher, as long as he preached that slavery was the right thing for Blacks (Blackwell 1991; Pinkney 2000).

During slavery, some slaves, usually the house servants, were allowed to worship with Whites, but were seated in the balconies, galleries, or in a separate area on the main church floor. During these services, Whites used the church as a vehicle to further instill within the slaves that slavery was a "Godly" condition and that they should accept their status, which would eventually get them into Heaven. Most of the sermons were delivered by white preachers. When Blacks were allowed to preach, they too had to instill within the slaves to accept their "godforsaken" status. Most black preachers accepted this fate and conformed to the wishes of the slave masters, especially when Whites were observing their services (Blackwell 1991; Pinkney 2000).

Since black preachers were often forbidden to read and write during slavery, reading and understanding the Bible was nearly impossible. Most had to rely on their memory from sermons they heard from the white preachers. However, many were able to fall back upon the art of storytelling they did while in Africa. As a result, a folk religion developed during slavery, which gives black religion its unique style today. Yet, when Whites were not around some black preachers delivered a different sermon to the slaves, which contra-

dicted the white masters' wishes (Blackwell 1991; Pinkney 2000).

Unfortunately, if black preachers were thought to preach about or caught preaching about freedom, they could be flogged or jailed, and never allowed to preach again. Being insecure, Whites believed within their fears that if Blacks knew the truth about their enslaved status that they would rebel. Therefore, slaves had to be convinced of their enslaved status and made to believe that it was God's will. Slaves were told that the slave masters were instruments of God on earth. To encourage this belief, many planters allowed black churches on their plantations, but monitored the activities. As well, black preachers were manipulated to assist in this social control and Whites encouraged them to do so. Nonetheless, Christianity was used as another means to control Blacks, and was highly condoned by Whites to make sure Blacks stayed in their place. In the end, Christianity was quickly accepted among Blacks (Blackwell 1991; Pinkney 2000).

However, following several slave revolts led by preachers such as Nat Turner, the slave masters began to keep a careful eye over the slaves' religious activities. After Nat Turner's revolt, black preachers were distrusted and Whites began to scrutinize their services. Most white slave masters stopped slaves from preaching and used white preachers who totally taught that slavery was justified in the Bible. From that point on, Blacks were not allowed to read the Bible for themselves, and were only allowed to sing and pray in their services. Their sorrows could be heard in their spirituals which still showed their displeasure with white Christianity's obvious approval of slavery, as well as their plans to somehow get freedom (Blackwell 1991; Pinkney 2000).

Free black preachers had a better chance at preaching in the North and some preached to black and white congregations. However, as tensions began to mount as a result of interracial church attendance, and racist treatment of Blacks was evident, the black church as a separate entity emerged in the late 1770s. As a result, Methodist, Protestant Episcopal, and Baptist churches were all in existence by the early 1800s. It is important to note that free Blacks in the northern churches assisted slaves in the southern churches by helping escaped slaves on the Underground Railroad. Many northern churches served as abolitionists' centers to assist in the movement to abolish slavery (Blackwell 1991; Pinkney 2000).

Despite the oppression and racism in the south, black southern churches still revitalized many African traditions and developed a desire to be free on earth as well as be granted a place in Heaven when their work was done on earth. This desire led to not only slave revolts but also to separating Blacks and Whites who attended church together in the north. Southern black Baptists initiated the move for separation when, in 1779, George Liel founded a black Baptist Church in Savannah, Georgia. Although it was risky to separate from Whites, especially since some Whites would imprison the preachers and flog black church members, black churches still survived (Blackwell 1991; Pinkney 2000).

In the North, Richard Allen led the separation of churches between Blacks and Whites in Philadelphia, Pennsylvania. He established the Bethel African Methodist Episcopal (AME) Church in 1794, which became the first AME independent church in America. This church and other AME churches became the most effective entities among black Methodists. Other effective churches also came about such as the African Methodist Episcopal Zion (AMEZ) Church in 1796, which was known for its leadership in political activity and for its most effective leader, Reverend Adam Clayton Powell, who later became a legislator (Blackwell 1991). As a result of these early black churches, they continued to spread throughout the country, especially since Blacks were still facing prejudice and racism in the white churches (Blackwell 1991; Pinkney 2000).

After the Civil War and during the very brief period of Reconstruction, when Blacks enjoyed a short-lived freedom as "citizens," black churches provided social structure and social services to the newly freed slaves, as well as provided shelter from white supremacy and blatant racism. Black churches were also at the forefront of founding schools and colleges for Blacks. Many early black politicians were associated with the black church and later served in the Legislature, Freedmen's Bureau,

and other federal positions. Indeed, the black church continued to be at the center of the black community during Reconstruction, the Jim Crow Era, The Civil Rights and Black Power Movements, and is currently still at the heart of the black subculture (Blackwell 1991; Pinkney 2000).

Yet, between 1896 and 1950, black religion saw the development of new sects and cults which sprouted from other denominations associated with the black churches. Many of these sects and cults came into existence to preserve some of the African traditions such as emotionalism. They also wanted to become totally free from white Christianity. Some of these included The Church of God in Christ, which practiced spiritualism and allowed members to have a "good feeling" about themselves; The Church of God, who were Black Jews and believed that they were the "True Jews of the Bible," and that white Jews were frauds; Father Divine's Peace Mission that supported the poor; and the Nation of Islam, that advocated self-help and self-dependence among Blacks. In some of these sects and cults, women could also be ministers (Blackwell 1991; Pinkney 2000).

During The Civil Rights Movement of the 1950s and 1960s, the black church became the center of most of the activities centered on non-violence. Many great leaders emerged from the roots of the black church and included Reverend Martin Luther King, Jr., whose name became synonymous with the movement; Reverend Ralph Abernathy; Reverend Fred Shuttlesworth; Reverend Jesse Jackson; Reverend Charles Steele; and many other great reverends. The black church was thought to have provided total institutional support of The Civil Rights Movement, and allowed Blacks to vent frustrations through singing, praying, and shouting. The church was also the place where strategies were planned and the vehicle through which these strategies were executed. Blacks could engage in open discussions of the issues and pressures that were oppressing them. Unfortunately, not all black churches participated in The Civil Rights Movement, and some seemed more concerned about life after death than with current issues (Morris 1984; Blackwell 1991; Pinkney 2000).

broom "jumping" = sweep away singleness, symbolize family

After The Civil Rights Movement and since the 1970s, the church has become more active and responsive to the current needs of its members and black people in general. During the 1990s, social cohesion and unity became the dominant role of the black church. Members and non-members still expected the church to provide assistance with personal issues, financial setbacks, a sense of direction, support with prejudices and discrimination issues, and other types of stressors. Without a doubt, the black church still provides a sense of self-worth and makes people feel good about themselves as well as serves as the center of the black community (Blackwell 1991; Pinkney 2000).

At the beginning of the twenty-first century, most Blacks were Baptist or Methodist. However, it is hard to specify exact numbers of church affiliations since the census does not directly collect these data. Nonetheless, the Baptist denomination claimed more black members than all the others combined. After the Civil War, the black Baptist Church exploded in growth, as Blacks used their newly found freedom to worship on their own without the control of Whites overseeing them. During this time, women in the Baptist Church had major roles in stimulating the black community (Pinkney 2000).

In fact, women of the Baptist faith have been the majority of black Christians in America. Within the Baptist faith itself, women make up more than half of the membership. However, due to sexism, most women do not hold leadership positions within the church, yet they perform most of the supporting roles of the church such as running Sunday schools, visiting the sick and shut-in, running nurseries, organizing programs, and many more duties and activities (http://findarticles.com/p/articles/mi_m1077/is_1_61/ai_n15770848/?tag=content;col1).

Over the years, black churches have endured criticisms from the black community. The southern black church met some criticisms for losing touch with the real issues facing Blacks in the larger society such as racism and equality. Instead, it seemed more interested in the "other world" issues, particularly once Blacks have left the earth and gone to Heaven or the great beyond. Whereas the northern black church did address these issues, but over time became less emotional in its services. In other words, the "Africanisms" were lacking in the northern churches (Pinkney 2000).

Yet, within the black subculture and throughout history, religion has had a tremendous impact on black Americans. Although African slaves were not Christians when they were first brought to America, many became Christians, and today the majority of African Americans are still Christians. The three largest black religious bodies are Baptist, Methodist, and Pentecostal. Still, there are some African Americans, such as the Black Muslims, who are not Christians and have indeed rejected Christianity. In fact, some Blacks still question why African Americans continue to embrace the religion of their white oppressors (Blackwell 1991; Pinkney 2000).

THE BLACK CHURCH CULTURE

The black church is an amazing entity, with a powerful culture of its own. For instance, the rural Baptist Church in "any rural town, USA," usually starts with the Saturday evening meal preparation for the Sunday service(s). On any given Saturday evening, black women are busy preparing food for the Sunday church services and socializing with each other. The next day, Sunday school may begin at 9:30 AM followed by the traditional 11 AM service, and in some cases a 2 PM service. Each church service starts with a song by a deacon and then others join in, then a deacon prays, and members are in tuned by saying Amen. A member reads a scripture from the Bible, then the big choir or youth choir sings, then members' testimonies are given (can be rather lengthy). Next, the sermon is delivered by a charismatic preacher who performs with humming and getting the members excited with "the word." Some members shout, faint, talk in tongue, catch the holy spirit, and comments like amen, preach, yes Lord, etc., follow or occur during the sermon (Pinkney 2000).

Some preachers are long-winded and the sermon can last for an hour or longer. To signal the end of the sermon, the preacher starts a song and others join in, the offering is collected, then more songs, next are announcements, and then the benediction at the end of the service. However, some churches may have a second sermon with a different preacher, so the church services can be further extended well into the day. If this is the case, then food is served mostly by the women ushers of the church, although many church members contribute to the food. Therefore, Sundays are almost always focused on the church. As well, other auxiliary services such as revivals, pastor anniversaries, church anniversaries, Christmas and Easter programs, youth programs, and others are also mostly planned and executed by women in the church (personal observations of a black church community).

In the black community, the church is so prominent that those who feel they are not living right will not attend; ironically, they are seen as the ones who should attend. People feel shame and embarrassed to let others know when they have blatantly sinned or "not living right," and therefore, will not go to church. They see it as a way to respect God by not going into his "house" full of sin; such as drinking the night before or doing and selling drugs in the community. These same individuals will run and hide from the preacher so that they will not have to be "accountable" at the moment, since they plan to "get right with God," at some later date. Whereas, at the same time, some who go to church every Sunday, still engage in the deviant behaviors of those who do not go to church at all. They too, will try to hide certain behaviors from the preacher when he is around (personal observations of a black church community).

In fact, the black preacher is seen as the most influential "Man of God" in the black community and is given the utmost respect among Blacks. He is called upon to render "Godly services" to the parishioners and in the community as a whole. He performs services during happy times, such as christening of children, baptisms, and weddings as well as during sad times, such as funerals. Communion is also a big event in churches where members symbolically partake in eating bread or crackers (representing the flesh of Jesus) and drinking a red juice (representing the blood of Jesus) to show their acceptance of Jesus Christ as their savior (personal observations of a black church community).

However, the baptism is the most important ritual among all Christians. It represents spiritual cleansing and a willingness to accept Christ as one's personal savior. It is at the center of the Baptist faith and involves the preacher fully dipping the member into the water for a quick second or two. It can be done in creeks, rivers, ponds, or pools and usually the other members of the congregation will attend and praise the Lord (personal observations of a black church community).

In regard to weddings, many black weddings are traditional but some have started to embrace African traditions such as "jumping the broom." Jumping the broom was an African ceremony that was practiced by Blacks during slavery when marriages among slaves were not legal. Today, jumping the broom may be a part of the traditional wedding ceremony. It is symbolic in that the couple who jumps the broom will be bound in marriage. It also symbolizes fertility and prosperity for the couple. As well, it means that the couple will sweep away their single lives, former problems and other sins, and by jumping over the broom, they will begin a new life as husband and wife. At the end of the wedding ceremony, the couple jumps over the broom that is placed in front of them when they turn to face the audience. The "jump" symbolizes the beginning of a new life (http://www.african-weddings.com/jumping_the_broom).

Jumping the broom itself was not an actual part of slavery instead it was a part of African culture practiced in African rituals even before slaves practiced it in America. It is still used in some parts of West Africa, where most of the slaves were captured and brought to America. In the African culture, the broom has both symbolic and spiritual significance. It was used by Africans in a tribal marriage ritual of putting sticks on the ground to represent the spot for the couple's new residence. The broom straws symbolizes the family, the handle of the broom symbolizes the Almighty, and the ribbon symbolizes the tie that binds the couple in marriage (http://www.african-weddings.com/jumping_the_broom).

Like weddings, funerals are also quite unique in the black community, and many funerals today still embrace African traditions. Many African American traditions of death originated from the Bakongo and the LaDogaa African tribes and have been passed down through older generations of Blacks, beginning in slavery and even practiced today. Many of the customs are viewed as superstitions and manifested in religious beliefs and practices. This is especially the case in the South, and specifically in the Sea Islands of Georgia and South Carolina, which are still strongly rooted in Africanisms, and most culturally associated with the African countries of Angola and Sierra Leone. However, African cultural traditions are also found in other parts of the country (http://northbysouth.kenyon.edu/1998/death/deathhistory.htm).

Therefore, when a loved one is dying or dies in the black community, it is a very sad but joyous time, as the celebration is often thought of as a grand time since the deceased will be going home to live with the Lord. Usually family members and friends are called to come home as soon as possible to see the dying person before death. Once the person dies or "passes," which is the preferred term that some Blacks use to mean that the person has gone on to the next phase of his or her life, and that their spirit and soul have left their bodies; the funeral arrangements can take up to two weeks, depending on the amount of time needed for all pertinent family members to get home in time (http://northbysouth.kenyon.edu/1998/death/deathhistory.htm).

Then, based on some of the African traditions and superstitions, when someone dies in the black community, a unique rites of passage takes place. Once the family members and friends are notified and begin to come home for the funeral, a series of events take place. First, the weather is carefully watched so that the funeral can be planned for a sunny day in hopes that the rain will stay away so that the deceased's soul can go to heaven. If it rains with lightning and thunder then the devil will come for the deceased's soul. So, most funerals are planned for a sunny day (http://northbysouth.kenyon.edu/1998/death/deathhistory.htm).

Sometimes it can take up to a week before the funeral takes place, but it is not unusual for it to take up to two weeks, depending on the family circumstances. A wake is held the night before the funeral for those who cannot make the funeral but would like to pay last respects to the dead and view the body. The deceased can also be viewed at the funeral parlor before the wake or the funeral. During the time leading up to the funeral, people gather at the main home of the deceased to comfort the family by bringing food and visiting the family members during this time of grief (http://northbysouth.kenyon.edu/1998/death/deathhistory.htm).

The funeral is the climax of the week of mourning and grieving. Usually the hearse leads the funeral procession and will drive through the yard of the deceased one last time so that the deceased's spirit and soul can visit their home for the last time before going on to glory and their final resting spot. If this does not happen, then it is believed that the deceased's spirit will not be at peace, and they will return to visit their home and will remain restless in their graves. After that, the immediate family members fall in line in their cars with the headlights turned on and follow the hearse to the church for the funeral. Once at the church, all family members line up behind the immediate family to go into the church. The funeral is one of the most emotional events of hurt, pain, grief, crying, and sometimes fainting that one could imagine (personal observations of a funeral service in the black community).

At the end of the funeral, the cars once again line up behind the hearse and the immediate family members to go to the burial site. At the site, a few words are said and the deceased is laid to rest. Other superstitions may also appear at the burial site. For instance, the bodies must be buried with feet facing to the east so that on Judgment Day the deceased can rise and properly pass on, otherwise, the deceased may remain on earth and their spirit will wander and not rest in peace (http://www.nasponline.org/resources/principals/culture_death.aspx). It is also believed by some that items can be buried with the dead for specific meanings; such as burying the dead with a switch in their hand so that the dead can continue to haunt an individual who killed him/her and whip them with the switch and/or show up to them in ghostly form. After the burial, family and friends either gather again at the church or at the deceased's home for food and refreshments. Grieving often continues for many days, weeks, months and even years (personal observations of funeral rituals in the black community).

Today, in 2012, the black church continues to serve as the center of the black community and is often found all over communities. There can be as many as three or more churches within the same neighborhood, and often on the same street; some within walking distance. In college towns, students may also attend church and contribute to the membership. Some churches or ministries are even on college campuses or adjacent to them. Many church-related schools still require their students to attend chapel. Nonetheless, freedom of religion has seen many mixed race churches emerge, as well as a few Blacks opting to attend white churches. Mega churches are also popular and earlier services are becoming the norm rather than just the traditional 11 AM service.

Regretfully, however, hatred, racism, and other sinful acts have led to church burnings all over the country, but particularly in the South. During the 1990s, more than 150 cases of church burnings were investigated by federal agencies and many more were investigated by local agencies. Even though not all of the burnings were of black churches, historical suspicions arise when a small, black, rural church is burned. The dark past of African Americans is quickly brought to light whenever a black church is burned. It is a horrifying reminder of what has happened to black churches in the past by white racists and the Ku Klux Klan, especially during The Civil Rights Movement (Booth 1996). Still, in spite of these burnings of black churches, Blacks' spirits and souls remained true to their faith.

Yet, these churches, or sacred houses of worship, like other social institutions have also experienced different types of social behavior and social interactions. Unfortunately, some have conflicts and many have become corrupted as a result of gossip, jealousy, and dirty secrets like adultery, child molestations, and other "Unchristian-like" behavior. Preachers have sinned or conned members out of millions of dollars like using

BLACK CHURCH BURNINGS AND BOMBINGS

Since the Ku Klux Klan and other hate mongers' bombing of the Sixteenth Street Baptist Church in Birmingham, Alabama, in 1963, which killed four black girls, black church bombings and burnings have since been associated with hatred and racism, especially in the South. Even before this infamous church burning, in January 1957, four black churches were bombed in Montgomery, Alabama. A year later, in 1958, both Birmingham, Alabama, and Memphis, Tennessee, had black church burnings. The next year, in 1959, another black church was burned in Roscoe, Georgia. In the 1960s, these church burnings continued in Pine Bluff, Arkansas, when a church was bombed. However, in 1964, Meridian, Mississippi, saw black churches being attacked. In that same year in Vicksburg, Mississippi, two people lost their lives in a church that was used to register black voters when the church was bombed. In 1968, Meridian had two additional black churches bombed and torched. In the 1990s, the trend of burning and bombing black churches returned. Between 1992 and 1996 there were more black churches burned than during the entire Civil Rights Movement. In fact, from January 1995 through July 1996 some seventy-plus black and mixed churches were burned. Amazingly, more churches were burned during this short span than during the previous five years combined (Simmsparris, 1998). Hence, to burn a church of any racial background is eerily symbolizing that hatred and racism have no limits on the length they would go to emphasize white supremacy; even burning a "house of God" has no bearing on their level of hatred. Where will they go on Judgment Day?

"prayer cloths," that members received after sending in monetary donations, as was the case with the popular "Reverend Ike," whose slogan was "You can't lose with the stuff I use" (Lehmann-Haupt 2009).

Some churches have also become a fashion show to see who can outdress each other. The "crowns" or hats are still very much a part of the dress code. Still most blacks have not lost hope and faith in their religious beliefs and many families expect family members to keep the family's religion. Without a doubt, the black church will continue to be the heart and soul of the black community.

SIGNIFICANT FACTS IMPACTING AFRICAN AMERICANS

(Potter and Claytor 1994; Weems 2012)

- The African Methodist Episcopal Church approved of ordaining women as deacons in 1948, and as elders in 1956.

- Black women comprise about 12% of the clergy.

- Fifty percent of female ministers are found in Holiness and Pentecostal Churches.

- In 1984, Leontyne Kelly was elected by the United Methodist Church as the first black woman bishop of any denomination in the country.

- In 1989, The Episcopal Church elected Barbara Harris, a black female, as the first female bishop in the Episcopal Church.

- In 2000, Vashti Murphy McKenzie was elected to Bishop in the African Methodist Episcopal Church; the first female bishop in a mainstream black denomination.

- Absalom Jones was the first black ordained Episcopal priest in America.

- Sojourner Truth, author of "Ain't I a Woman," was a member of the Mother A.M.E. Zion Church that was founded in 1796, and had the first black congregation in New York City. The church also served as a station along the Underground Railroad.

- James W. C. Pennington was the first Black to earn a Doctor of Divinity Degree.

- James Augustine Healy was the first black Catholic priest in the United States.

- Bishop Henry McNeal Turner was appointed by President Lincoln as the first black chaplin of the United States Army.

- Henry Highland Garnet was the first black minister to preach before the U.S. House of Representatives.

DISCUSSION QUESTIONS

1. Why did Whites force Blacks to become Christians?

2. What role did religion play in the lives of slaves?

3. What role does religion play in the lives of African Americans today?

4. Describe the importance of the black church in the black community.

5. What other African traditions are still present in the black church today?

6. Describe the role of the black preacher during slavery and today.

7. Why are most women not in leadership roles in the black Baptist church?

8. Why do some Blacks continue to embrace the religion of their oppressors during slavery?

1. Become a participant observer in a Sunday church service of a rural black church. Describe the experience after your visit.

2. Compare and contrast black and white church services.

3. Conduct an assessment of church attendance by college students and write up the results.

Name _____

TEN THOUGHTS ACTIVITY

1. List 10 thoughts on what comes to mind when you think of Southern Baptists.

    _____

    _____

    _____

    _____

    _____

    _____

    _____

    _____

    _____

    _____

2. List 10 thoughts on what comes to mind when you think of the black church.

    _____

    _____

    _____

    _____

    _____

    _____

    _____

    _____

    _____

    _____

3. List 10 thoughts on what comes to mind when you think of God.

_____

_____

_____

_____

_____

_____

_____

_____

_____

_____

SUGGESTED RESOURCES

A Common Destiny: Blacks and the American Society. 1989. National Academy Press.

Haywood, Chanta M. *Prophesying Daughters.* 2003. University of Missouri Press.

http://gbgm-umc.org/advance/Church-Burnings/

http://www.african-weddings.com/jumping_the_broom

http://www.christiantimelines.com/aa_church.htm

http://www.nytimes.com/2009/07/30/nyregion/30ike.html

REFERENCES

Blackwell, James E. 1991. *The Black Community Diversity and Unity,* 3rd ed. New York: Harper Collins, Publisher.

Booth, William. "In Church Fires, a Pattern but No Conspiracy," *The Washington Post,* June 19, 1996, A01.

Ebony Pictorial History of Black America, Volume 1, 1971, Nashville, TN: The Southwestern Company.

http://findarticles.com/p/articles/mi_m1077/is_1_61/ai_n15770848/?tag=content;col1

http://northbysouth.kenyon.edu/1998/death/deathhistory.htm.

http://www.african-weddings.com/jumping_the_broom

http://www.nasponline.org/resources/principals/culture_death.aspx

Lehmann-Haupt, Christopher. "Reverend Ike, Who Preached Riches, Dies at 74," *The New York Times,* July 29, 2009. Retrieved January 20, 2012 from http://www.nytimes.com/2009/07/30/nyregion/30ike.html

Morris, Aldon D. 1984. *The Origins of the Civil Rights Movement.* New York: The Free Press.

Pinkney, Alphonso. 2000. *Black Americans,* 5th ed., New Jersey: Prentice Hall Publisher.

Potter, Joan, and Constance Claytor. 1994. *African American Firsts.* New York: Pinto Press.

Shepard, Jon M., Narayan Persaud, and Brenda Hughes. 2009. *Sociology,* 10th ed. Thomson/Wadsworth, Publisher.

Simmsparris, Michele M. "What Does it Mean to See a Black Church Burning? Understanding the Significance of Constitutionalizing Hate Speech," 1 University of Pennsylvania Journal of Constitutional Law 127–151, Spring 1998.

Weems, Renita J. "Black America and Religion," Ebony FindArticles.com, retrieved January 20, 2012.

CHAPTER 6

Politics and the Military

Since the 1970s, Blacks have freely attended and participated in public accommodations, exercised voting rights privileges, elected capable Blacks to public administrations, and enlisted in the military. In fact, Blacks have recently enjoyed significant accomplishments in politics and in the military, and have risen to top posts within both areas. The appointment of General Colin Powell as the Secretary of State by the Republicans in 2001 and the historical election of the nation's first black president, Barack Obama, by the Democrats in 2008, show that if given the opportunity, Blacks can serve at the highest levels in America. However, like other social institutions, Blacks have not always enjoyed the freedom of politics and the military in America. Therefore, this chapter examines these social institutions as they relate to African Americans.

POLITICS

During slavery Blacks were considered property, had no citizenship, and no political participation in the United States. However, immediately after The Civil War, they were briefly involved in the country's political process and freely voted during Reconstruction. During the early part of Reconstruction, Blacks' political participation was the best it had ever been than in any other time in American history. They significantly contributed to southern politics. Indeed, several Blacks assumed top posts in politics and one even served as Acting Governor of Louisiana, P. B. S. Pinchback. Unfortunately, no black person ever served as governor during Reconstruction. However, there were two black lieutenant governors and several black representatives in the United States Congress. In many instances, Blacks were the numerical majority in several southern states like Mississippi and South Carolina, but never had the opportunity to control any of these states, although they registered and voted in greater numbers than Whites (Franklin 1965; Bennett 1969; *Ebony* 1971; Pinkney 2000).

Since President Abraham Lincoln was a Republican and had latently freed the slaves, nearly all Blacks in America were also Republicans. However, Lincoln's successor, President Andrew Johnson, a Democrat disguised as an independent, was a racist who vetoed every bill designed to help Blacks. Fortunately, Congress overrode his vetoes and many bills were passed that served in the best interest of Blacks. It was clear to Congress and abolitionists that President Johnson had no intentions of helping Blacks. Indeed, the Democratic Party was first associated with the slave states and did not serve in the best interest of Blacks (Franklin 1965; Bennett 1969; *Ebony* 1971; Pinkney 2000).

Unfortunately, as mentioned in Chapter 3, the dreadful Compromise of 1877 came about as the result of the disputed election of Republican President Rutherford B. Hayes in 1876 by Congress. This was the worst political stance that came about during Reconstruction that would literally nearly overturn everything that had been accomplished for Blacks within the very short period after the Civil War. In fact, during the compromise, the Republican Party abandoned Blacks and threw them "under the bus," to their former slave masters in the South. However, the Republican leaders thought that the Compromise of 1877 was the only way to avoid another civil war. Nevertheless, this compromise gave white southerners the muster they needed to "get Blacks back in their place" (Franklin 1965; Bennett 1969; *Ebony* 1971; Pinkney 2000).

The reality of the Compromise of 1877 removed the remaining military troops from the South, giving the South absolute home rule and other negotiated favors. Perhaps the most dreadful favors promised the South was political autonomy, and that there would be no intervention in southern matters pertaining to race and policy. In exchange for these favors, the southern leaders promised that the constitutional rights of Blacks would be adhered to and that Blacks would be protected. Federal politicians were well aware of southerners' intentions of how they wanted to restructure the South, but still appeared to be more interested in politics than in the rights of Blacks. Thus, within a short span of time, almost all of the accomplishments for Blacks during Reconstruction had been overturned and southern Whites were determined to disfranchise them and shut them out of the political process (Franklin 1965; Bennett 1969; *Ebony* 1971; Pinkney 2000).

At the same time, Blacks were still experiencing some freedom as American citizens. Nevertheless, Blacks quickly realized that any rights that had been given them were only on paper and nothing more (Curran and Renzetti 1987). So, after a very brief period of political participation Blacks in the South were faced with policies and practices designed to preserve white supremacy. These included poll taxes, literacy tests in order to vote, white primary elections which excluded Blacks, and grandfather clauses which only allowed voting to those and their descendants who had been eligible voters before the Civil War. As a result of these measures, Blacks were quickly becoming disfranchised in the South and by the early 1900s, all Blacks in the South were systematically disfranchised and not allowed to vote or participate in politics (Franklin 1965; Bennett 1969; *Ebony* 1971; Curran and Renzetti 1987; Hraba 1979; Kitano 1985; Parrillo 1985; Feagin 1989; Pinkney 2000).

During the systematic disfranchisement of Blacks in the South, there was no need for them to be affiliated with any political parties since they could not participate in any way. Meanwhile, American politics began to shift and the platforms of the two major political parties began to change as the country embraced other social changes like the Great Depression and two world wars. Still Blacks were not allowed to participate in the country's political process. However, due to the social condition of the country and the realization that Whites were becoming a large part of the poor in America, at least one president and first lady took notice and interest in the plight of the poor (Blackwell 1991; Pinkney 2000).

Both Democratic President Franklin D. Roosevelt and First Lady Eleanor Roosevelt developed an interest in the general welfare of poor people with specific attention on the condition of Blacks. President Roosevelt was the only president to serve three complete terms with the fourth term cut short by death. During his administration (1933–1945), Blacks re-engaged in the political process and made a major leap to the Democratic Party, thus abandoning the Republican Party, which had earlier abandoned them. Since this major transition from the Republican Party, most Blacks have remained Democrats to this day (*Ebony* 1971; Bausum 2009).

President Roosevelt also had a very special relationship with his "Black Cabinet," whose formal name was the Federal Council of Negro Affairs. This cabinet consisted of an informal group of black community leaders and activists who apprised the president of the needs of the black community. Known for his "New Deal" approach to America, which consisted of a variety of social services for America's poor, President Roosevelt and the First Lady Eleanor Roosevelt were icons in the black community. They were specifically interested in and addressed the specific needs of Blacks, who had been relatively neglected since the Reconstruction Era (Pinkney 2000). By the mid-1930s, there were over 40 Blacks employed in federal executive positions and in the New Deal agencies. The First Lady was very instrumental in making sure the needs of Blacks were addressed, and she was a personal friend of the great educator, Mary Mcleod Bethune, one of the "Black Cabinet" members (http://www.oxfordaasc.com/public/features/archive/1008/index.jsp).

Other presidents, mostly Democrats, followed Roosevelt's lead and were either directly or indirectly sensitive to Blacks in America. These included Harry S. Truman, who continued Roosevelt's agenda and also integrated the military; Dwight D. Eisenhower, who was a Republican during the Civil Rights Movement but was in favor of freedom and equality for Blacks, and stated that "there must be no second class citizens in this country" (Bausum 2009, 157). He also sent federal troops to Little Rock, Arkansas, to enforce integration of the public schools, as a result of the *Brown v. Board of Education* Supreme Court ruling.

President John F. Kennedy became very popular among Blacks during the heat of the Civil Rights Movement when he was elected. He was committed to peace and justice and was very sensitive to the civil rights issues of Blacks, including the right to vote. He publicly supported racial equality in America. After his assassination in Dallas, Texas, President Lyndon B. Johnson continued and supported his civil rights agenda. He, too, envisioned fairness for all Americans, including the right to vote, and his efforts brought major improvements in the lives of Blacks and other minorities as well as the poor on nearly every social condition they faced. Unfortunately, the Vietnam War overshadowed all the domestic good he had done for the country and he did not seek reelection (Bausum 2009).

The Republicans then gained control of the presidency toward the end of The Civil Rights and The Black Power Movements with the elections of Richard Nixon and Gerald Ford. However, given the embarrassment of Nixon's administration and the Watergate scandal, which later forced him to resign, becoming the first president to do so, Ford assumed a tainted presidency and the Republicans lost the public's trust. Fortunately for Blacks and other minorities, Democratic President

James E. (Jimmy) Carter was elected after Gerald Ford and was known for criticizing racial discrimination—particularly, favoring Whites over Blacks and other minorities (Bausum 2009).

However, Republicans would return to the White House a few years later with a vengeance, with the election of the oldest president to assume office, Ronald Reagan. Reagan's gift to Black Americans was the signing of a Bill to make Dr. Martin Luther King's birthday a national holiday. Republican President George Bush assumed the presidency after Ronald Reagan and focused mainly on war issues in Iraq. However, good news came to the black community again, with the election of one of the most popular and one of the youngest presidents to assume office, Democratic President William (Bill) J. Clinton. Clinton was very sensitive to the issues facing the black community and issues impacting Blacks in the larger society (Bausum 2009). He was well-respected among Blacks in America.

Clinton's administration was followed by the election of Republican President, George W. Bush, who, like his father, President George Bush, also focused mainly on war issues. However, his presidency saw the uniting of diverse cultures and races in America, as Americans pulled together without regard to color or "racial issues" in support of the war with Afghanistan and the hunt for Osama bin Laden, who was behind the bombing of the World Trade Center, which killed hundreds of Americans of all races (Bausum 2009). However, it would be the next Democratic President, Barack Obama, who would render the capture and killing of Bin Laden, thus, bringing the races together once more to focus on a common foe (http://www.nytimes.com/2011/05/02/world/asia/osama-bin-laden-is-killed.html?pagewanted=all).

Finally, President Barack Obama made history when he became the first black president of the United States of America on November 4, 2008 (Bausum 2009). His run for the top post in the nation brought out a record number of black voters, including elderly black voters who had not voted since the Civil Rights Movement. However, the excitement around the possibility of history being made aroused people from all walks of life to participate in the voting process, including first time voters and a record number of black male voters. At the conclusion of his historical election, emotions ran high in the black community, as Blacks were overcome with joy, tears, and disbelief that "one of their own," a black man, was finally President of the United States of America (http://www.thegrio.com/politics/obama-campaign-focuses-on-black-vote-targets-hbcus.php).

Although Booker T. Washington was the first black man to dine at the White House, President Barack Obama and First Lady Michele Obama and their children are the first Blacks to live there. Ironically, Barack grew up during The Civil Rights and Black Power Movements, which were the periods in U.S. history that would subsequently pave the way for his presidency 40-plus years later (Bausum 2009). Although President Obama became the first black president of the United States, he was not the first to campaign for the top spot. Others who paved the way for him included Shirley Chisholm in 1972, Reverend Jesse Jackson in 1984 and 1988, Lenora Fulani in 1988, and Carol Moseley Braun in 2004 (http://www.oxfordaasc.com/public/features/archive/1008/index.jsp).

MILITARY

Since the president of the United States is also the commander in chief of the Armed Forces, the political arena is very closely related to the military. In fact, many of the founding fathers and other presidents had military experience before taking the top post in America. However, although voting is a factor in the election of presidents, many times voters do not have any control over matters that are decided at the highest levels of the political social structure in America, such as declaring war. These types of decisions are usually made by the president and other legislators without the input of voters (Shepard, Persaud, and Hughes 2009).

Since the beginning of America's history as an independent nation, and having fought for its own freedom, Blacks have played a pivotal role in the battles, whether as slaves or as freedmen. For several centuries, Blacks have been patriotic to a country that has not always respected them as loyal contributors and protectors, and sometimes not even viewed them as human beings. Yet, Blacks have fought to defend the nation, when the nation did not fight to defend them. Even though Blacks

were treated as second class citizens, they bravely fought in segregated military units to protect the honor of the United States of America. Over the years, they have fought in every war since the American Revolutionary War against England (Blackwell 1991).

Nonetheless, fighting for the country was still not enough to grant Blacks equal rights in America as they continued to experience racism and discrimination both in America and abroad, as they fought for a country that condoned unfair treatment of them. Although Blacks fought for America just like Whites did, they were still treated as inferior in the military. In fact, many racial conflicts between black and white servicemen took place on military bases in the United States as well as abroad, even on naval ships. Ironically, although Blacks and Whites were protecting the same country against foreign enemies, they were also fighting among themselves in a racial battle for equality (Blackwell 1991). It appeared that Blacks were good enough to sacrifice their lives for a country that treated them as inferior, but not good enough to be respected as citizens and heroes during or after the fact. Like other parts of American society, the military was a microcosm of this society, in that unequal treatment in this institution was the same as in any other.

Unfair treatment of Blacks in the military was made clear in the very first war in which black Americans participated—the Revolutionary War against England (1775–1783). Although Whites were reluctant to allow Blacks to fight in the war, some 5000 black men fought for America's freedom throughout the war. In the end, America ultimately received its freedom, although only some of the country's citizens were freed. The others (Blacks) were not even considered "American citizens," and obviously did not need to be free. Still, freedom was the hope and dreams of free Blacks and slaves who thought that if the colonies won their freedom, that this would also mean that they too would be free (Altman 1997). Unfortunately, it would take another war on American soil before this freedom was realized for Blacks.

Due to the slave masters' fear of "all black" troops, it was the policy of the colonies' Continental Army to not allow Blacks to fight in the Revolutionary War. The colonists were afraid that slaves would rebel and would be disloyal to the slave owners. However, as the war continued, the British offered to free all slaves who joined their armed forces. Hence, twenty thousand black men fought for the British during this war. Following suit, the Continental Army decided to also allow Blacks to join their armed forces. In fact, by 1779, the Continental Congress recommended that slaves be recruited to serve in the Continental Army. Unfortunately, when the war ended, the Americans demanded that slaves who fought with the British be returned to their masters. Fortunately, the British refused to abide by this demand and evacuated about 14,000 black soldiers. Indeed, about 1,100 went on to help the British develop the colony of Sierra Leone in Africa (Altman 1997).

As time went on, it seemed that America's deep "dark" secret (slavery) was being exposed to the rest of the world, especially since the country won the war with England for its own freedom. Although this was successfully accomplished, it still did not dawn upon the American forefathers, who seemed to be hypocrites at the time that "freedom was still an issue" in America and that only "white Americans" were freed while "black Americans" were still slaves. It did not matter that Blacks too, had fought in the Revolutionary War, and that one of them, Crispus Attucks, was even the first to die for America's freedom (Altman 1997).

Obviously, the shame on America had become too much to bear, so in 1808 both England and the United States outlawed the slave trade, but from the beginning there was little enforcement. As the unprotected West African coastline, along with the persistent demand for slave labor, and the enormous profits for the slave masters all combined to keep the triangular trade intact until the bloodiest event in American history took place—the Civil War, which finally brought a temporary end to America's shame and freed the slaves as a result (Stampp 1965; *Ebony* 1971; Hraba 1979; Parrillo 1985; Kitano 1985; Feagin 1989).

Initially, black men were not allowed to serve in the military during the Civil War (1861–1865). However, after January 1, 1863, when the Emancipation Proclamation freed most of the slaves, and as a result allowed for Blacks to serve in the Army, thousands of black men quickly tried to enlist. This was done in spite of the reality that they could have been shot or enslaved if

caught, which was Confederate policy. Yet, during the war over 200,000 Black men eventually enlisted in the Union Armed Forces. Of these, about 38,000 died and thousands more were wounded or missing in action after the war (Altman 1997; *Ebony* 1971).

Indeed, many black men fought bravely and honorably for their country during the Civil War, including an all-black group of former slave men, known as the First South Carolina Volunteers, that was organized in 1862 by Union General David Hunter. During that same year, Robert Smalls, a slave from Beaufort, South Carolina, hijacked the Planter, a Confederate ship in the Charleston, South Carolina, harbor and successfully delivered it to the Union Forces. He later served in the United States Congress during Reconstruction (Altman 1997; *Ebony* 1971). Subsequently, an all-black school in Beaufort, South Carolina, was named for him during the mid-1900s, and today it is an integrated middle school (http://www.robertsmalls.org/). Nonetheless, only 24 black men were given the Congressional Medal of Honor for their services (Altman 1997).

The honor and dignity of black men were never major concerns in the United States Armed Forces. They were continuously given the least desirable duties, the worst jobs to perform, and the least amount of respect or recognition for performing them. Other forms of discrimination included the salaries of black servicemen in comparison to white servicemen. Not surprisingly, black men were paid less than white men, had less than adequate equipment to train with, and received inferior medical care while in the same military (Altman 1997; *Ebony* 1971).

It was disheartening to have experienced some of the things that black men experienced in the military. Yet, they continued to fight for America as America continued to slap them in the face with discrimination and racism. Sadly, black men were often at a crossroads with their own conscience in performing their duties with pride and integrity. One such ordeal involved the Frontier Wars, which were fought mainly against Native Americans, another powerless minority group in America. Blacks were often put on the frontlines of fighting the Native Americans to protect the white settlers (Altman 1997; *Ebony* 1971).

Fighting the Frontier Wars made Black's progress in the military extremely hard and unrewarding, as they continued to risk their lives for their white oppressors by fighting against another minority group that was also oppressed by Whites. Nonetheless, a year after the Civil War ended, in 1866, The Reorganization Act allowed four black regiments to be established: the 24th and 25th Infantry and the 9th and 10th Calvary. These regiments were later known as the Buffalo Soldiers and many were veterans of the Civil War. They were given duties west of the Mississippi River, and ordered to protect the white settlers from being attacked by Native Americans. Likewise, black men also fought in the Spanish-American War, and some lost their lives when a battleship sank in Havana, Cuba, in 1898. Some also fought in the Philippine Islands (Altman 1997; *Ebony* 1971).

Further, against the wishes of the southern Democrats who initially blocked the drafting of Blacks in World War I (1917–1918), Blacks still participated in this "Great War." During this war, over 350,000 black men served in the military and about 100,000 of them served overseas. Up to this point, Blacks had served in every major war involving the United States, yet they continued to be treated unequally; serving in segregated forces including combat units, receiving inferior medical care, and having to endure inferior recreational facilities. Obviously, it was clear that the United States had no intentions of honoring or respecting their contributions to war efforts.

In fact, other countries were more appreciative of black Americans than their own country. In 1918, France bestowed its highest military honor upon Henry Johnson of the famous 369th Infantry. He was the first United States soldier to be awarded France's Croix de Guerre honor (Altman 1997). Sadly, as the black war veterans returned "home" to racism in the United States, many received a violent and hostile welcome and appreciation for their sacrifices in World War I, the "Great War" or "The War to End All Wars." Unfortunately, between 1914 and 1920, of the 382 known lynching of Blacks, many of the victims included World War I veterans. In fact, some of them were lynched while still wearing their uniforms (Ebony 1971). Evidently nothing had changed in America in terms of race relations.

As wars began to intensify around the world, the United States military remained segregated, although there was a slight increase in black officers during World War II. As World War II commenced and dreadfully wore on, it became the worst war the world has ever witnessed, with racism in Germany at the center of the controversy, as Adolph Hitler set out to exterminate the Jews. Simultaneously, racism and discrimination continued to pose an extremely serious problem for the United States military, despite the fact that 1,000,000 Blacks served in World War II. Racial tensions intensified among American Armed Forces at home and overseas. For example, 258 black sailors were court-marshaled and 50 of them were imprisoned for refusing to load live ammunition after an explosion killed 320 people, including 202 Blacks at Port Chicago, California. The Navy later confessed that racial prejudice and discrimination were factors in this case (Altman 1997).

Another incident of courage involved a black sailor named Dorie Miller, who was assigned the duties of a mess attendant in the Navy, but later became a Pearl Harbor hero. While performing his mess duties, the Japanese attacked his battleship on December 7, 1941. Upon realizing what was happening around him, Miller then took the captain of the sinking ship to a safer place, then quickly went back to the deck. Despite having no formal combat training, he began firing an unmanned machine gun which took down two Japanese aircrafts. He continued firing until his ammunition ran out, and then he abandoned ship. Despite this courageous deed, the racist Navy refused to recognize him or to even identify him for months. However, the black Press continued to run the story until the Navy finally decided to identify him and then awarded him a medal. As well, in 1942, President Franklin D. Roosevelt nominated him for the Navy Cross, and he became the first black sailor awarded the Cross, which is the Navy's second highest honor (http://www.oxfordaasc.com/public/features/archive/1008/index.jsp).

Likewise, racism was blatantly present in the Army against a black squadron of pilots who were trained at Tuskegee Institute in Tuskegee, Alabama. They were known as the Tuskegee Airmen and more affectionately known as the Red Tails, since their planes were readily identified by the red color on their aircrafts' tails. The first cadets graduated three months after the bombing incident at Pearl Harbor but the Army initially discriminated against them and would not deploy them outside of the United States. However, as the tensions grew and desperation set in with the war efforts, the Army finally deployed them in 1943 and shipped them to North Africa. Still, racism in the military nearly caused them to be recalled, but the squadron's commander, Benjamin O. Davis, Jr., testified that they were capable of the mission. Commander Davis became the first black General of the Air Force. He was the son of General Benjamin O. Davis, Sr., the first black General of the Army, and indeed of the military (Altman 1997; http://www.biography.com/people/benjamin-o-davis-jr-37840).

One year later, in 1944, the first Tuskegee Airmen, the 99th, merged with three more black squadrons and together they formed the 332nd Fighter Group. Under Davis' command, the Tuskegee Airmen undertook more than 1500 combat missions, shot down more than 100 enemy airplanes, destroyed 150 other planes on the ground, and sank a German destroyer and other boats at sea. In the end, only 66 aircraft casualties were among them. Overall, the Tuskegee Airmen were famous for not losing a single United States bomber plane to the enemy aircrafts, as they successfully carried out 200 escort missions during the war (Altman 1997).

The Tuskegee Airmen won over 100 Distinguished Flying Crosses and three Distinguished Unit Citations. Shattering the racist beliefs of the 1940s, their intellectual ability, bravery, courage and stellar performance in World War II dispelled the myth and doubts that black servicemen were not competent or disciplined enough to serve America in combat units. As a result, United States General George Marshall stated that black military men were just as capable of fighting and equally entitled to defend America as were white servicemen. Apparently this was a notion that could be tied to the beginning of the Civil Rights Movement that was to further evolve in the 1950s and 1960s (http://www.oxfordaasc.com/public/features/archive/1008/index.jsp).

Black women were also added to the United States military during World War II with the creation of the Army Auxiliary Corps (WAAC) in 1942. In 1943, it became the Women's Army Corps (WAC) and was part of the regular Army. Black women mostly had support duties such as delivering supplies to combat soldiers. Of notable distinction was the first black female officer ever and highest ranking black female in the military during World War II, Major Charity Adams. She commanded the first black female unit (the 6888th Central Postal Directory Battalion) overseas, who were responsible for delivering mail to millions of American troops in Europe (http://www.oxfordaasc.com/public/features/archive/1008/index.jsp).

Although the Army allowed Blacks to enlist, they were still mostly commanded by Whites, and served in all-black regiments. The Navy, however, assigned the most menial tasks on the ships to Blacks in segregated units. Initially, the Marine Corps did not even allow Blacks to enlist "among the few good men." Overall, segregation existed at every military base in the United States (http://www.livinghistoryfarm.org/farmingin the40s/life_18.html).

Finally, after World War II, in 1948, President Harry S. Truman issued Executive Order 8891, which desegregated the United States military. The Air Force was the first to immediately desegregate its military forces. The others reacted less hastily, resulting in the last army units being integrated in 1954. This was also the year that the Civil Rights Movement was picking up momentum with the onset of the *Brown v. Board of Education* ruling during the same year (Altman 1997). The integration of the military was an indirect spark that ignited the trail for the Civil Rights Movement to travel.

When the military integrated in the late 1940s, this integration was realized mostly during the Korean War (1950–1953). Still, much discrimination and racism continued in the military. With each subsequent war, Blacks tried so hard to prove their patriotism to America, but kept getting doors slammed in their faces, as racism continued to keep America diseased for years. These racial barriers and tensions were still present in the military during the dreaded Vietnam War (1961–1975) when Blacks accounted for about 10% of the United States military (Altman 1997; Blackwell 1991). This was also a time of great racial tensions in the United States as a whole.

However, change began to take place within the United States military with the more recent wars like the 1991 Persian Gulf War with Iraq. Twenty percent of the United States troops in the Gulf's combat zones were black. As well, of notable accomplishment during this time, was the Chairman of the Joint Chiefs of Staff, General Colin Powell, a black man, who later became Secretary of Defense in 2001 under President George W. Bush (Bausum 2009; Altman 1997). In 2001, things had certainly improved for Blacks in the military and with black and white race relations in the country overall. This was evident when the World Trade Center was bombed by terrorists and America went to war with Afghanistan. Race did not seem to be a factor for Blacks and Whites at that time, since they both had a common enemy—Al Qaeda terrorists and their Taliban supporters (http://robt.shepherd.tripod.com/black-heroes.html).

These united "race" fronts continued among the United States Armed Forces as the country went back to war with Iraq in 2003. At that time, the United States was engaged in two overlapping wars. In 2011, President Barack Obama brought the military troops home and ended the war with Iraq (http://www.usatoday.com/news/world/iraq/story/2011-12-15/Iraq-war/51945028/1). As well, President Obama also ordered the capturing and destruction of Osama bin Laden, who was the number one enemy of America for about 10 years during the war with Afghanistan (http://www.nytimes.com/2011/05/02/world/asia/osama-bin-laden-is-killed.html?pagewanted=all).

Without a doubt African Americans have made great strides in politics and in the military since it was desegregated about 60 years ago. However, Blacks are still grossly underrepresented in the higher military ranks. Recent data revealed that Blacks made up about 17 percent of the military, but made up only 9 percent of the officer ranks. Further examination of the military officers' ranks revealed only one black out of 38 four-star generals or admirals. Only ten black men were four-star ranked (five in the Army, four in the Air Force, and one in the Navy). Overall, the Army has been in the forefront in regard to black officers with almost twice as many over the last 30 or more years, as the other military branches. Black soldiers represented

Image © Akva, 2012. Used under license from Shutterstock, Inc.

PRESIDENT BARACK OBAMA

In 2004, the state of Illinois saw for the first time in United States history two black men from the two major political parties campaigning against each other to be the next U.S. Senator: Democrat Barack Obama and Republican Alan Keyes. When the dust settled on November 2, 2004, Barack Obama became the fifth black U.S. Senator in the country's history. After a successful term as senator, Barack entered the presidential race. On June 3, 2008, he received enough delegates to be the presumptive Democratic Party nominee after the state primaries. On August 28, 2008, Obama accepted the Democratic nomination for President of the United States of America. On November 4, he was elected the nation's 44th President. On January 20, 2009, Barack Obama was sworn in as the 44th President of the United States of America, becoming the first black person to ever be elected president of the world's greatest and most powerful nation. On October 9, 2009, President Barack Obama was awarded the Nobel Peace Prize (http://www.biography.com/people/barack-obama-12782369).

up to12% of all Army officers in comparison to between 4% and 8% in the Navy, Air Force, and the Marine Corps (http://www.huffingtonpost.com/2008/07/23/black-military-officers-r_n_114474.html).

Currently, there are about 400,000 Blacks out of about 2.1 million active duty military forces. Of this number, most Blacks are found among the enlisted ranks. Within the military, African Americans have more management positions than they do in the wider society. Further, the military still has race relations issues, but they are not as pronounced as in the other social institutions in America (http://www.huffingtonpost.com/2008/07/23/black-military-officers-r_n_114474.html).

Moreover, during the last three decades the percentages of Blacks in the military have increased (13% in the Navy, 17% in the Air Force, 20% in the Marine Corps, and 30% in the Army). Each of the four branches has its own story to tell with regard to Blacks. However, the Army has always been ahead of the other branches, with the Navy being last in its recruitment of Blacks. Impressively, Blacks comprise ten percent of Army officers today, which is twice as many as the Air Force and Marine Corps and three times as many as the Navy. Indeed, the United States Military has served Blacks well over the last 60 years, just as Blacks have served the military well over the years (http://www.theatlantic.com/past/docs/unbound/flashbks/black/moskos.htm).

Significant Facts Impacting African Americans

(http://www.oxfordaasc.com/public/features/archive/1008/index.jsp)

- Hiram Rhoades Revels was the first black U.S. Senator from Mississippi in 1869.

- Blanche Kelso Bruce was the first black U.S. Senator from Mississippi to serve a full term in the U.S. Senate in 1875.

- John Willis Menard was the first Black elected to the U.S. House of Representatives from Louisiana in 1868; although he never served.

- Joseph Hayne Rainey from South Carolina was the first Black to serve in the U.S. House of Representatives in 1870; he was elected four times.

- Edward Brooke from Massachusetts was the first Black elected to the U.S. Senate since Reconstruction in 1966.

- Shirley Anita Chisholm was the first black woman elected to Congress in 1968; she served in the House of Representatives.

- Carol Moseley Braun was the first black female U.S. Senator in 1992.

- Adam Clayton Powell from New York was elected to the U.S. House of Representatives in 1945.

- John F. Conyers Jr. is the longest serving black member of the U.S. House of Representatives since 1965.

- Barbara Jordan was elected the first black U.S. Representative from Texas in 1972.

- Mike Espy became the first black U.S. Representative from Mississippi since Reconstruction in 1986.

DISCUSSION QUESTIONS

1.   Why did Whites not want Blacks to enlist in the military?

2.   What role did the slaves play in the military?

3.   What role does voting play in the lives of African Americans today?

4.   Describe the importance of the military in the black community today.

5.   Describe the social factors impacting the election of the first black president of the United States.

6. What was the role of the Tuskegee Airmen during World War II?

7. What was the role of black women in the military during World War II?

8. Why did Blacks continue to fight for a country that did not appreciate their efforts and loyalty?

9. When and why did Blacks switch to the Democratic Party?

1. Imagine what it would be like if Blacks were disfranchised today; record your thoughts.

2. Compare and contrast the military service of Blacks and Whites.

3. Conduct an assessment of political issues among college students on your campus and write up the results.

Name _____

TEN THOUGHTS ACTIVITY

1. List 10 thoughts on what comes to mind when you think of Blacks and politics.

   _____

   _____

   _____

   _____

   _____

   _____

   _____

   _____

   _____

   _____

2. List 10 thoughts on what comes to mind when you think of Blacks and the military.

   _____

   _____

   _____

   _____

   _____

   _____

   _____

   _____

   _____

   _____

3. List 10 thoughts on what comes to mind when you think of President Barack Obama.

_____

_____

_____

_____

_____

_____

_____

_____

_____

_____

SUGGESTED RESOURCES

A Common Destiny: Blacks and the American Society. 1989. National Academy Press.

Carter, Cynthia Jacobs. *Freedom in My Heart.* Washington, DC: The National Geographic Society.

Desegregation of the Armed Forces. The Truman Library. Available at: Gardner, Michael R., George M. Elsey, Kweisi Mfume. 2003. *Harry Truman and Civil Rights: Moral Courage and Political Risks.* Carbondale, IL: SIU Press.

http://www.wwnorton.com/college/history/ralph/workbook/ralprs36b.htm.

http://www.army.mil/africanamericans/timeline.html

http://www.bcbst.com/about/diversity/Color_of_Blood-Military_Integration_Time_Line.pdf

http://www.biography.com/tv/classroom/black-history-timeline

http://www.trumanlibrary.org/whistlestop/study_collections/desegregation/large/index.php?action=chronology

Sitkoff, Harvard. "African Americans, American Jews, and the Holocaust." In *The Achievement of American Liberalism: The New Deal and Its Legacies.* Ed. William Henry Chafe. New York: Columbia University Press, 2003, 181–203.

REFERENCES

Altman, Susan. 1997. *The Encyclopedia of African American Heritage.* New York: Facts on File, Inc.

Bausum, Ann. 2009. *Our Country's Presidents.* Washington, DC: National Geographic Society.

Bennett, Lerone, Jr. 1969. *Before the Mayflower: A History of Black America.* Chicago: Johnson Publishing Company, Inc.

Blackwell, James E. 1991. *The Black Community Diversity and Unity,* 3rd ed. New York: Harper Collins, Publisher.

Curran, Daniel J., and Claire M. Renzetti. 1987. *Social Problems: Society in Crisis.* Boston: Allyn and Bacon.

Ebony Pictorial History of Black America, Vol. 1. 1971. Nashville, TN: The Southwestern Company.

Feagin, Joe R. 1989. *Racial and Ethnic Relations,* 3rd ed. Englewood Cliffs, NJ: Prentice Hall.

Franklin, John Hope. 1965. *From Slavery to Freedom,* 2nd ed. New York: Alfred A. Knopf.

Hraba, Joseph. 1979. *American Ethnicity.* Itasca, IL: F. E. Peacock.

http://robt.shepherd.tripod.com/black-heroes.html

http://www.theatlantic.com/past/docs/unbound/flashbks/black/moskos.htm

http://www.biography.com/people/barack-obama-12782369

http://www.biography.com/people/benjamin-o-davis-jr-37840

http://www.thegrio.com/politics/obama-campaign-focuses-on-black-vote-targets-hbcus.php

http://www.huffingtonpost.com/2008/07/23/black-military-officers-r_n_114474.html

http://www.livinghistoryfarm.org/farminginthe40s/life_18.html

http://www.nytimes.com/2011/05/02/world/asia/osama-bin-laden-is-killed.html?pagewanted=all

http://www.oxfordaasc.com/public/features/archive/1008/index.jsp

http://www.robertsmalls.org/

http://www.usatoday.com/news/world/iraq/story/2011-12-15/Iraq-war/51945028/1

Kitano, Harry H. 1985. *Race Relations,* 3rd ed. Englewood Cliffs, NJ: Prentice Hall.

Parrillo, Vincent A. 1985. *Strangers to These Shores: Race and Ethnic Relations in the United States,* 2nd ed. New York: MacMillan.

Pinkney, Alphonso. 2000. *Black Americans,* 5th ed. New Jersey: Prentice Hall Publisher.

Shepard, Jon M., Narayan Persaud, and Brenda Hughes. 2009. *Sociology,* 10th ed. Thomson/Wadsworth, Publisher.

Stampp, Kenneth. 1965. *The Peculiar Institution: Slavery in the Ante-bellum South.* New York: Alfred A. Knopf, Publisher.

CHAPTER 7

Community: Geographical Location, Family, and Health

The black community has always existed in America, and the family has always been a vital institution to its existence, despite the fact that slavery ripped the black family apart. Like other aspects of society, the black community evolved as a response to historical events which led to its very unique cultural development. Within the black community's subculture, there are many positive and negative social issues, social problems, social conditions, and social dilemmas. Some of these impact the geographical locations, families, and health of black Americans and their communities. Therefore, this chapter examines the geographical locations of the black community, the families within them, and the health conditions of these families.

The black community as an independent entity literally sprang up overnight, as soon as Blacks were convinced that slavery had ended in America. At that point, most Blacks who wanted to be free simply left the fields and immediately walked off of the plantations. Many just wandered directionless into the bliss of freedom. Most had no place to go but into the thin air, yet they did just that. While others quickly tried to flee north to find family members and other loved ones. Unfortunately, many were elderly, in bad health, were suffering from starvation, and had no other choice but to return to their ex-slave masters for mere survival. Whites knew this and certainly took advantage of their precarious situation and condition (Franklin 1965; Bennett 1969; *Ebony* 1971; Pinkney 2000).

THE BLACK COMMUNITY AND GEOGRAPHICAL LOCATION

The first "black flight" occurred when Blacks fled the slave plantations, gladly leaving their "homes" on "the quarters." Recall from Chapter 2 that field hands and other slaves lived in small, dismal, often windowless, leaky cabins that had just the basics such as a stove and which seemed little more than a "dog" house. Often slaves slept on the cold, sometimes muddy dirt floors. These cabins were near the big house and were referred to as slave quarters or "the quarters" (Stampp 1965; *Ebony* 1971). So, they obviously did not leave much of a "home" anyway, and they could sleep on the cold ground on their own.

Though barely out of institutionalized slavery, the majority of Blacks were understandably impoverished. Unfortunately, this poverty would haunt them for many years to come. Plus, land reform plans (i.e., 40 acres and a mule) were never carried out, and most former field laborers became sharecroppers (Franklin 1965; Bennett 1969; *Ebony* 1971; Curran and Renzetti 1987; Hraba 1979; Kitano 1985; Parrillo 1985; Feagin 1989; Pinkney 2000), which was merely advanced slavery.

Moreover, ever since the Civil War, Blacks began leaving the South as fast as they could, often not realizing or knowing where they would end up. Blacks in rural areas moved to cities, Blacks in the South moved to the North, and many Blacks even moved to countries in Africa. In the 1870s, some went to the Southwest and others went on to the West. For instance, Oklahoma was a place in the Southwest where Blacks wanted to establish a nationalist, separate state and in 1891, the all-black town of Langston, Oklahoma, was established (*Ebony* 1971). Further, the Midwest, despite its cold climate, became very attractive to Blacks. For example, about 50,000 Blacks left the South and settled in Kansas. As well, some went on to Iowa, where a black utopia, Buxton existed (Gray 1984). Moreover, in 1895, about 197 Blacks boarded a ship in Savannah, Georgia, and went to the African country of Liberia (*Ebony* 1971).

By the early 1900s, approximately 90% of all Blacks still resided in the South. About 75% were living in rural areas under extreme oppressive and impoverished conditions. However, between 1916 and 1918, it is estimated that between a half million to 2 million Blacks left the South in what is commonly called the "Great Migration." Most of them migrated from Mississippi, Alabama, Georgia, and the Carolinas, and settled mostly in Michigan, New York, Pennsylvania, Ohio, and Illinois. These migrations escalated in response to better economic opportunities in the North and legally enforced racial discrimination in the South (Franklin 1965; Bennett 1969; *Ebony* 1971; Turner, Singleton, and Musick 1984; Hraba 1979; Kitano 1985; Parrillo 1985; Feagin 1989; Pinkney 2000).

Despite the overt racism in the South, over time the North became far more racially segregated. In fact, today in 2012, the Northeast and the Midwest are the most racially segregated regions in the country. When Blacks migrated to the North, they remained in close proximity to each other in the cities, thereby creating the black urban north and the black urban ghettos. When the Second Great Migration occurred between

1940 and 1970, more than 5 million Blacks left the South and headed north and west. They went to the large urban cities and stayed in communities that were vacated by white flight. As Blacks moved in the new neighborhoods, Whites moved further and further away. Whites tried to avoid living around Blacks so that their property value would not drop and so that they would not be forced to integrate with them (http://www.blackdemographics.com/citiesstates.html).

This racial segregation in neighborhoods was realized through a number of different ways including governmental policy, zoning, redlining, blockbusting, and blatant racist tactics. Thus housing discrimination has always been a serious social problem for Blacks in America. For example, in the beginning the Federal Housing Administration (FHA) implemented discriminatory policies. They were in favor of racially segregated neighborhoods and discouraged the approval of housing loans to those not in racially segregated areas of communities. Residential zoning was also used to separate the races by exclusively restricting the entrance of certain racial groups into a particular neighborhood, and to further determine where certain racial groups will be contained (Blackwell 1991; http://www.blackdemographics.com/citiesstates.html).

Redlining was also used, which literally involved red lines drawn on a map that indicated where enclaves of blacks were located in an area of town, and then banks would deny loans to Blacks or charge higher fees for loans and other banking services. When redlining was the practice of the day, it was used excessively to discriminate against inner city blacks.

Blockbusting was another tactic used by white realtors, which made Blacks and Whites victims. It involved scaring and encouraging Whites to sell their homes at a loss just to get out of the neighborhood quickly since Blacks were rapidly moving in, which meant that white property values would quickly depreciate. Once the Whites bought into this scheme and moved away, prices were raised on the properties and then sold to Blacks at enormous prices, ridiculous interest rates, and other pathetic pitfalls. The realtors made a profit of course from both Blacks and Whites (Blackwell 1991; http://www.blackdemographics.com/citiesstates.html).

Finally, when all else failed, Whites resorted to racist acts of violence against Blacks to keep them out of their neighborhoods. This violence was nationwide and from coast to coast. It could include anything from racist threats and graffiti to cross burnings on the lawns of Blacks, to physical and violent attacks on Blacks. This violence, coupled with little police protection forced many Blacks to leave neighborhoods where they were unwanted. Nonetheless, this type of violence saw an increase in the 1980s and is still present in some neighborhoods even in 2012 (Blackwell 1991; http://www.blackdemographics.com/citiesstates.html).

Nonetheless, America has still found a way to remain segregated, whether on a volunteer basis or not. For instance, Detroit, Michigan, is the nation's most segregated metropolitan area. Blacks comprise almost 90% of the city's population but more than 95% of the suburbs are white. Other highly segregated metro cities include Gary, Indiana; Milwaukee, Wisconsin; Chicago, Illinois; Cleveland, Ohio; Buffalo, New York; Newark, New Jersey; New York, New York; Cincinnati, Ohio; and St. Louis, Missouri. These cities also have a significant black population (http://www.blackdemgraphics.com/citiesstates.html).

States with significant black populations include California, Illinois, and New York. New York still has the largest number of Blacks in the country with roughly three million. However, southern states like Florida, Georgia, and Texas each has almost 3 million Blacks. As well, a little more than half of the population in Washington, DC, is black (51%). Other states with high percentages of Blacks include Mississippi (37%), Louisiana (32%), Maryland (30%), South Carolina (28%), Alabama (27%), North Carolina (22%), and Virginia (20%) (http://www.blackdemographics.com/citiesstates.html).

Interestingly, after the Second Great Migration in 1970, 47% of Blacks lived outside of the South. Further, more than 80% lived in urban areas regardless of the geographical location. Ironically, by the 1970s is when a reverse migration took place among Blacks, and they began to move back to the "New South" in great numbers. In general, their return simply followed the same routes that their predecessors took when they first migrated north during the first migration. Those Blacks who left the eastern areas such as New York City went back to the Carolinas; those leaving places like Cleveland, Ohio, and Detroit, Michigan, went back to Alabama and Georgia; those leaving Chicago, Illinois, and St. Louis, Missouri, went back to Mississippi and Tennessee; and those leaving Los Angeles, California, went to Texas. As a result, the South has seen a significant increase in its black population. As of 2010, more than half of all Blacks resided in the South (http://www.blackdemographics.com/citiesstates.html).

THE BLACK FAMILY

Without a doubt, slavery victimized the black family by ripping apart husbands, wives, and children. Some families were destroyed during the capturing and kidnapping of slaves, even before Blacks were brought to America. Having been stripped of their African culture, including their names, Blacks had no real identities, other than the forced names of their masters, which many have kept to this day. Once in America, slaves could not legally marry and, therefore, their families were not recognized as a traditional family structure (Stampp 1965; *Ebony* 1971). In spite of this, many slaves still performed their own marriage ceremonies by "jumping the broom." Jumping the broom was an African ceremony that was practiced by Blacks during slavery when marriages among slaves were not legal. The broom straws symbolize the family; the handle of the broom symbolizes the Almighty, and the ribbon symbolizes the tie that binds the couple in marriage (http://www.african-weddings.com/jumping_the_broom).

Perhaps the most devastating destruction of the black family though, resulted from the tearing apart of slave families right before their eyes. The heartless and ruthless masters did not care about preserving slave families. Mothers begged and cried mercilessly as their children were sold away from them, never to be seen again. Husbands also watched brokenheartedly as their wives were sold away from them. Many times this was done on the spur-of-the-moment and without any warning

(Stampp 1965; Andrews and Gates 1999; Sirimarco 2007).

Therefore, it is clear that the black family structure has always differed from the white family structure in the United States, beginning with slavery. It is evident that the black single-parent family structure was first created by Whites and forced upon Blacks in society, since Whites routinely and constantly broke up black families by separating fathers, mothers, and children (Stampp 1965). During slavery this was the norm for Blacks as far as Whites were concerned. Yet, today, Whites are now concerned that this is a deviant family structure based solely on the black subculture and its "deviant" ways (Blackwell 1991). Whites see themselves as having no part of this creation, yet it was the white social structure that created and condoned black single-parent families since the dawning of time when slaves first touched the American soil.

Despite slavery's victimization of the black family, Blacks were always concerned about their families and tried as hard as they could to keep their beloved families intact. In fact, after slavery ended, many Blacks were able to find and reconnect with their families, forming strong, intact, two-parent families in the black community. As a result, the black family structure was and still is composed of single and two-parent families, as well as strong extended families. However, during the 1980s and into the 1990s, the black family was said to be in crisis and was predicted to vanish (*Ebony* 1986).

Although the single-parent, female-headed household is now the most common family structure in the black community (Shepard et al. 2009), this is not to say that two-parent families have vanished. In fact, the black family did not vanish but has undergone a structural transition. Further, a family does not necessarily have to be composed of two white parents, two white children, and have a white picket fence around the yard. Instead, it may also consist of one black mother, two or more black children, and no fence around the yard. The black father may not be present in the home, but it is usually for structural rather than cultural reasons. Just because he is not in the home does not necessarily mean that his family does not exist (*Ebony* 1986).

By the early 2000s, 62% of all black families were headed by a single parent, and most of these were female-headed families (Shepard et al. 2009). This increase in single-parent, female-headed households is directly related to the increase in divorces, parent separations, or those who have never married. Whatever the reason, children usually remain with the mother. These children are more likely to live in poverty than children living in two-parent families (Shepard et al. 2009).

Poverty in the black community has always been an extremely harsh reality in society. From the onset of slavery and right up to the present, this impoverished condition has plagued the black community all over the country. Although poverty has improved among Blacks, the rates are still high relative to their numbers in the total population (about 15%). In 2009, the poverty rate for Blacks was 26%. When examining the rates within the race, 41% of female-headed families with children are impoverished, as compared to only 7% of two-parent families (http://www.blackdemographics.com/housing_poverty.html).

Further, poverty has a dismal impact upon housing in the black community. It is a challenge for many working-class and lower-class Blacks to get housing that they can afford. A lot of Blacks rent their housing, more than half, and of that number 53% spend a sizable amount (30%) of their incomes on rentals. This becomes a struggle for many Blacks who spend a lot of their income for rental housing, and then can barely make it from paycheck to paycheck (http://www.blackdemographics.com/housing_poverty.html).

To make matters worse in the black community, other structural conditions disguised as black cultural norms impact the black family. Many feel that issues in the black community are impacted by cultural conditions, when in fact they are structural issues impacting upon cultural conditions. For example, black men have been granted a cold life in America. From slavery to present, black men have been oppressed, disrespected, and feared at the same time. They have also been rendered powerless from the time of their arrival in America. Indeed, they have had to endure some of the most degrading experiences associated with being a man. For instance, having to endure the pain of knowing and seeing female slaves physically, mentally, and sexually abused by white slave owners, yet there was nothing they could do to protect their mothers, wives, sisters, or daughters from this abuse. This oppression has angered and frustrated black men throughout the years, but they have been socialized in America to internalize these emotions (*Ebony* 1986).

Black men are not born "as the lowest on society's value scale," but they quickly learn from society that they are not "valued," and many of them face this lesson in society's institutions. They have been treated as less than men as they witnessed slavery ripping them apart from their families at the white man's discretion. Throughout the years, and even today, they are still being ripped apart from their families at the Government's discretion. For example, the Government's Welfare System in America is a double-edged sword in terms of the black family. Though intended to help the black family survive, the Welfare System is simultaneously destroying the black family by the way it is structured. This structure has been partially responsible for forcing black men to leave their families. The system latently punishes some two-parent families. For instance, in order for some two-parent families to receive certain types of aid, one of the parents must be disabled. Unfortunately, this and other Welfare policies and guidelines force the fathers to walk away so that mothers can receive the federal aid needed to support the remaining members of the family (*Ebony* 1986).

Simultaneously, as black men are being forced out of their homes by the government, they are faced with extreme unemployment. Since society's norms dictate that men are responsible for supporting their families, this expectation places a lot of stress on black men who cannot live up to these expectations. The inability to financially support their families often frustrates and causes black men to lose their self-esteem, and as a result serves as a reason why many black men never marry in the first place. When they are unable to support their families, many are overwhelmed by feelings of worthlessness and they feel useless to their families. They may even blame their families for their misfortune in society. Then they often seek refuge in other ills of society such as drugs, crime, and even domestic abuse. Some might even seek religion as a last resort to their oppression. Yet, some black men, as a result of the other ills they encounter, may find a long-term or permanent home in another government institution—prison (*Ebony* 1986).

On the other hand, some black men care deeply about their families, especially their children and often use their children as a boost to their egos and self-esteem. Some even believe that the number of children they have is somehow a testament to their manhood. Thus, sex is often the only thing that some oppressed people use to feel good about themselves. Sometimes, sex leads to fathering children and the cycle continues. Nonetheless, if fathers take their children seriously, children can be used as a great boost to their self-esteem. Especially for those who cannot contribute to the financial stability of their children's lives, they can at least contribute to the nurturing of them. They can give the babies a bottle, change their diapers, or take them for a walk in the fresh air. At the same time, it would not hurt to tell the babies and the children that "he" loves them (*Ebony* 1986).

Sadly, the grim reality is that some black fathers, for whatever reason, some of which they have no control, either walk away from their homes and families, are forced to walk away from them due to welfare laws, or never had any intentions of being a part of the family in the first place. Unfortunately, when the father leaves, this without a doubt contributes to the weakening of the strong black family. Without him in the home, some of the paternal nurturing values are not transmitted to the children. Despite the reason for black fathers leaving, it is their children who suffer. Children often model behavior of their parents, who are their first teachers, and can learn about gender relationships and responsibilities from observing their parents. If the father is not around, regardless of the reason, children can internalize his absence as the norm, and in the future are likely to behave and conform to the same way that their parents did (*Ebony* 1986).

When black men walk away from their families because of low self-esteem, poverty, unemployment, government laws, or when they refuse to accept fatherhood responsibilities, this places an enormous demand and a tough burden with a bitter pill to swallow upon black women. The black family suffers a tremendous blow when black men turn their backs on their women and children and walk away from them. The black women must become both mother and father to their children, a role that they have played since the beginning of slavery in America (*Ebony* 1986).

Indeed, black women are some of the strongest women and best jugglers in the world. They have been responsible for being the head of the black family and raising everybody's children; theirs, those of other slaves, and those of the slave masters for at least 300 years in America. Though they have been successful at this function, it has left them with a tremendous responsibility and an incredible condition to endure. Although slave women were forced to have children by the slave masters, were bred with other slave men and had their children, slave women were not allowed to have husbands (Staples 1986). Unfortunately, this situation did not end with slavery (Rodgers-Rose 1980), but continued throughout history and even today in 2012 black women are still taking care of children and many still do not have husbands.

Over the years, black women have been less likely to marry than any other women in America. Although many contribute this issue to black men now marrying white women, this is, however, not the case on a large scale. Only about 10% of black men marry women of other races. Still, this is more than twice as many black men as compared to black women, with about 4% marrying outside of their race (http://www .blackdemographics.com/housing_poverty.html).

Yet, through the years black women have had more contact with the white world than black men. In fact, black women have been more accepted and appreciated by Whites than black men, particularly those who have served as "mammies" and nurses for Whites. Many black women have literally raised the white children that they took care of over the years, from slavery until the present. Some have even lived in the homes of Whites to take care of them and their children. Some became like family, and were seen as more than "the help." Sadly some black women had to take care of white children all day while their own children were

being taken care of by someone else. This was done, however, not by choice but by necessity, in order to make ends meet for their own families. As a result, more doors, although mostly back doors have been opened for them than for black men. Whites feel more at ease and less threatened with black women than they do with black men (Bernard 1966).

Nonetheless, structural conditions still play a major role in the life chances of black females (*Ebony* 1986). In the United States' society, low education leads to low level occupations, which then leads to low income. Indeed, black women face double jeopardy in terms of race and gender, garnering two strikes; triple jeopardy when uneducated is thrown into the equation, yielding a strikeout. But the game is not over yet, still others are faced with a fourth jeopardy with discrimination in the job market. The game must now add a new strike in order to accommodate the misfortune that confronts some black women in America.

Further, black women do not receive equal pay for equal work and many are given the dead end jobs with no chance of promotion. To some, it is better to stay at home and get government benefits than working for pennies, although many black women prefer to work. In reality, black women do not fare a whole lot better than black men in the job market, given the evils that confront them. For instance, black mothers are confronted with both racism and sexism in the job market while simultaneously taking care of a family, many times alone. For those who are educated, too, many are suffocating with loneliness and unhappiness as they continue to battle the social structure for higher paying occupations. Some are so busy dealing with that aspect of their lives that they end up spending most of their younger years chasing the American Dream. Many often miss out on the opportunity to have children and then find themselves at the midnight hour of the childbearing clock. Unfortunately, many end up alone without children and without husbands (*Ebony* 1986).

On the other hand, many black women do have children and are excellent mothers. They may have to be "every woman," but that comes naturally since they have been functioning in that role for hundreds of years (Rodgers-Rose 1980). Some highly educated women are opting to have children at an older age, even in their forties, and some are opting to not have children at all. Some simply prefer their careers to children. Regardless of their preferences, generations of black mothers and fathers have worked hard to provide opportunities for their children that were denied to them. Unfortunately, a lot of black children are raised without knowing their fathers, let alone their fathers' occupations (*Ebony* 1986).

However, many black children are faced with insurmountable obstacles that block their opportunities for success. Many are constantly being born into poverty-stricken families and neighborhoods, attending the poorest schools, and have no vision for the future (*Ebony* 1986). Every day young black teenage girls and younger girls are abandoned by their mothers, ignored or forgotten about by their fathers, miseducated by their teachers, discounted among the politicians, and abused by insensitive males who get them pregnant and leave them. Too often they are just babies themselves and know very little about babies, let alone being mothers. They confront a rude awakening when they realize what it is like to be a black mother in America (*Ebony* 1986).

Nonetheless, society has tended to place all of the blame for the problems of black children and youth on the "dysfunctional" black family structure, specifically female-headed families. However, there is no consistent evidence that suggests that female-headed families produce wayward, delinquent, or uneducable children. Just because a single mother has to work, and sometimes works more than one job to support her family, does not necessarily mean she rejects, neglects, or abuses her children. Indeed, the quality of time spent with her children may be far more important than the quantity of time spent with children. There are some two-parent families that do not have much time to spend with their children either, due to their careers. Many times babysitters, many who are unrelated to the families, spend the bulk of the time with these children while the parents are both busy with their own careers (Gray-Ray and Ray 1990).

In addition, the extended family is the backbone of the black community and ensures the survival of the black family (Hill 1972). For instance, black single mothers depend on extended family members such as their mothers, sisters, nieces, aunts, as well as some of the males in the family to assist them with providing free or inexpensive child care. Many also depend on fictive kin (those who are just like family and often consider themselves as family, like a real good friend or neighbor) to assist with caring for black children. However, both single and married middle-class black mothers also are heavily involved in the extended family network including child care, financial assistance, and emotional support (Harriette McAdoo 1978; Rodgers-Rose 1980).

As well, perhaps the biggest support system in the black community is grandparents. They play a very significant and highly respected role in the lives of black children (Allen 1985). Many black children live with their grandparents, and sometimes their parents also live there as well. It is not uncommon for multigenerational family structures to exist in the black community. Many grandchildren are absorbed into the grandparents' households. In fact, grandmothers have the highest rate of absorption of black children (Heiss 1975; Hill 1972). Grandmothers are extremely important to black children and are affectionately known as "Big Mama." Black children enjoy going to "Big Mama's" house, especially on Sundays.

Moreover, black families differ in the types of discipline they administer to their children. Black middle-class parents are less likely to use physical punishment and more likely to use verbal punishment than are black working-class parents. Hence, working-class parents are often criticized for being ineffective parents for using physical punishment with their children. However, many black working-class parents frequently combine spankings with emotional nurturance, as evidenced in the old saying that "it will hurt them more than it will hurt the child," to have to spank their children (*Ebony* 1986).

This combination of spankings and affection may be more effective than the strategies used by middle-class black families such as threatening to withdraw love or some material object to control the child. It is often observed how well-behaved, and emotionally healthy working-class black children are as compared to black middle-class children. In fact, black male youth usually place mothers and grandmothers at the utmost spot in their lives, and would do anything to protect them, especially if they are single parents. Many young men feel that they must take on the father role of protection since there is no father in the home (*Ebony* 1986).

HEALTH IN THE BLACK COMMUNITY

The extended black family, fictive kin, and multigenerational support have always been staples in health care in the black community (Johnson & Barer 1990) from slavery until the present. During slavery, Blacks had no access to health care and had to depend upon themselves for medical treatments and homemade remedies. Although it was in the best interest of the slave masters to protect their "property" (slaves), many did not take the health care of Blacks seriously. In fact, many slave owners manumitted, or freed their elderly slaves, to avoid having to take care of them until death (Genovese 1974). Many slave owners simply left them to defend for themselves in hopes that they would die. However, since the elderly are highly respected among members of the black community, other slaves would often do what they could to assist the elderly with health issues; usually with some type of roots or herbal remedy.

Slaves depended upon the help and services of root doctors to help with their healing needs. Today, some members of the black community still depend upon root doctors to assist with health and a variety of other needs such as fighting evil spirits or to change a person's luck. The roots could take the form of a doll, colorful stoness or simply be roots of plants. A root's color had meaning as well: red caused evilness to someone, blue fought evil and helped save love relationships, and black roots meant death (www.stanford.edu/group/ethnoger/african.html). Some Blacks also believe in faith healing for treating illnesses, such as prayers and laying hands on individuals (Mitchell 1978).

Nonetheless, slave owners would do what they could to get the most economical benefit from every slave. If the slave could not be insured, or if the slave's life was less than the insurance on the slave, then often the slave was left defenseless and left to wither in old age. Other times, if the older slaves stood a possibility of being sold or traded, they were "doctored up" to look younger and the slave owner would then lie about the age of the slave in order to make a profit on the sale (www.stanford.edu/group/ethnoger/african.html).

Legally, slave owners had to provide food for the slaves or they could be fined and the slaves would be sold. However, this rarely occurred since slaves had no legal rights. Slaves received unhealthy and poor nutritional food rations once a week such as salt pork, a few pounds of bacon, and some corn (Stampp 1965; *Ebony* 1971). Today in 2012, the diet of some African Americans is still unhealthy, and has led to health conditions such as obesity. Although the nation is experiencing a crisis with obesity, this crisis has a greater impact in the black community. Black women have the highest obesity rates in the country, with 79% of them being overweight or obese. As well, black men also have a high rate of obesity at 72% (http://www.blackdemographics.com/health.html).

Sadly, the black culture promotes unhealthy eating habits as seen in the way Blacks prepare their food which tends to be fried, rich, salty, full of fatty calories, but awesomely delicious, such as macaroni and cheese and collard greens cooked with salt pork, just as in slavery. The black diet is more commonly referred to as "soul food." Another problem is the convenience of fast food restaurants found within the wider society. These eating habits are a direct contributor to many other health issues in the black community. The Centers for Disease Control and Prevention has documented that obesity is a chronic disease (http://www.blackdemographics.com/health.html).

Other health issues in the black community include hypertension, more commonly known as high blood pressure. Like obesity, Blacks have the highest rates of hypertension in the country. Statistically, about 21% of black men and 44% of black women have hypertension. Some of this can be contributed to the soul food diet, but stress is another major contributor to high blood pressure. Many Blacks experience a tremendous amount of stress in their everyday lives just dealing with social, economical, and environmental issues that are present on a daily basis in their neighborhoods. A lot of this stress is dealt with through smoking cigarettes, which is another horrible condition found among Blacks. Although over the years cigarette smoking has been on the decline among black males since 1974, still 26% of them continue to smoke, and they tend to smoke more than white men, white women, and black women (http://www.blackdemographics.com/health.html).

Another frightening health concern that is ravaging through the black community is HIV and full-blown AIDS. In the beginning most associated HIV and AIDS with being gay or homosexual, and using infected drug needles. However, more Blacks are also getting the virus through heterosexual contact. A lot of the blame for this has been placed on men on the "down-low," who pretend to live straight lives with wives and children, but engage in sexual activities with other men. As well, many black men leaving prisons and re-entering their communities may contribute to this AIDS epidemic, since many of them may have engaged in homosexuality while in prison. Unfortunately, unprotected sex is still a huge problem in the black community among the young and the old alike (http://www.blackdemographics.com/health.html).

In addition, black men's health is also impacted by their environments, life chances, and lifestyles. In their later years, they are least likely to benefit from retirement and social security payouts, although they may have contributed to both while they were employed. Even more frightening is the life expectancy rate for black men, who are least likely to live beyond the age of 70. In fact, the average black man dies earlier than age 70. This statistic is compounded by their high rates of homicides and death due to HIV and AIDS (http://www.blackdemographics.com/health.html).

Although most Blacks are able to maintain good mental health, many still take it for granted in the black community (http://www.stanford.edu/group/ethnoger/african.html). Many Blacks underestimate the seriousness of mental illness and may write off such serious mental disorders like depression as "just the blues," or "down on their luck." Blacks are less likely to seek medical treatment for mental illness and often rely on prayer as a way to cope with stress. Many feel that they will be labeled a nut or wacko if the community knew that they got mental health treatments. Therefore, many mentally ill individuals freely roam around the neighborhood and interact with others with the understanding by others that these individuals are "crazy." Some may even terrorize their communities forcing people to be afraid for their own lives, not knowing when they may come into contact with the mentally ill person, or when the person is "not in their right mind."

Mental illness has been a serious, overlooked aspect of health care in the black community by both Whites and Blacks. Psychiatrists used to think that black Americans as a race did not have high rates of depression because of their oppressed condition in society, which served as a buffer against depression. It was thought that depression was not a factor for Blacks since they did not have much to lose and therefore did not have to be depressed about anything (Prange & Vitols 1962). These prejudicial notions about Blacks often led to the inaccurate diagnoses of depression and other mental illnesses that they may have had (Adebimpe 1981; Poussaint 1983; Williams 1986; http://www.stanford.edu/group/ethnoger/african.html).

Nonetheless, poverty and other stressful conditions impact the mental health of Blacks which can result in serious psychological problems. Many are in serious need of mental health treatment, especially those with schizophrenia who might get misdiagnosed with something else, because it could be mistaken for some other emotional distress. For those Blacks who do get treatment, they are more likely to discontinue their treatment and less likely to follow-up with their doctors. As well, even though substance use is lower among Blacks than Whites, alcohol and drugs kill more Blacks than any other disease or illness in the country. Further, the suicide rate for Blacks is lower than that for Whites. In 2005, the suicide rate for black men was five times that of black women (http://healthyminds.org/More-Info-For/African-Americans.aspx).

Moreover, the death rate for Blacks is related to the conditions found in the black subculture, such as inadequate or no health care insurance. Many Blacks do not have access to health insurance or health care. This results in less access to preventive health care as well as mental health care, which many insurance plans do not cover or slightly cover, leaving Blacks more vulnerable to diseases and illnesses such as cancer, of which they are more likely to die. The main causes of death among black Americans in 2007 in ascending order were heart disease, cancer, stroke, diabetes, unintentional injuries, homicide, chronic lower respiratory diseases, kidney disease, HIV disease, and Septicemia which is a serious blood infection (http://www.blackdemographics.com/health.html).

Nonetheless, when facing the inevitability of death, some Blacks still have a very hard time in letting go of loved ones. They would prefer to keep their loved ones as long as possible regardless of their health conditions. Many will remain in the hospital rooms around the clock switching out with other family members to make sure their loved ones are comforted and protected until the very last breath is taken. They often believe that only God knows when he will call their loved ones to Glory, and they will not allow the medical staff to pull the plug. Some may not even want to let their loved ones know what the medical diagnosis is for fear that the news might make them give up on life and meet an early death. Indeed, Blacks are less likely to complete a living will with an advance directive of what to do in the case of terminal illness (Mouton 2000). When the doctors give up on a family's loved one, and the family is allowed to decide to take their loved ones home to die, many often choose that option. Up until the late 1990s, most black elders stayed in their homes or in the homes of their children instead of being sent to a nursing home to die (www.stanford.edu/group/ethnoger/african.html).

Clearly the black community has more than its share of social issues, social conditions, social problems, and social dilemmas. While this chapter only touched on a few of them, with the major focus on the working class segment, the next chapter will focus on social class with emphasis on the black middle class. Education and employment will be the main point of focus to further the discussion on imagining and understanding the African American Experience.

Significant Facts Impacting African Americans

(Potter and Claytor 1994)

- Dr. David J. Peck was the first Black American to earn a medical degree in the country.

- Dr. Rebecca Lee Crumpler was the first black female to earn a medical degree.

- Dr. Ida Gray was the first black female dentist in the United States.

- Dr. Daniel Hale Williams was the first physician to perform open heart surgery in America.

- Dr. Charles R. Drew was the first to preserve blood and blood plasma in the country.

- Dr. Alexa Canady was the first black female neurosurgeon in America.

- Dr. Benjamin S. Carson was the first neurosurgeon to separate Siamese twins.

- Dr. Joycelyn Elders was the nation's first Black Surgeon General.

- Dr. Regina Benjamin became the nation's Surgeon General under President Barack Obama.

BLACK MEDICAL OPPRESSION: THE TUSKEGEE SYPHILIS EXPERIMENT "BAD BLOOD OR BAD RESEARCH"

The Tuskegee Experiment at Tuskegee Institute in Tuskegee, Alabama, was perhaps the worst dehumanizing, unethical, and racist medical research in the country. This despicable experiment began in 1932 and was only supposed to last for six months, but lasted for forty years, ending in 1972. For four decades poor black men, mostly illiterate sharecroppers in Alabama, were involved in a research experiment, which literally had intentions of watching them die (Jones 1993)! The study involved 600 men, 399 were infected with Syphilis and 201 were not (http://www.cdc.gov/tuskegee/timeline.htm). The study itself was never designed to treat the infected men, rather its purpose was to trace the etiology of the disease to determine how it affected Blacks. Sadly, the men were never told they had Syphilis or what the disease would do to them. Instead they were told they had bad blood. They were never given proper healthcare, only aspirin in the beginning. They were told and led to believe that they were patients in a government study of "bad blood," and that they would receive free medical exams, free meals, and "burial insurance," for participating. Little did they know the real reason for the ironic burial insurance was their own ultimate death. In 1947, even after Penicillin was proven to be effective for treating Syphilis, the unethical researchers still did not administer the drug to the men. Dreadfully, the men had Syphilis for decades, which is a horrible disease caused by a bacteria that is sexually transmitted. Pregnant mothers who are infected can pass the bacteria to their babies which can lead to skin and organ problems in babies, or even result in stillborn deaths. If left untreated in adults, it can lead to serious medical conditions including blindness, skin sores and rashes, organ failures, and even death (www.cdc.gov) which was the ultimate goal of the study. For years, unethical researchers watched men suffer, infect their families, deteriorate, and die from Syphilis. Finally in 1968 a whistle-blower, Dr. Peter Buxtun raised concerns about the unethical study and in 1972 the study finally ended. In 1973, a class action lawsuit was filed on behalf of the study participants, which resulted in a $10 million out-of-court settlement, lifetime medical benefits, and burial services for those who were still alive in 1974. A year later, family members were added to the program's settlement. In 1997, President Bill Clinton issued a national apology for the unethical medical experiment. In 2004, the CDC funded a $10 million cooperative agreement with Tuskegee University National Center for Bioethics in Research and Health Care. Sadly, on January 27, 2009, the last surviving widow died (http://www.cdc.gov/tuskegee/timeline.htm).

DISCUSSION QUESTIONS

1. How can the black family be strengthened?

2. How can the black community be strengthened?

3. Should the Government provide universal health care for impoverished minorities?

4. What can black men and black women do to reduce the tension between them?

5. How can black children be saved from a life of poverty?

6. Why do older Blacks not trust medical research experiments?

7. How does the government contribute to the creation of single-parent families?

8. What is meant by "soul food" in the black community?

9. How can Blacks improve their health?

10. What has caused black men to be so frustrated in America today?

ACTIVITIES/FIELD EXPERIENCES

1. Imagine what it would be like if all Blacks left the South; record your thoughts.

2. Why do Blacks continue to live in the South?

3. Compare and contrast the life chances and lifestyles for Blacks in the North and the South.

4. Research and construct your Family Tree as far as you can go.

TEN THOUGHTS ACTIVITY

1. List 10 thoughts on what comes to mind when you think of black men.

   _____

   _____

   _____

   _____

   _____

   _____

   _____

   _____

   _____

   _____

2. List 10 thoughts on what comes to mind when you think of black women.

   _____

   _____

   _____

   _____

   _____

   _____

   _____

   _____

   _____

   _____

3. List 10 thoughts on what comes to mind when you think of black children.

_____

_____

_____

_____

_____

_____

_____

_____

_____

_____

SUGGESTED RESOURCES

A Common Destiny: Blacks and the American Society. 1989. National Academy Press.

http://www.ahrq.gov/research/disparit.htm for research on racial disparities in health care.

http://www.scholarworks.umass.edu/cibs/vol3/iss1/2/ for research on the black family.

Wesley, Nathaniel. 2010. *Black Hospitals in America.* Tallahassee, FL: NRW Associates Publications.

REFERENCES

Adebimpe, V. R. 1981. "Overview: White norms and psychiatric diagnosis of black patients." *American Journal of Psychiatry,* 138(3), 279–85.

Allen, Walter R. 1985. *Beginnings: The Social and Affective Development of Black Children.* Hillsdale: Lawrence Erlbaum Associates.

Andrews, William L., and Henry Luis Gates, Jr., eds. 1999. *The Civitas Anthology of African American Slave Narratives.* Washington, DC: Civitas Counterpoint, Publisher.

Bennett, Lerone, Jr. 1969. *Before the Mayflower: A History of Black America.* Chicago: Johnson Publishing Company, Inc.

Bernard, Jessie. 1966. *Marriage and Family Among Negroes.* New Jersey: Prentice Hall.

Blackwell, James E. 1991. *The Black Community Diversity and Unity,* 3rd ed. New York: Harper Collins, Publisher.

Curran, Daniel J., and Claire M. Renzetti. 1987. *Social Problems: Society in Crisis.* Boston: Allyn and Bacon.

Ebony. 1986. "Black Love and The Extended Family Concept Should Be Priorities." (August) 158–59.

Ebony Pictorial History of Black America, Volume 1. 1971. Nashville, TN: The Southwestern Company.

Feagin, Joe R. 1989. *Racial and Ethnic Relations,* 3rd ed. Englewood Cliffs, NJ: Prentice Hall.

Franklin, John Hope. 1965. *From Slavery to Freedom,* 2nd ed. New York: Alfred A. Knopf.

Genovese, E. D. 1974. *Roll Jordan Roll: The World the Slaves Made.* New York: Pantheon Books.

Gray, Phyllis. 1984. *Buxton, Iowa: A Black Utopia in the Midwest.* Unpublished Masters Thesis. Iowa State University, Ames, Iowa.

Gray-Ray, Phyllis, and Melvin C. Ray. 1990. "Juvenile Delinquency in the Black Community." Youth and Society 22(1):67–84.

Heiss, Jerold. 1975. *The Case of the Black Family: A Sociological Inquiry.* New York: Columbia University Press.

Hill, Robert B. 1972. *The Strengths of Black Families.* New York: Emerson Hall.

Hraba, Joseph. 1979. *American Ethnicity*. Itasca, IL: F. E. Peacock.

http://www.african-weddings.com/jumping_the_broom

http://www.blackdemographics.com/citiesstates.html

http://www.blackdemographics.com/health.html

http://www.blackdemographics.com/housing_poverty.html

http://www.cdc.gov/Tuskegee/timeline.htm

http://www.healthyminds.org/More-Info-For/African-Americans.aspx

http://www.stanford.edu/group/ethnoger/african.html

Johnson, C. L., & Barer, B. M. 1990. "Families and networks among older inner-city blacks." Gerontologist, 30(6), 726–33.

Jones, James. 1993. *Bad Blood: The Tuskegee Syphilis Experiment*. New York: The Free Press.

Kitano, Harry H. 1985. *Race Relations*, 3rd ed. Englewood Cliffs, NJ: Prentice Hall.

McAdoo, Harriette Pipes. 1978. "The Impact of Upward Mobility of Kin-Help Patterns and the Reciprocal Obligations in Black Families." Journal of Marriage and the Family 40:761–76.

Mitchell, F. 1978. *Hoodoo medicine: Sea Island herbal remedies*. Berkeley, CA: Reed, Cannon and Johnson.

Mouton, C. P. 2000. *Cultural and religious issues for African Americans*. In Braun, Pietsch, & Blanchette, (Eds.) *Cultural Issues in End-of-life Decision Making*. Thousand Oaks, CA: Sage.

Parrillo, Vincent A. 1985. *Strangers to These Shores: Race and Ethnic Relations in the United States*, 2nd ed. New York: MacMillan.

Pinkney, Alphonso. 2000. *Black Americans*, 5th ed., New Jersey: Prentice Hall Publisher.

Potter, Joan, and Constance Claytor. 1994. *African American Firsts*. New York: Pinto Press.

Poussaint, A. F. 1983. "The Mental Health Status of Blacks," in J. D. Williams (Ed.), *The State of Black America*. New York: National Urban League.

Prange, A. J., & Vitols, M. M. 1962. "Cultural aspects of the relatively low incidence of depression among Southern Negroes." *The International Journal of Social Psychiatry*, 8(2), 104–12.

Rodgers-Rose, La Frances. 1980. *The Black Woman*. Newbury Park, CA: Sage Publications.

Shepard, Jon M., Narayan Persaud, and Brenda Hughes. 2009. *Sociology*, 10th ed. Thomson/Wadsworth, Publisher.

Sirimarco, Elizabeth. 2007. *American Voices From The Time of Slavery*. New York: Marshall Cavendish Benchmark, Publisher.

Stampp, Kenneth. 1965. *The Peculiar Institution: Slavery in the Ante-bellum South*. New York: Alfred A. Knopf, Publisher.

Staples, Robert. 1986. *The Black Family—Essays and Studies*. California: Wadsworth Publishing Company.

Turner, Jonathan H., Joyce Singleton, Jr., and David Musick. 1984. *Oppression*. Chicago: Nelson-Hall.

Williams, D. H. 1986. "The Epidemiology of Mental Illness in Afro-Americans." *Hospital and Community Psychiatry*, 37(1), 42–49.

CHAPTER 8

Social Class, Education, and Employment

It has been shown throughout the foregoing chapters how the legacy of slavery in America has impacted nearly every aspect of the black community. This is also vividly evident in America's central social institutions such as the educational system, and in social conditions such as employment. Just as Blacks developed a burning desire to reunite black families, after the end of the Civil War, they also developed an urgent, strong sense of need to become educated, even against all odds. Without a doubt, the major handicap for most newly freed slaves was that most of them were illiterate and could not read, write, or comprehend written materials, since they were forbidden to become educated during slavery. Whites knew this and certainly took advantage of their precarious situation and conditions. Yet, for every Black person who was lynched or burned alive, a business genius was eventually created (*Ebony* 1971).

Although slavery relegated the great masses of African Americans to the lowest rung on the social status ladder, thereby creating a caste system of seemingly "untouchables," (Hraba 1979), there was still a minute population of free Blacks who had a superior social class to slaves but an inferior social class to Whites. The very first United States Census in 1790 counted nearly 60,000 free Blacks in the nation with about 27,000 in

the South and 32,000 in the North. Maryland, Virginia, and Pennsylvania, respectively, had the largest number of free Blacks in the year right before the onset of the Civil War, in 1860 (*Ebony* 1971).

Free Blacks tended to dwell in the cities since it was there that they had the best life chances for education, employment, and thus social mobility. Regardless to where they lived though, free Blacks almost had it as tough as slaves in many states. Some states had ridiculous laws which severely limited the economic development of free Blacks. For instance in the early 1800s, somewhere between 1818 and 1830, some states, particularly the state of Georgia, made it illegal for Blacks to own real estate; to buy or sell alcoholic beverages; and free Blacks could not buy goods on credit without the permission of their white guardians (*Ebony* 1971).

Other examples of the degradation of free Blacks in America included some states chasing them out of the state once they became free. Many states also made free Blacks post bonds to ensure the state that they would not become an economic burden on the public. Free Blacks were even made to support America's institutions without being able to reap the benefits that their labor and money helped to create and support. For instance, in 1859, free Blacks in Baltimore had to pay school taxes but their children were forbidden to attend the public schools for which they paid taxes. Further, perhaps the most ridiculous laws of them all were the ones passed by some states which made it easy for Blacks to re-enslave themselves, as an alternative to bearing the burdens of being free. Sadly, it was a very difficult task for free Blacks to remain free, yet some states intentionally added to this difficulty by attempting to eliminate the free black social class in general (*Ebony* 1971).

SOCIAL CLASS

In spite of all odds against free Blacks in society, there has always been a black middle class in America, although quite different from the white middle class, yet, similar in many ways. During slavery, the black middle class was mostly those Blacks of lighter complexion, mulattos, including those who could pass for being white. Many of these Blacks were accepted by Whites and were given the better jobs than dark-skinned, free Blacks. Although light-skinned free Blacks were treated much better than dark-skinned free Blacks, they still experienced segregation from Whites, and in some cases were also shunned by other Blacks. As a result, light-skinned free Blacks created their own destiny through developing their own schools and business opportunities. As well, just like Whites, many light-skinned Blacks also discriminated against dark-skinned free Blacks. For example, it was not uncommon for some black institutions of higher learning to require that photos be submitted as part of the application for admissions packets. This, of course, was to ensure that not too many dark-skinned Blacks would be accepted (*Ebony* 1971; BlackDemographics.com).

Although the precarious black middle class existed to some extent, most were still relegated to living in the black community among the working-class and lower-class Blacks. However, after the Civil Rights and Black Power Movements, the black middle class witnessed an exponential growth. With the gradual demise of the skin tone differential, Blacks became more educated, got better paying and professional jobs, and some moved into better middle class white neighborhoods, as well as established their own middle class neighborhoods (BlackDemographics.com).

Nonetheless, many members of the black middle class, about 38% of the black population as of 2010, are still in a precarious position. Although many had incomes between $35,000 and $100,000 annually, some still lived from paycheck to paycheck. This was also the case for some working-class Blacks, but at a different income level. If some middle-class Blacks were forced to be without a paycheck for several consecutive months, many might lose their middle-class status or be forced to live beyond their means, in a state of denial that their financial situation had changed (Blackdemographics .com). Given the reality of the recession during the second decade of the twenty-first century, this denial might become a fast reality.

EDUCATION

Unfortunately, Blacks were not allowed to become educated during slavery, and as a result started out in America with a severe handicap in the literacy arena. Regrettably this handicap continues to haunt African Americans even in 2012. However, a few free Blacks were educated and some helped to educate the slaves whenever the opportunity presented itself, but the majority of the masses of Blacks were not educated. Nonetheless, some slaves secretly self-educated, or a few Whites riskily took a chance on educating them (*Ebony* 1971).

As early as the Revolutionary War period, educational opportunities for Blacks were developed. In New York, the Manumission Society started a school for a few Blacks, the African Free School in 1787. By 1820, it enrolled about 500 students. In the decade right before the Civil War, there were about one thousand Blacks in southern schools in New Orleans and over a thousand Blacks in northern schools in Baltimore, Maryland. By the time the Civil War started, there were over thirty thousand Blacks in schools nationwide. Still, getting an education in America was not always easy for Blacks. Black codes and laws in the South prohibited them from being educated. It was also difficult to get educated in other parts of the country such as the Midwest, the West, and in the North. Several states had laws which did not allow Blacks to attend the public schools, such as Ohio, Indiana, and Illinois. When they did provide separate schools, they did not adequately fund the schools for Blacks (*Ebony* 1971).

In the North, efforts to allow Blacks to be educated were also met with extreme rejection. For example, in Canterbury, Connecticut, white villagers attempted to burn a school for black females started by a white Quaker female teacher, Prudence Crandall, in 1833. Despite her conviction and successful appeal for starting a school for Blacks, Whites still continued to attack the school, which was eventually closed so that the students would not be harmed. Yet the most extreme case occurred in Canaan, New Hampshire, in 1835 when Noyes Academy opened as an integrated school. Whites first failed in an attempt to attack the school, but in retaliation, rounded up men from other villages as well as about 100 oxen which dragged the school a half mile into a swamp (*Ebony* 1971).

Despite white resistance to Blacks being educated, some Blacks attended some of the nation's top schools in higher education even before the Civil War, such as Bowdoin College in Maine. In 1826, John B. Russwurm graduated from this school, making him the first African American student to graduate from an American College. Blacks also attended Harvard, Oberlin, and other white institutions before the Civil War. At least two black institutions of higher learning were also started in the North before the Civil War; Lincoln University in Pennsylvania in 1854 and Wiberforce University in Ohio in 1856. However, before either of them, Cheyney University of Pennsylvania was founded in 1837 as the Institute for Colored Youth, making it the oldest historically black university in the United States. (*Ebony* 1971).

Immediately following the Civil War, Blacks, both young and old alike, flocked to schools in the South to receive an education. However, most Blacks still lived on farms and were sharecroppers, which meant that the children also helped on the farms. Only a few of these children were actually enrolled in school, and those who did enroll, could only attend for a short while. Of course, these schools were far from being ideal, as most were one room shacks that were grossly overcrowded, the teachers were not well educated themselves, and many were incompetent (Pinkney 2000) yet, Blacks did what they had to do to help get themselves educated. Education became the most important goal Blacks set for themselves and teachers were given the highest respect in the black community (*Ebony* 1971). Still, by the early 1900s, only a little over half of the black children between ages 6 and 14 were in school. However, by the last few decades of the 1900s, major changes had occurred for black children in the educational arena, as most of them were enrolled in school across the nation (Pinkney 2000).

Nonetheless, before the success of the overwhelming majority of black children attending school by 1990 (Pinkney, 2000), the road to educational equality was incredibly rocky, especially during the Civil Rights Movement of the 1950s and 1960s when school desegregation became the law of the land. Although the United States Supreme Court outlawed school segregation in America's public schools in the *Brown v. Board of Education* ruling in 1954, many states, especially in the South, simply ignored it or dragged their feet with enforcing it. As a result, black students continued to attend segregated, underfunded schools that were inferior to schools that white students attended. Most of the black schools had inadequate facilities and equipment, and used furniture and books that were passed down from the white schools. Those areas that were forced to comply in a timely manner pretended to do so by integrating the public schools while simultaneously creating white private schools and academies to avoid having to go to school with Blacks. Other instances were riddled and spoiled with violent outbreaks as was the case in Little Rock, Arkansas, with the integration of Central High School (*Ebony* 1971; Pinkney 2000).

Sadly, many African American students still find themselves subjected to segregated, inferior schools that are located within their own neighborhoods. Many of these schools employ uncertified teachers, and use teachers who are not qualified to teach in the areas for which they are hired. The classes are too big and some of the teachers are not concerned with the learning abilities of some of the students (Crone 2011). Unfortunately, many of these schools are found in areas outside of the South, particularly in the northern and Midwestern inner cities. Interestingly, the South has gone from having the most segregated schools to now having the most integrated schools (Pinkney 2000).

THE TALENTED TENTH AND THE MIS-EDUCATION OF THE NEGRO

Two great African American male graduates of one of the nation's most prestigious universities, Harvard University, in the early 1900s, spoke about the importance of educating "Negros" (African Americans) "the right way." These men were William Edward Burghardt (W. E. B.) Du Bois, the first black Harvard Ph.D., and Carter G. Woodson, the second black Harvard Ph.D. (*Ebony* 1971). Both scholars contributed monumental knowledge during their time and through their writings, that are still very relevant today. If some of their teachings had been rigorously applied throughout the black community, as well as throughout the nation as a whole, perhaps the outcome for Blacks in terms of education would have been a lot better a lot sooner.

First, Du Bois described the "Talented Tenth," a concept he coined in 1903, as those few Blacks who were the most educated and intelligent of the race, and who were the critical factor in uplifting the masses of Blacks in America. Further, meaning that Blacks, like any other race, were going to have to help and save themselves. He crusaded for the creation of a black college educated elite group of individuals to become leaders and teachers of the masses of Blacks, while emphasizing their heritage. The Talented Tenth idea was warmly embraced by most educated Blacks, especially those who rejected the teaching of Booker T. Washington, who encouraged Blacks to accept their inferior status and get a vocational trade (Altman 1997).

Du Bois further described racial barriers in the educational system in the United States, and particularly in the North. He stated that most Blacks could not be properly educated in white institutions and that those Blacks in the North who were admitted to them, were simply tolerated but were not educated. Instead, they were crucified. Further, Blacks on white college campuses were barely recognized in classes, in cafeterias, or even on the campus. In some of the Ivy League schools, such as Harvard and Yale, Blacks were admitted but certainly not wanted or welcomed. In fact, Princeton did not even accept black students (historyisaweapon.com).

Indeed, Blacks were being mis-educated as was described in Du Bois' statement that Blacks must know their history in America, which they seldom learned in white institutions. He further advocated that Blacks must read books by black authors and scholars and that they should study intelligently from the black point of view about issues and historical events such as slavery, Reconstruction, and economic development. Although he was not advocating for segregated schools, he did suggest a separate black school in which black students could be treated like human beings and taught by black teachers who understood the black experience in America (historyisaweapon.com).

Carter G. Woodson, known as the "Father of Black History," went on to coin the phrase and further extend the discussion of "the mis-education of the Negro." In his book of the same title, he blasted the educational system in America, and described the vicious cycle that occurs when mis-educated people graduate from schools, and then go on to teach and mis-educate others. He was mostly concerned about black children and youth who were most vulnerable to this mis-education, since it tended to begin very early in life and become deeply rooted in their minds. This then could cause deep-seated insecurities, intra-racial issues, and interracial problems (historyisaweapon.com).

Woodson was further concerned about the mis-education of black children who were not being taught the truth about their race and its contributions to American society. The fact that most history books paid little to no attention to the history and achievements of Blacks in America troubled Woodson and he set out to improve this travesty. The information that was presented about Blacks depicted them in insignificant, subordinate, and oftentimes subhuman roles. Some books even made it seem as if the Whites did Blacks a favor by bringing them from Africa and civilizing them in white America, even if nothing more than making them slaves. To Whites this was better than the heathenism of Africa. Woodson was disgusted by this brainwashing of black children, which made them to believe that they were inferior to the white race and could never be equal. It was pathetic to think of the despicable knowledge that was being taught to black children, tinting their impressionable minds for many years to come (historyisaweapon.com).

Even worse, the mis-education of black children continued to be passed down from generation to generation denying black children the real truth about their race and culture. This could do great damage to their self-esteem by making them believe that their destiny was that of "nothingness and nobodyness." It was Woodson's goal, to which he dedicated his academic career, to provide black children and youth access to true education of the historical and cultural contributions of their race. It was his hope that this real education would dispel the myths and lies provided them through the mis-education of them by Whites. He felt that the truth would instill race pride and race knowledge in the minds and souls of black children. In doing so, their self-esteems would be heightened, in knowing that they are "somebody" (historyisaweapon.com).

Mis-education of white children also occurred and to some extent, is still occurring in America. Unfortunately, they too were not taught the truth about black history and contributions to America, and thus did not have the real picture of Blacks in society. This caused them to be ignorant of black Americans, and many of them had nothing to fall back on, except stereotypes; particularly those that suggested that Blacks were inferior to Whites. Therefore, those stereotypes were ingrained in their psyches without any other means to combat this misconception. Some teachers simply did not know black history themselves, because they were never taught it, or some simply chose to disregard the topic altogether, especially the teaching of slavery. It may be concluded then, that in general, Americans, regardless of race or ethnicity, may be mis-educated.

HISTORICALLY BLACK COLLEGES AND UNIVERSITIES (HBCUS)

During the time when Whites would not allow black students to enroll in traditionally white institutions (TWIs), Blacks built their own colleges to address their educational needs. These institutions of higher learning became known as historically black colleges and universities (HBCUs). Most were established before 1964 with the sole purpose of educating Blacks in America (education.stateuniversity.com). Right after the Civil War, most of them were started to meet the demands of educating the newly freed slaves, and at the same time, to keep them out of the white institutions. The subsequent segregated, dual system of higher education was highly influenced by the *Plessy v. Ferguson* Supreme Court Decision which ruled that separate but equal schools were not unconstitutional (*Ebony* 1971). Nonetheless, this decision increased the number of HBCUs (education.stateuniversity.com).

The fact that HBCUs were never equal to traditional white schools obviously was not a concern to the U.S. Supreme Court Justices; particularly since most HBCUs had very little resources and finances of which to operate. Further, in terms of governmental funding, HBCUs were never treated as being just as important as the white schools on any dimension. Still, it was nearly 60 years before the Supreme Court reversed its earlier *Plessy v. Ferguson* decision in 1954, and ruled in the *Brown v. Board of Education* of Topeka, Kansas, case that separate and equal schools were unconstitutional (*Ebony* 1971).

With the *Brown v. Board of Education* case in 1954, which was successfully argued before the United States Supreme Court by then-attorney Thurgood Marshall, who eventually became the first black U.S. Supreme Court Justice, states were mandated to dismantle their unequal, segregated dual system of higher education. This of course was met with a lot of resistance and even violence at some schools in the South such as The University of Mississippi and The University of Alabama (*Ebony* 1971). This dismantling also had an impact on some of the HBCUs that were either merged with white universities or dissolved completely. This was a result of some who viewed HBCUs as also being segregated institutions of higher learning. This debate continues even in 2012, of whether or not HBCUs are still needed now that Blacks can freely attend public institutions of higher learning (education.stateuniversity.com).

However, those in favor of HBCUs are adamant that they still play a major role in society and are of extreme historical significance to African Americans, particularly since they were the only institutions of which Blacks could attend and receive an education in America during extreme and legal segregation. In fact, many outstanding African Americans who have made tremendous contributions to society graduated from HBCUs. Plus, although black students have the freedom to attend any institution of higher learning of their choice, some are still opting to attend HBCUs. Even though most black college students attend predominantly white schools, about 85%, HBCUs still continue to produce about 26% of black students earning the Bachelor's degree (education.stateuniversity.com).

Further, HBCUs continue to address a major issue still found in the black community, the mis-education of some black youth. Some black students enter college having attended poorly funded and badly structured high schools, which mis-educated them on both their African heritage and on basic fundamentals necessary to function in America. As a result they come to college with severe deficiencies, of which many are not even aware that they have, not having been taught any differently. Since HBCUs are inherently aware of this travesty, many programs are offered to assist the students with these deficiencies. As a result, black students at HBCUs tend to have higher grade point averages and are more socially adjusted and comfortable than black students at white universities (education.stateuniversity.com), who may also have to contend with racism and discrimination. HBCUs have a way of instilling a sense of black pride within their students which increases their self-esteems. Thus, HBCUs are staples within the black community.

In 1904, Mary Jane McLeod Bethune, an incredible educator, started her own school, the Daytona Normal and Industrial School for Negro Girls in Daytona Beach, Florida, with just $1.50 and five female students. Within a couple of years, the enrollment grew to 250 students, and became known as Bethune-Cookman College. It is now known as Bethune-Cookman University (*Ebony* 1971; Altman 1997). Currently, there are over 100 HBCUs (Pinkney 2000) that are still in existence, proudly serving black students and instilling within them their rich cultural heritage of which both Du Bois and Woodson advocated.

CURRENT STATUS OF BLACKS AND EDUCATION

African Americans have come a very long way in terms of being educated in the United States. Sadly, the fact that they were not allowed to become educated during slavery has severely handicapped the race for many years to follow. For without an education in a capitalistic, middle class society such as the United States, life chances are crippled for those met with this fate. Yet, Blacks still survived this insurmountable obstacle and, by 2010, about 82% of them age 25 and older graduated with a high school diploma. As well, by 2010, 3.8 million black students were in college, and for those who had graduated from college, 18.2% of them age 25 and older have a Bachelor's Degree. Further, for this age group, 1.5 million Blacks had advanced college degrees such as a master's or doctorate. However, black females led the way in achieving degrees at any level with at least 60% awarded to them in 2007–2008 (BlackDemographics.com).

Unfortunately, there is an urban legend circulating about there being more black men in prison than in college. Although this urban legend has been very misleading and overwhelmingly and inaccurately stated, many still believe it is true. In dispute of this twisted truth, according to data gathered by the government, more "young" black males are in college than are in prison, indeed twice as many, even though some studies have found that in general more black men, regardless of age are in prison than in college. However, the salient variable in this college-prison misconception is "age," and more specifically traditional college age, 18–24. Among this age group, more young black males are in colleges and universities than are in the nation's prisons (BlackDemographics.com).

EMPLOYMENT

Unfortunately, most Blacks were slaves upon their arrival in the United States of America and therefore not employed for many long years. Instead, they provided the free labor that helped to strengthen the country's economy. Even after slavery, many Blacks were still not employed, but this time due mostly to racism than to slavery. For those who did find work, many continued to do the same kinds of jobs that they did as slaves. Most became sharecroppers and continued to work for white farmers for pennies or at a loss when crops were lean. However, there were a few free Blacks in all states who were required to work. Yet, Whites made it difficult for them to do so by only allowing them to work in certain jobs. There were laws in some states restricting the type of cash crops that Blacks could sell such as corn, wheat, and tobacco. In spite of these obstacles, some free Blacks still managed to live quite comfortably on their incomes, and some had affluent lifestyles and occupations such as dentists, teachers, caterers, and had many other businesses (*Ebony* 1971).

However, one business that was exclusively intended to assist blacks with their financial needs was the Freedman's Savings and Trust Company, which was a black bank established by Congress right after the Civil War in 1865 to help the newly freed slaves. Although most of the accounts were less than $50, that was a huge amount for some Blacks and was in many cases, their life savings at that time. Unfortunately, due to bad investments and mistakes with loans and defaults, the bank began to experience a downfall. In hopes of saving the bank, Frederick Douglass became the president and invested his own money in an attempt to save it, but the bank still collapsed and was shut down on June 28, 1874 (*Ebony* 1971; Altman 1997).

Not surprisingly, Congress did not refund those Blacks who had lost their money and for many, their total life savings under the demise of the bank. Fortunately though, Senator Blanche Bruce was successful in his efforts to assist about half of the Blacks who lost their

funds to get at least some of their money back. This traumatic experience with banks left a bad taste in the mouths of many Blacks and left them distrustful of banks for many years thereafter (Altman 1997). Even today, many elderly blacks refuse to put their money in banks, opting to use cigar boxes, under the mattress, or freezers instead.

During the decades from the Civil War to the Civil Rights Movement, roughly about 100 years, Blacks continued to struggle economically. Although the Civil Rights and Black Power Movements resulted in the removal of legal obstacles to employment opportunities, thus opening up jobs once closed to Blacks, most of these jobs continued to be menial and unrewarding with no chance of promotion or advancement. In addition, Blacks continue to suffer economically from racism. Further, new industry, especially those with the better jobs, tends to locate in areas with the fewest number of Blacks in their population (Swanson 1988; Walker 1977; Rosenfeld, Bergman, and Rubin 1985; Bullard 1989). As a result, counties and towns that are majority Black have a very difficult time attracting new industry.

Traditionally, economic development has been controlled by certain elite groups that are sometimes hard to identify. They, unfortunately, have an impact on whether industry will be allowed to locate in a particular area. Firms that are perceived to be competitive with existing ones will rarely be sought. Fearing an upset of the existing status quo, firms that may improve conditions for Blacks will also be met with resistance (Rungeling, Smith, Briggs, and Adams 1977).

Strategies, such as unionization, that have benefitted Whites and to some extent, middle-class Blacks, may not work in some parts of the country. The problem of racism in labor unions is just as bad as it is anywhere else in the job market. Traditionally, labor unions were mostly segregated. Although the general policies of the American Federation of Labor (AFL) and the Congress of Industrial Organizations (CIO) do not discriminate, these policies are often discriminatory at local levels (Turner, Singleton, and Musick 1984; Feagin 1989). Because labor unions are the main avenues for entry into most skilled and unskilled blue-collar jobs, racism in the unions had detrimental consequences for Blacks. This is particularly profound because the vast majority of Blacks who are employed are blue collar workers, and in need of labor union protection (Turner et al. 1984).

In areas where most of the labor force is relatively unskilled and Black, unions may or may not be beneficial. The fact that stronger labor unions imply higher wages is encouraging, but the reality that most of the labor force in some areas is unskilled is distressing. Generally, unskilled workers may end up gaining nothing with union membership because, if a union contract forces a business to raise its wages, then inevitably the business may attempt to retaliate by eliminating workers either through automation, direct layoffs, or attrition (Naylor and Clotfelter 1975). This can be devastating to poor Blacks, and may cause more harm than good.

Elites in certain areas generally gain economically from discriminating against Blacks (Becker 1971; Glenn 1963; Thurow 1969; Szymanski 1976), and therefore would most likely try to continue this practice. For example, some areas are composed of a dual labor market: one for Blacks and one for Whites. Blacks are often found in low-paying, dead-end jobs that are undesirable to Whites such as frontline factory workers in a popular food industry; whereas, Whites are found in more prestigious positions with better wages, such as managers in the same popular food industry (Bonacich 1976; Feagin 1989; Szymanski 1976).

The prejudice attitudes of some white employers cause them to resist hiring Blacks, even when they could use them to produce greater profits for less pay. Because of these attitudes, white workers have a greater chance of benefitting from white employers' discrimination against Blacks (Reich 1971). On the other hand, some employers actually prefer to hire Blacks, so that they can exploit them to increase profits and decrease labor costs. In this sense, white employers gain, but white workers lose. Therefore, white workers resist this practice because they fear job displacement or lower wages. Thus, this practice causes the working class, both white and black, to be at odds with each other, and increases the chance of racial conflict between them. This type of manipulation stems from elite groups having the power to control employment opportunities in certain areas. Exploitation of this sort will be harder to eradicate

since it is built into the economic structure (Thurow 1969; Bonacich 1976; Feagin 1989; Szymanski 1976; Glenn 1963).

Also, wage differentials exist in some areas. It is no secret that racism restricts Blacks to low-paying jobs. In addition, Whites earn more than Blacks in the same occupations. These differences will continue to exist as long as little attention is directed at investigating equal opportunity cases (Runeling et al. 1977; Naylor and Clotfelter 1975). The time has come for policymakers to pay attention to the areas of the country where the most disadvantaged laborers are found (Lyson 1988). This includes areas which are highly populated with unskilled Blacks. Wilson (1985) described the situation precisely by stating that the current position of Americans today is a classic case of the rich getting richer (Whites) and the poor getting poorer (Blacks).

Moreover, the federal-assisted programs and antidiscrimination policies such as Affirmative Action of the 1960s and '70s helped primarily middle-class Blacks. They were not designed with the problems of lower-class Blacks in mind, who, are not only faced with racism, but also with social class discrimination and economic oppression. Therefore, these programs and policies were mostly ineffective in parts of the country where there is no viable black middle class. As such, Affirmative Action programs, in their original forms, were somewhat irrelevant to the problems of these areas. Especially since many of the low-paying, undesirable jobs do not cause racial competition between Whites and Blacks, because these jobs are commonly referred to as "Black" jobs (Wilson 1985).

In fact, the condition of Blacks in rural places like the Mississippi Delta probably worsened during the period of antidiscrimination policies and federal-assisted programs. This is mainly due to the fact that these policies and programs did not specifically address the fundamental causes of poverty, underemployment, and unemployment among Blacks. Even if all racism in economic development were eliminated, unless there was a serious charge to eliminate structural barriers to meaningful employment, the socioeconomic status of Blacks in places like the Delta will not improve significantly. Nonetheless, the lack of economic opportunities for Blacks in these areas suggest that they are likely to remain in economically oppressed areas, their children will continue to attend economically depressed school systems, and the pool of uneducated and unskilled black laborers will continue to expand (Wilson 1985). These factors will also continue to discourage industrial development in these areas.

Some people in certain areas argued that Affirmative Action Programs did not work because of the already strained race relations between Blacks and Whites. However, economic development will never advance much beyond the present situation if something is not done to improve the life chances of the disadvantaged Blacks in America. Further, in many circumstances, Whites have discriminated against Blacks simply because of racism, and the fact that it has been the norm not to hire or promote them. Another factor that was present in the minds of some Whites in the country was that Affirmative Action Programs involved "reverse discrimination," in which there is discrimination against qualified Whites, who may be arbitrarily excluded (Curran and Renzetti 1987).

Still another factor is the sentiment that Whites today should not be held responsible for their ancestors' past actions. This may be valid, but they are responsible for their own actions of prejudice and discrimination, since some continue to operate through institutionalized racism. They also continue to reap the social and economic benefits associated with exploiting Blacks.

CURRENT STATUS OF BLACKS AND EMPLOYMENT

As in education, over the years, black women have been the most successful in the overall job market. This is most likely related to their higher levels of educational attainment. In 2010, thirty-four percent of black women as compared to 23% of black men were employed in management or professional jobs. Many Blacks are also heavily employed with the federal government, especially since the federal government was one of the first work force areas to integrate based on race. Still, the black unemployment rate at the beginning of 2012 was 14%, almost twice as high as the national rate of 8% (BlackDemographics.Com).

Besides being heavily concentrated in the federal government positions, Blacks are also entrepreneurs. For example, Sarah Breedlove, better known as Madam C.J. Walker, became the first black woman to own a million-dollar empire in the hair and beauty business in the early 1900s. She opened her own factory in Indianapolis, Indiana, and employed thousands of black women, trailblazing the way and hope for other black businesses (Altman 1997). Since her time, blacks have continued to persevere in the business world. In fact, there were close to 2 million black-owned businesses in America in 2007. During that time, about 4 out of 10 black-owned businesses were in the health care and social services areas such as maintenance and laundry services. In the nation's capital, Washington, DC, Blacks owned 28% of all businesses, which was the highest in the nation, followed by Georgia with 20%, and Maryland with 19%. However, New York City had the most black-owned businesses in the country, accounting for about 8% of all businesses owned by Blacks in America (BlackDemographics.Com).

Given the aforementioned discussion of the socioeconomic status of African Americans, it is obvious that an identifiable middle class does exist in America, and that Blacks have come such a long way from the caste system of slavery to get where they are today. However, the next chapter will explore an even higher social class of African Americans, several of whom are among some of the wealthiest individuals in America. Chapter 9 will examine this upper echelon group of African Americans by focusing on the entertainment sectors of the black community.

"ICONS" IN THE AFRICAN AMERICAN EDUCATIONAL COMMUNITY

The United Negro College Fund (UNCF)

In 1944, Frederick Douglass Patterson established the United Negro College Fund (UNCF) to help support black students and black colleges. With the motto, "a mind is a terrible thing to waste," each year UNCF provides financial support to over 60,000 students who

DR. CARTER G. WOODSON, FATHER OF BLACK HISTORY

Dr. Carter G. Woodson, son of former slaves was an extraordinary historian and educator, who authored many books regarding African Americans. He holds the unique distinction of being **the only black person of slave parents to earn a doctorate degree in America.** In 1912, he earned a Ph.D. from Harvard University. A few years later, in 1915, he was one of the founding members of the Association for the Study of Negro Life and History (ASNLH). Its purpose was to educate everyone, but particularly African Americans, about the history and contributions of Blacks in America. Carter was thoroughly assured that education was the key to helping and advancing the African American race. Shortly after the founding of the ASNLH, he started the Journal of Negro History. In 1926, Carter began Negro History Week in hopes of promoting a greater awareness of African American history and achievements. The month of February was chosen because it contained the birthdays of Frederick Douglass and Abraham Lincoln, who were both very prominent figures in black history. The success of Black History Week gave way to the development of Black History Month in 1976. Since then, Black History Month has been successfully celebrated annually. In an effort to reach ordinary people about black history and culture, Carter published the Negro History Bulletin in 1937. Dr. Carter authored many books including *The Education of the Negro Prior to 1861; The Negro Church; A Century of Negro Migration; Negro Makers of History;* and his most widely acclaimed, *The Miseducation of the Negro* (Altman 1997).

are attending one of its 38 member colleges and universities through scholarships and internships. This financial assistance provides support to students from low- and working-class families that could not otherwise afford to send their children to college. UNCF also provides operating funds for the small, private colleges that are affiliated with the organization. To show its commitment to the importance of education for all Americans, the UNCF sponsors an annual televised campaign, "UNCF, An Evening of Stars," to help raise money to support the students and the schools that they serve (http://www.uncf.org/sections/WhoWeAre/SS_AboutUs/aboutus.asp).

The Tom Joyner Foundation

Tom Joyner is one of the most influential black men in the United States. A native of Tuskegee, Alabama, he is the son of a Tuskegee Airman, and a graduate of Tuskegee University with a major in sociology. Using his sociological imagination and exercising an amazing understanding of the black community's educational needs, he created The Tom Joyner Foundation in 1998, which earmarks and awards funds for students and schools that have depleted their funds. This foundation has raised more than $60 million to help fund students in financial need, and to help keep them in the nation's historically black colleges and universities. Each month a different HBCU is selected to receive support from the Foundation. The Foundation exists to "super serve" the black community. For more information visit blackamericaweb.com or email TJF@blackamericaweb.com (http://www.blackamericaweb.com/content/tom-joyner).

The National Black Graduate Student Association, Inc (NBGSA)

The National Black Graduate Student Association, Inc was founded at the end of the first National Black Graduate Student Conference held at the University of Michigan, Ann Arbor, in 1989. Organized by the great, bright vision of five graduate students, the conference attracted attendees from all over the country, with a theme to address some of the issues facing the black community. The goal of the conference was to provide black graduate students a forum for professional development, while providing a venue for social and networking opportunities among them. Dr. Todd Shaw became the first national president of the NBGSA. The organization administers an e-mentoring program, The Dr. Todd C. Shaw E-Mentoring Project which is intended to link NBGSA members with professionals and/or other graduate students who will provide support, guidance, and encouragement to mentees for their academic, professional, and social development. The national headquarters is located at Howard University in Washington, DC (http://nbgsa.org/index.php/dr-todd).

The National Pan-Hellenic Council, Inc., and the Divine Nine

The National Pan-Hellenic Council, Inc. was organized on the campus of Howard University in 1930. Its purpose is to coordinate the mutual interests of the nine Black Greek Sororities and Fraternities, affectionately known as "The Divine Nine." The Council promotes social interaction through various meetings and forums designed to inform and engage cooperative initiatives for a networking exchange among members and the general public, through public service activities in the black community.

The Divine Nine Includes the Below Member Organizations:

1906 Cornell University Alpha Phi Alpha Fraternity

1908 Howard University Alpha Kappa Alpha Sorority

1911 Indiana University Kappa Alpha Psi Fraternity

1911 Howard University Omega Psi Phi Fraternity

1913 Howard University Delta Sigma Theta Sorority

1914 Howard University Phi Beta Sigma Fraternity

1920 Howard University Zeta Phi Beta Sorority

1922 Butler University Sigma Gamma Rho Sorority

1963 Morgan State University Iota Phi Theta Fraternity

(http://www.nphchq.org/mission.htm)

Adhiambo School

Adhiambo is a private African and African American centered institute for preschoolers to fifth graders, located in Jackson, Mississippi. The aim of the school is to motivate the children through positive cultural images, as well as to provide sound academic programs. Adhiambo seeks to strengthen the children's attitudes of self-determination through providing a thorough understanding of their African and African American heritage. The children are well prepared and grounded in knowledge of little known black history facts as well as versed in mainstream educational knowledge. It is located at 3424 Robinson Street, Jackson, Mississippi, 39209-0392; phone: 601-922-1184. Adhiambo is owned and directed by Mahari and Azma Butler (http://www.privateschoolreview.com/school_ov/school_id/15369).

DISCUSSION QUESTIONS

1. Are HBCUs still needed in America today?

2. How can HBCUs be strengthened?

3. Why are more black students attending traditional white colleges and universities than HBCUs?

4. What businesses are most needed in the black community and why?

5. Describe the black middle class in America.

6. Why do many elderly Blacks not trust banks today?

7. What is meant by the mis-education of the Negro?

8. Explain why white Americans are also mis-educated in America?

9. How can Blacks improve their social class status?

10. Why was education so important to Blacks immediately after the Civil War?

11. What was it like being a "free" black during slavery?

1. Imagine what it would be like if all Blacks had had the same opportunity to be educated in America just like Whites. Record your thoughts.

2. Design an effective anti-discrimination program in terms of education and employment opportunities that is applicable to society in the twenty-first century.

3. Compare and contrast the life chances and lifestyles of working class, lower class, and middle class Blacks in America.

4. Research and list all 100-plus HBCUs; include their founding date, original name, and current location; include any unique information.

TEN THOUGHTS ACTIVITY

1. List 10 thoughts on what comes to mind when you think of black students on white college campuses.

   _____

   _____

   _____

   _____

   _____

   _____

   _____

   _____

   _____

   _____

2. List 10 thoughts on what comes to mind when you think of white students on black college campuses.

   _____

   _____

   _____

   _____

   _____

   _____

   _____

   _____

   _____

   _____

3. List 10 thoughts on what comes to mind when you think of the future of America's black children.

_____

_____

_____

_____

_____

_____

_____

_____

_____

_____

SUGGESTED RESOURCES

A Common Destiny: Blacks and the American Society. 1989. National Academy Press.

Allen, Walter R. 1992. "The Color of Success: African-American College Student Outcomes at Predominantly White and Historically Black Colleges." *Harvard Educational Review* 6(2):26–44.

Fleming, Jacqueline. 1984. *Blacks in College.* San Francisco: Jossey-Bass.

Franklin, John Hope. 1980. *From Slavery to Freedom: A History of Negro Americans.* New York: Knopf.

REFERENCES

Altman, Susan. 1997. *The Encyclopedia of African-American Heritage.* New York: Facts on File, Inc.

Becker, Gary S. 1971. *The Economics of Discrimination.* Chicago: University of Chicago Press.

Bonacich, Edna. 1976. "Advanced Capitalism and Black/White Relations in the United States: A Split Labor Market Interpretation." *American Sociological Review* 41:34–51.

Bullard, Robert, ed. 1989. *In Search of the New South: The Black Urban Experience in the 1970s and 1980s.* Tuscaloosa, AL: University of Alabama Press.

Crone, James A. 2011. *How Can We Solve Our Social Problems?* 2nd ed. Los Angeles: Sage.

Curran, Daniel J., and Claire M. Renzetti. 1987. *Social Problems: Society in Crisis.* Boston: Allyn and Bacon.

Ebony Pictorial History of Black America, Volume 1. 1971. Nashville, TN: The Southwestern Company.

Feagin, Joe R. 1989. *Racial and Ethnic Relations,* 3rd ed. Englewood Cliffs, NJ: Prentice Hall.

Glenn, Norval. 1963. "Occupational benefits to Whites from Subordination of Negroes." *American Sociological Review* 28:443–8.

Hraba, Joseph. 1979. *American Ethnicity.* Itasca, IL: F. E. Peacock.

http://education.stateuniversity.com/pages/2046/Historically-Black-Colleges-Universities.html

http://nbgsa.org/index.php/dr-todd

http://www.blackamericaweb.com/content/tom-joyner

http://www.blackdemographics.com/employment.html

http://www.historyisaweapon.com/defcon1/misedne.html

http://www.nphchq.org/mission.htm

http://www.privateschoolreview.com/school_ov/school_id/15369

http://www.uncf.org/sections/WhoWeAre/SS_AboutUs/aboutus.asp

Lyson, Thomas A. 1988. "Economic Development in the Rural South: An Uneven Past—an Uncertain Future." In *The Rural South in Crisis: Challenges for the Future*, 265–74. Edited by Lionel J. Beaulieu. Boulder, CO: Westview.

Naylor, Thomas H., and James Clotfelter. 1975. *Strategies for Change in the South*. Chapel Hill: The University of North Carolina Press.

Pinkney, Alphonso. 2000. *Black Americans*, 5th ed. New Jersey: Prentice Hall Publisher.

Reich, Michael. 1971. "The Economics of Racism." In *Problems in Political Economy*, 107–13. Edited by David M. Gordon. Lexington, MA: Heath.

Rosenfeld, Stuart A., Edward M. Bergman, and Sarah Rubin. 1985. *After the Factories: Changing Employment Patterns in the Rural South*. Southern Growth Policies Board: Research Triangle Park, North Carolina.

Rungeling, Brian, Lewis H. Smith, Vernon M. Briggs, Jr., John F. Adams. 1977. *Employment, Income, and Welfare in the Rural South*. New York: Praeger Publisher.

Swanson, Louis E. "The Human Dimension of the Rural South in Crisis." In *The Rural South in Crisis: Challenges for the Future*, 92–98. Edited by Lionel J. Beaulieu. Boulder, CO: West View.

Szymanski, Albert. 1976. "Racial Discrimination and White Gain." *American Sociological Review*, 41:403–14.

Thurow, Lester. 1969. *Poverty and Discrimination*. Washington, DC: The Brookings Institution.

Turner, Jonathan H., Joyce Singleton, Jr., and David Musick. 1984. *Oppression*. Chicago: Nelson-Hall.

Walker, James L. 1977. *Economic Development and Black Employment in the Nonmetropolitan South*. Austin, TX: Center for the Study of Human Resources, The University of Texas.

Wilson, William Julius. 1985. "The Black Community in the 1980s: Questions of Race, Class, and Public Policy." In *Majority and Minority*, 4th ed., 490–501. Edited by Norman R. Yetman. Boston: Allyn and Bacon.

CHAPTER 9

Artistic Expressions, Literary Works, and Entertainment

Up to now, the foregoing chapters have traced the fate of Blacks from a caste system of slavery to a working-class status, improving to a middle-class status, and then finally, to a few of them entering the upper class in American society. This upper-class status of Blacks is heavily composed of some of the best superstar entertainers in the world. These individuals have earned millions, and many of them are among some of the wealthiest individuals in America. This chapter examines this upper echelon group of African Americans as well as focuses on the artistic expressions and literary works of the black community.

However, like Blacks in other areas of American society, these upper-class Blacks have also experienced prejudice, discrimination, and racism in America. They were not always accepted into society, as if it were color-blind. Therefore, this chapter continues to thematically insist that regardless of social class status in America, "race" still matters. Further, many literary authors have expressed the "black experience" in their writings and black visual artists have also expressed the "black experience" in their artistic portraits and paintings of black culture.

ARTISTIC EXPRESSIONS

Beginning with the Great Pyramid and the Great Sphinx of the city of Giza, in the country of Egypt, on the great continent of Africa, slaves and Blacks have built some of the most incredible sculptures the world has ever known. The Sphinx is an awesome statue that has a man's head, which represents divine power, and a lion's body which represents physical strength. It is estimated to be about 5000 years old. In the same area of Giza is the Great Pyramid, which is a four-sided massive structure covering about 13 acres with an original height of 482 feet. It is thought to be the biggest stone building ever built in the world. It was built as a tomb for Khufu, an Egyptian ruler, somewhere between the third and thirteenth dynasties. It is still considered one of the Seven Wonders of the World (Altman 1997).

African art itself is also some of the most amazing sculptures on earth. Yet, like other aspects of African and African American contributions, students in America are not readily exposed to African art. Many learn about Michelangelo and Picasso, but few learn about African Ife sculptures. Art is a significant part of many African rituals and celebrations and is indeed a major aspect of African culture. Oftentimes the artist or sculptor was in tune with him or herself as well as with nature and ancestor spirits. Dead ancestors were very highly respected and their spirits lived on in sculptures and masks. Therefore, the history and cultures of the African diaspora are reflected in their art and sculptures (Hendricks 1971).

These traditional African art and sculptures have influenced others around the globe, including African Americans. Although many Africans brought to America as slaves had no time to further develop their natural talents, many were indeed gifted. Some of them became craftsmen and carved tools, furniture, and other items. Many Blacks were also blacksmiths and masters at what they did. Many of their items are still displayed in museums (Hendricks 1971).

Despite slavery and racism in America, African Americans still succeeded as artists, painters, and sculptors. After the Civil War, some worked other jobs but continued their arts and crafts whenever they had time. Some of these artists were recognized for merit and include Robert M. Douglas, Jr. and David Bustill Bowers. However, Edward W. Bannister was the first black artist to be widely recognized in exhibitions of his work. He won a prize in 1876 in Philadelphia, Pennsylvania, for his painting titled "Under the Oaks." Yet, Henry O. Tanner became the best-known African American artist of that time and went on to become internationally known. Many of his art works were based on biblical themes and were widely accepted abroad. His works were found in European museums and in Chicago and New York City's art galleries (Hendricks 1971).

Although many black artists left the United States or were forced out due to racism, many stayed and some received general recognition for their artwork. These included William Harper and Laura Wheeling Waring. However, during the 1920s and 1930s, the Harlem (New York) Negro Renaissance created a major wave of black artists in America. This period reflected an awareness and definition of black culture in society. Some of the best known artists of this time who had their art works in major galleries and museums included William H. Johnson, Jacob Lawrence, Georgette Seabrook, Horace Pippin, and many more great

artists of the time. Many others went on to become Art professors at colleges and universities (Hendricks 1971).

During the Civil Rights and Black Power Movements of the 1950s and 1960s, many black artists' works centered on a rich black heritage and expressions of "blackness," clearly dealing with the black experience in America. These artists included greats such as Harper Phillips, Gregory Ridley, Robert Carter, Reginald Gammon, Lloyd Toone, Faith Ringgold, Vincent Smith, Benny Andrews, Russ Thompson, Bob Thompson, and many others who painted the "black experience" in America (Hendricks 1971). Nonetheless, this was a trying time for black artists, especially women. For example, Elizabeth Catlett moved to Mexico City but was still investigated by the United States House Un-American Activities Committee. She was best known for her sculpture "Homage to My Young Black Sisters" in 1968. Yet, in 1972, at age 80, artist Alma Woodsey Thomas was the first black female to have solely her work displayed at the Whitney Museum (http://www.history.com).

More recent artists have also addressed the "black experience" in America, such as Betye Saar, Kara Walker, and Lawrence Jacobs. Saar's work directly depicted racism in America. One of her most famous art works, "The Liberation of Aunt Jemima" dealt with the prejudice of the infamous syrup bottle which stereotyped black women as domestics (http://www.history.com) by the way she was dressed on the bottle, with the rag on her head. The liberated picture featured her with a smile and a different hairstyle. Walker's work has also brought her much fame as her artwork focused on disturbing scenes of life in the antebellum South. As well, Lawrence Jacob's paintings shed light on black life in general with the "Life in Harlem" and "War" artwork being among some of his best (http://www.history.com).

LITERARY WORKS

African Americans are natural storytellers following in the great tradition of African Griots, who were given the utmost respect in the African communities (Bennett 1969). These black storytellers have also sculpted words of expressions into poetry. Indeed, some of the greatest and most well-known poets in America are of African descent. The first known storyteller, Lucy Terry, a slave who came to America as a young child, became a poet as a teenager when she wrote a poem about Native Americans and Whites in battle at the Bars. Her only published poem, "Bars Fight," was written in 1746 but did not get published for nearly 150 years—in 1893. This accomplishment made her the first black poet in America (Potter and Claytor 1994).

Phillis Wheatley, though, became the most well-known black female poet of her time. She was the first black to publish a volume of poetry in America. Like Lucy Terry, Phillis was also a young slave child who was brought to America on a slave ship. Both were brought to Massachusetts. However, Phillis was fortunate enough to be owned by the Wheatley's who provided her a general education and encouraged her to pursue her poetry. In 1773, she went to England with her master's son and published her first book of poems there, and became the first black person to have a book published. Yet, perhaps the biggest honor for her was the opportunity to meet the first president of the United States, George Washington. She wrote a poem of congratulations for him when he became the commander-in-chief of the military in 1775. He then invited her to visit him at his headquarters (Potter and Claytor 1994).

Other great African American writers and poets succeeded Terry and Wheatley. They had many achievements including those of Paul Laurence Dunbar, who was the first black poet to receive national recognition for his book titled *Lyrics of Lowly Life* in 1896, which was one of the most popular books of poetry, which also made him the most important poet of that time. Other historical periods such as the Harlem Renaissance Era, roughly between 1919 and 1930, saw an amazing torrent of some of the most prolific writers of all time. Harlem, a thriving city in New York, was the place to be for any black talent. This era promoted black talent as a way to fight the insurmountable racial challenges facing Blacks at that time (Altman 1997).

Many incredible African American writers followed the early pioneers. These include James Weldon Johnson who, along with his brother John Rosamond John-

son, in 1900 wrote the song, "Lift Every Voice and Sing," which became known as the black national anthem. Other masterpieces include the works of the Harlem Renaissance's poet laureate, James Mercer Langston Hughes. He published his first book of poetry, *The Weary Blues* in 1923, followed by several other publications. More importantly, Hughes has a personal and significant tie to the "black experience" in America. He lived with his grandmother, whose husband Lewis Sheridan Leary had been killed among those fighting for the abolition of slavery with John Brown at Harpers Ferry, West Virginia. His grandmother told him stories of black heroes and would then cover him with his grandfather's bloodstained shawl while he slept at night (Altman 1997).

Other great books include Nathan Eugene "Jean" Toomer's *Cane*, which was published in 1923, and considered one of the most important novels of the Harlem Renaissance. Toomer was the grandson of P. B. S. Pinchback, who was the U.S. Senator from Louisiana during the Reconstruction period in America, and who briefly served as Acting Governor of Louisiana. Another classic was Countee Cullen's *Color*, a book of poetry published in 1925. He was also married to the great writer, W. E. B. Du Bois' daughter, Nina. Other classic works include Zora Neale Hurston's 1937 novel, *Their Eyes Were Watching God*; and Richard Wright's most famous 1940 novel, *Native Son*, which dealt with northern racism (Altman 1997).

More classic literary works continued during the turbulent years of the Civil Rights and Black Power Movements. These include Gwendolyn Brooks' 1950 book, *Annie Allen*, which was a book of poetry for which she won a Pulitzer Prize. Her books focused on issues of ordinary black people such as black youth, violence, and racism. As well, Ralph Waldo Ellison's 1952 novel, *Invisible Man* was thought to be one of the best books of the twentieth century. It addressed the character of an unnamed man, who tried unsuccessfully to get white Americans to "see" him as an individual regardless of his racial background. The book won the National Book Award in 1952 (Altman 1997).

Next was James Baldwin's classic in 1953, *Go Tell It on the Mountain*, which described the role of the

Christian church in the black community. In 1958, author Lorraine Hansberry wrote the play, *A Raisin in the Sun*, which focused on a black family that tried to move into a white neighborhood. She became the first black woman to have a Broadway play, which won the New York Drama Critics Circle Award for Best Play, 1958–1959. In 1965, author Claude Brown wrote his autobiography, *Manchild in the Promised Land*, which highlighted his life in a Harlem gang (Altman 1997).

The 1970s continued the amazing tradition of great black prolific writers in America. The multi-talented Maya Angelou is one of America's most famous writers, who had been very active in the Civil Rights Movement decades earlier. In 1970, one of her autobiographies, *I Know Why the Caged Bird Sings* was published. In 1972, she was the recipient of the Pulitzer Prize for her poetry book, *Just Give Me a Cool Drink of Water 'fore I Diiie*. In 1993, she had the honor of reading her poem, "On the Pulse of Morning," at the inauguration of President William "Bill" Clinton (Altman 1997; Potter and Claytor 1994).

As well, author Toni Morrison published her first novel, *The Bluest Eye* in 1970 and her second, *Sula* in 1973; and in 1977, published *Song of Solomon*, for which she won the National Book Critics' Choice Award. In 1988, her nationally acclaimed novel, *Beloved* made her a Pulitzer Prize winner (Altman 1997; Potter and Claytor 1994). In 1971, Ernest J. Gaines wrote his most famous novel, *The Autobiography of Miss Jane Pittman*, which focused on the life of a slave woman who lived to participate in the Civil Rights Movement of the 1960s. The novel was later turned into a television movie starring the amazing Cicely Tyson. In 1976, author Alex Haley published his most famous book, *Roots*, which traced his family history in America to his African roots. *Roots* won the National Book Award in 1976 and became a television mini-series in 1977. In that same year, Haley won a Pulitzer Prize for his famous book (Altman 1997).

The 1980s and beyond showcase African American prolific writers who continue to produce major literary works, many of which became movies. These include Alice Walker, whose third novel, *The Color Purple*, which focused on the life of a black woman who was mistreated by most but who survived in spite of it. The book won the Pulitzer Prize in 1982 and was later turned into a major movie (Altman 1997) starring superstars Whoopie Goldberg, Danny Glover, and Oprah Winfrey. In the 1990s, two of Terry McMillan's most prominent novels became major movies. In 1992, *Waiting to Exhale* was turned into a movie starring the great Whitney Houston, and in 1998, *How Stella Got Her Groove Back* was also made into a major hit movie starring the amazing Angela Bassett (www.terrymcmillan.com).

ENTERTAINMENT

Not only have African Americans excelled in artistic expressions and literary works, but they have also excelled in entertainment in America and, indeed, the world. Their music and dance styles, like those shown on the iconic "Soul Train" television dance show, hosted by Don Cornelius have been captivating. Their acting abilities have been extraordinary, such as those mentioned in the previous section. They have also excelled as talk show hosts (i.e., Arsenio Hall) and have some of the greatest comedians ever to tell a joke (i.e., Eddie Murphy). Many black entertainers are multi-talented and their contributions to the entertainment arena are unique and unmatched. Indeed, many are among the most famous and wealthiest individuals in America. Still, they too have had to endure the reality of America's racist society in some of the most demeaning ways imaginable.

Since the time of slavery, negative stereotypes of African Americans have persisted in America. Like slavery, when Blacks were considered less than human, and treated accordingly, this inhumane treatment also found its way into the entertainment world of white Americans as amusement for their pleasure. Racism and stereotypes of black entertainers were so extreme, that most could not even play themselves (Blacks) in entertainment roles. Whites would mimic black life through entertainment by performing in blackface. They would paint their white faces black with charcoal paste or burnt cork and would paint huge red or white lips around their mouths. Then they would perform in what became known as minstrel shows. Later, when

Blacks were allowed to perform for Whites, they too had to perform in blackface (http://black-face.com).

Unfortunately, these minstrel shows became the most popular source of entertainment in America between 1840 and 1890, which encompassed the Civil War and the Reconstruction Era. These shows allowed Whites to pretend to be black performers by singing black music, dancing like Blacks, speaking in a slave's dialect, and making cruel jokes about Blacks. Some of the amusement included stereotypes such as the "coon," who represented free Blacks, but who was seen as no better than the slaves. The buck, who was a large black man that was always lusting and chasing after white women; the Uncle Tom, who was a good, religious, and obedient to Whites black man; and the pickaninny who had huge eyes, nappy hair, big wide lips and always appeared to be eating watermelon. Fortunately, by World War I, this form of entertainment in America had run its course (http://black-face.com).

In spite of these dehumanizing minstrel shows, Africans and African Americans have been great performers for centuries. They have been musically gifted throughout their heritage in Africa as well as in America. African American music has evolved from slavery when they first sung the old Negro spirituals to the present-day various types. Spirituals developed because slaves were not allowed to sing or play African music. Therefore, their musical genius and prowess evolved from combining West African rhythms and slave owners' church hymns into their own unique "Negro Spirituals." Many spirituals contained coded messages in hopes of helping each other escape the horrors of slavery. The song, "Wade in the Water," is a good example since it alerted escaped slaves to wade in the water when rivers or streams were available so that slave hunting dogs could not pick up their scents (Altman 1997).

Gospel music, another unique form of African American religious music evolved from the old Negro spirituals that were sung by slaves. These songs are usually filled with emotional sounds like moaning and humming, clapping, stomping or dancing, and shouting out comments to the Lord. In the 1930s, Thomas A. Dorsey organized the first gospel choir. Some well-known gospel singers include Mahalia Jackson, and the

Reverend James Cleveland, who is considered the "Godfather of Gospel Music." In fact, many well-known entertainers began their talents by first singing gospel music. These include Aretha Franklin and the Staple Singers (Altman 1997).

Although the Blues are credited with being started by Blacks in the Mississippi Delta during the 1890s, the slaves' old Negro spirituals and the "call and response" songs gave roots to this type of music. Blues music stresses any aspect of life from poverty to racism. In 1920, Mamie Smith recorded the first Blues song, "Crazy Blues." Other Blues greats include Riley Ben (B.B.) King, also known as the "King of the Blues," and Gertrude Pridgett "Ma" Rainey, known as the "Mother of the Blues" (Altman 1997).

The Blues music gave birth to Jazz music, which also evolved as a distinct sound in 1890 in New Orleans, Louisiana, among the big black bands that played during Mardi Gras, a New Orleans favorite celebration. Some of the black Jazz greats include Joe Oliver, Duke Ellington, Sarah Vaughn, Nat King Cole, John Coltrane, Ella Fitzgerald, Louis Armstrong, and many others. However, Billie Holiday's song, "Strange Fruit," in 1939 reflected the horrors of black lynched victims hanging from trees like fruit. Later, mega superstar Diana Ross starred in the movie, "Lady Sings the Blues," which was based on Holiday's life (Altman 1997).

Rhythm and Blues, yet another African American musical creation during the 1930s, combined Blues and Jazz into a unique sound that ultimately influenced the development of Rock and Roll. Soul music evolved from Rhythm and Blues in the 1950s, and black music was then taken to a new level of insurmountable significance under Motown Records, a powerhouse founded by Berry Gordy, Jr. Both styles of music saw incredible talent emerge such as The Temptations, Gladys Knight and the Pips, Diana Ross and the Supremes, Smokey Robinson and the Miracles, The O'Jays, Earth, Wind, and Fire, Patty Labelle, Stevie Wonder, Marvin Gaye, and The Commodores (Altman 1997).

However, the two icons of Soul music are Diva Aretha Franklin and James Brown. Aretha Franklin was crowned the "Queen of Soul," and produced megahits such as "Respect" and "Chain of Fools." She also sang at the inauguration of President Barack Obama in 2008. James Brown, known as the "Godfather of Soul" was also an electrifying dancer. Brown's 1960s hit song, "Say it Loud, I'm Black and I'm Proud," became a major source that fostered black pride during the Civil Rights and Black Power Movements (Altman 1997).

Still, another form of African American music that became popular among a younger crowd is rap music, also known as hip hop, which contains rhyming lyrics on nearly anything the mind could imagine. The Sugar Hill Gang and Run DMC were great rap artists in the early stages of this musical form (Altman 1997). Rap music has inspired a whole new generation of artists such as Lil' Wayne and Nicki Minaj.

Blacks also made their marks on other types of music such as opera. Some of these greats include Leontyne Price, who was the first black to sing opera on television and Marian Anderson, who was denied the opportunity to sing at Constitution Hall in Washington, DC, because she was black. She later became the first black to sing at New York's Metropolitan Opera House in 1955 (Altman 1997).

As black music evolved into a staple in the American society, so too did black musical legends such as Michael Jackson, "The King of Pop," Whitney Houston, "The Voice," and Beyonce Knowles, who was crowned "America's Most Beautiful Woman," by People Magazine in 2012. Michael Jackson became a dynamic singer and dancer as a young child as the lead singer of the famous Jackson Five. As a solo artist, his 1981 mega smash hit, "Thriller," became the biggest selling album of all time. As an electrifying dancer, he created the moonwalk dance which became his signature dance in his performances (Altman 1997).

Like Michael, Whitney Houston also began singing as a child. Whitney had a voice unlike any other and was one of the greatest female singers of all time. According to the Guinness World Records in 2009, Whitney was cited as the most-awarded female entertainer of all time. Her signature song, "I Will Always Love You," became the best-selling song by a female artist in music

history (www.whitneyhouston.com). Sadly both Michael Jackson and Whitney Houston died in 2009 and 2012, respectively.

Currently, Beyonce Knowles is perhaps the most popular black singer in the world. While with Destiny's Child, the singing group of which she was the lead singer in the beginning of her career, she began her solo career and produced the megahit, "Crazy in Love." Other monstrous hits followed including "Irreplaceable," and "Single Ladies." Her music has earned her 16 Grammy Awards, several MTV Video Music, and American Music Awards (www.beyonceonline.com/us/bio).

African Americans have also excelled as actors and actresses in movies and on television, but in the beginning encountered some difficulty in finding roles suited for Blacks outside of the typical domestic and other stereotypical roles. For example, Hattie McDaniel, a very talented actress, played Mammy in the film "Gone with the Wind" in 1939. As a result, she became the first Black to win an Academy Award for "Best Supporting Actress." As well, Harry Belafonte and Dorothy Dandridge starred in movies in the 1950s. In 1954 they both starred in "Carmen Jones" which subsequently made Dandridge the first black actress nominated for an Academy Award for "Best Actress." In 1960, Harry Belafonte was the first black entertainer to receive an Emmy Award for his television show, "Tonight with Belafonte" (Potter and Claytor 1994).

The 1960s saw a few more very talented black performers in film and on television. In 1963, Sidney Poitier became the first black actor to win an Academy Award for "Best Actor" for his role in "Lilies of the Field." In 1992, he was honored with the American Film Institute's Life Achievement Award, becoming the first black to ever receive this honor. Further, William Henry "Bill" Cosby, Jr., a multi-talented entertainer as well as an author and philanthropist, became the first black in 1965 to star in a prime-time television show, "I Spy." However, he later starred in one of America's most popular shows of all time, "The Cosby Show," in which he played a medical doctor from 1984–1992. Over the years, Cosby has been the recipient of Grammy and Emmy Awards throughout his career. He has also written a "best seller" book, "Fatherhood," and in 1988 gave Spelman College a $20 million gift (Potter and Claytor 1994; Altman 1997).

Despite these early success stories of black actors and actresses, some African Americans continued to have a difficult time finding meaningful and positive roles during the subsequent years in the 1970s. During the 1970s there was specific attention on films aimed at black audiences, known as "Blaxploitation" films. These included "Superfly," "The Mack," "Shaft," "Foxy Brown," "Coffy," "Cleopatra Jones," and many others. Most of these movies dealt with crime, drugs, violence, and sex in inner cities. In these movies, usually the underlying causes of these problems were racism and exploitation of poor Blacks, which then allowed a super hero main black character to successfully rid the effected Blacks of the problem. However, by the 1980s, influential Blacks ultimately stopped these types of movies from being produced (http://black-face.com).

Since the 1970s, more favorable roles for African Americans began to appear. Blacks began to write, star in, direct, and produce their own movies and television shows. Several of these movies have already been mentioned during the Literary Works section of this chapter. Other great ventures include "The Oprah Winfrey Show," which ran successfully for 25 years beginning in 1986 to 2011. The weekday talk show became the number one show of its kind in the nation and in history, and made Winfrey one of the richest women in America. She has also starred in and produced many successful movies and television shows (Altman 1997; Potter and Claytor 1994).

Other multi-talented African Americans who are also actors, directors, and producers include Shelton "Spike" Lee and Tyler Perry. The 1980s and 1990s saw exceptional films about black culture by Spike Lee, who is known for tackling "hard to discuss" and controversial topics such as interracial relationships and "color" intraracial issues in the black community. Some of his films include "She's Gotta Have It," "School Daze," "Jungle Fever," "Do the Right Thing," and "Malcolm X," which starred the super talented Denzel Washington (Altman 1997).

Tyler Perry began his productions during the 1990s and has continued to the present. His signature character, "Madea," a comedic, sassy, domineering black woman, who is played by him, has brought him incredible fame. Madea was rated the 28th character of the 100 Greatest Characters of the last 20 years by Entertainment Weekly. In 2005, he released his first movie, "Diary of a Mad Black Woman." Other movies include "Why Did I Get Married," "Madea's Family Reunion," and "Meet the Brown's" (http://www.tylerperry.com/biography).

Blacks have continued to do well in the film entertaining arena and have won some amazing awards as a result. For example, in 1994, Angela Bassett won the Golden Globe Award for "Best Actress" for her role as the famed singer, Tina Turner in "What's Love Got to Do With It," which made her the first black woman to win this award (http://www.goldenglobes.org/browse/film/25779). Denzel Washington became the only black man to win Academy Awards for both "Best Lead Actor" in 2002 for his role in "Training Day" (oscar.go.com/oscar-history?year=2002), and "Best Supporting Actor" in 1990 for his role in "Glory" (oscar.go.com/oscar-history?year=1990). In 2002, Halle Berry became the first black woman to win an Academy Award for "Best Lead Actress" for her role in Monster's Ball (oscar.go.com/oscar-history?year=2002).

In sum, African Americans have become a staple in the entertainment world, as well as made their marks in the literary and visual arts arena. Although those in these higher status areas have had a much higher standard of living and better life chances, they too have had to endure the realities of racism and inequality in American society.

ON THE HORIZON IN THE BLACK COMMUNITY

Kebra Moore is using her music and inspirational messages to raise the awareness of the many sacrifices military service members and their families make daily. The primary goal is to show them appreciation for their service. Through the "Let's Say Thank You Campaign" the hope is to encourage these service members who are facing life changing injuries to focus on their abilities and not disabilities. On Christmas Eve in 1999, Kebra Moore was involved in a motor vehicle accident, which left her paralyzed in the lower extremities. Thus, she personally understands the many challenges associated with a sudden lifestyle change. Yet, she has not allowed this accident to stop her from living a life filled with passion and pursuing her goals. Kebra is a graduate of Claflin University, in Orangeburg, South Carolina, where she received her Bachelor's of Arts degree in music education. In spite of her injury and challenges, she is making a name for herself in the music industry. Kebra's song titled "He'll Make a Way" was featured on President Barack Obama's documentary soundtrack "BECOMING BARACK: Evolution of a Leader." She has appeared on Black Entertainment Television's (BET) hit show "Bobby Jones Gospel." Her single, "Beautiful" and video are being played na-

tionally and internationally. Kebra's working on her next production, "Under the Influence," which is set to be released in Fall 2012. For more information on Kebra and her music, please visit www.kebramoore.org.

Sonja Griffin Evans is an acclaimed international cultural artist and the owner of Gumbo Gallery in Pensacola, Florida. Gullah Cultural Artist Evans has trained under some of the most talented artists in the country. Sonja believes art should encourage and inspire as well as educate, preserve, and empower communities. Her passion and drive are to artistically record her culture and heritage via her painting as a way of preserving its imagery for future generations. She is an advocate for the creation of Art Ministries in community churches and advocates for the arts across the country. She has received extensive recognition for her contribution of her artwork to museums and non-profit organizations. With years of experience in sales, management, and as a professional artist, she is diligently focusing on building an art industry that will create generational wealth in black communities and provide an incubator, becoming a primary source of representation in support of multicultural artists. Sonja Griffin Evans is the founder of For Artists By Artists which is a nonprofit organization dedicated to promoting cultural diversity in the arts. Sonja is a member of the Teaspoon Foundation, Century, Florida, and President of the De Villiers Cultural Heritage Society, Pensacola, Florida. She also serves on the Board of Directors, National Cultural Heritage Tourism Center, and on the Board of Directors for the Florida Black Chamber of Commerce. Sonja Griffin Evans and the Gumbo Gallery have won many prestigious awards. She was recently named as a Mamie Till Mobley Woman of Courage Award Honoree (mother of Emmitt Till, the youth murdered in Mississippi in 1955), and was an Onyx Award Nominee. Evans has been featured on television, on radio broadcast, and in many publications. Her artwork is in prestigious private and corporate collections nationally and abroad (www.gumboartgallery .com, www.fabaarts.org, www.devilliersmuseum.com).

Courtesy Itbiell Yisreal

Kebra Moore

VISION

PRIDE

STRENGTH

RESPECT

FAITH

© Sonja Griffin Evans

Walk in the Light

EBONY
A Literary Staple in the Black Community

John Harold Johnson, founder of Johnson Publishing Company launched the first issue of the legendary *Ebony* magazine in 1945. Since that time, *Ebony* has become a literary staple in black America, and is the best-selling black magazine worldwide. Debuting at a time when the American society and its social institutions were still disrespectful to African Americans, their culture, and their history, *Ebony* provided popular and thoroughly researched information on the black community that other mainstream magazines chose to ignore. Under the extraordinary and fantastic editorial leadership of its executive editor, social historian Lerone Bennett, Jr., and author of the renowned book, *Before the Mayflower: A History of Black America, 1619–1962, Ebony's* topics ranged from successful entertainers to unpleasant civil rights events and anything in-between. It even featured a column written by Rev. Martin Luther King in the earlier days of produc-tion. In the 1960s as the Civil Rights Movement's turbulent years wore on, *Ebony* magazine brought the events to the black community each month. In 1955, *Ebony's* sister magazine, *JET* exposed to the world the disgusting and horrifying reality of black life in America when it published a close-up picture of Emmett Till, the brutally beaten black youth who was killed in Mississippi while visiting relatives. *Ebony* was at the head of the race with some of the most incredible stories in history that impacted black Americans. Indeed, when the unimaginable occurred in the 2008 election of the nation's first black president, President Barack Obama, *Ebony* published the first interview with the new president (www.newseum.org/news/2010/10/65-years-ago-in-news-history-the-birth-of-ebony-magazine.html; Altman 1997; http://www.blackpast.org/?q=aah/ebony-magazine).

DISCUSSION QUESTIONS

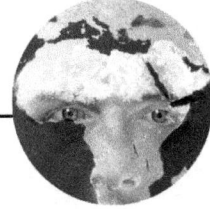

1. Are black entertainers subjected to racism that is still prevalent in society today?

2. Why is *Ebony* magazine a staple in the black community?

3. Imagine how demeaning it must have been for Whites to have portrayed Blacks in the blackface minstrel shows. Record your thoughts.

4. Describe the evolution of black music in society.

5. Why are black entertainers considered some of the most talented individuals in America and, indeed, the world?

6. What is so unique about *On the Horizon* entertainer, Kebra Moore?

7. Why is black visual art important in the black community?

8. What did most of the early writings of black authors and poets have in common?

9. Who do you think built the Great Pyramid and the Great Sphinx?

10. Does race still matter in America? Why or why not?

ACTIVITIES/FIELD EXPERIENCES

1. Draw a picture based on your imagination and understanding of the "black experience" in America.

2. Research and describe the top 25 black entertainers of all time in America.

3. What do you see when you look at the artwork presented in this chapter by artist Sonja Griffin Evans?

4. Read at least one of the literary works discussed in this chapter and write a one-page summary of its contribution and your understanding of the "black experience" based on the work.

TEN THOUGHTS ACTIVITY

1. List 10 thoughts on what comes to mind when you think of black visual artists in America.

   _____

   _____

   _____

   _____

   _____

   _____

   _____

   _____

   _____

   _____

2. List 10 thoughts on what comes to mind when you think of black literary works in America.

   _____

   _____

   _____

   _____

   _____

   _____

   _____

   _____

   _____

   _____

3. List 10 thoughts on what comes to mind when you think of black entertainers in America.

_____

_____

_____

_____

_____

_____

_____

_____

_____

_____

SUGGESTED RESOURCES

The Apollo Theater

http://www.apollotheater.org/

Black Entertainment Television

http://www.bet.com/

Motown Records

http://www.motown.com/

Soul Train

http://soultrain.com/

REFERENCES

Altman, Susan. 1997. *The Encyclopedia of African-American Heritage.* New York: Facts on File, Inc.

Bennett, Lerone, Jr. 1969. *Before the Mayflower: A History of Black America.* Chicago: Johnson Publishing Company, Inc.

Ebony Pictorial History of Black America, Volume 1. 1971. Nashville, TN: The Southwestern Company.

Hendricks, Geoffrey. 1971. "African Art." In Rhoda L. Goldstein, ed., 36–48. *Black Life and Culture in the United States.* New York: Thomas Y. Crowell Company.

http://www.beyonceonline.com/us/bio

http://www.blackpast.org/?q=aah/ebony-magazine

http://black-face.com

http://www.history.com

http://www.newseum.org/news/2010/10/65-years-ago-in-news-history-the-birth-of-ebony-magazine.html

http://www.tylerperry.com/biography

oscar.go.com/oscar-history?year=1990

oscar.go.com/oscar-history?year=2002

Potter, Joan, and Constance Claytor. 1994. *African American Firsts.* New York: Pinto Press.http://www.goldenglobes.org/browse/film/25779

www.devilliersmuseum.com

www.fabaarts.org

www.gumboartgallery.com

www.imdb.com/name/nm0000932/bi

www.kebramoore.org

www.terrymcmillan.com

www.whitneyhouston.com

CHAPTER 10

"Black" in America

Throughout the book, it has been shown how slavery significantly impacted the African American experience. It has also been shown how racism, an unfortunate staple in America, has also impacted the African American experience. Without a doubt slavery and racism have reinforced each other, and together have unleashed paralytic toxins upon the experiences of Blacks in America since they first set foot on the American soil. Yet, in spite of these toxins, and an excruciatingly painful experience, African Americans still found a way to survive against "all" odds. Therefore, this chapter concludes this discussion, and focuses on the remaining aspects of the "Sociology of the Black Experience" in the United States. It describes what it means to be **"BLACK"** in America by discussing "the good, the bad, the ugly, and the magnificent" in the black culture.

DEMOGRAPHICS OF AFRICAN AMERICANS

Interestingly, when the first U.S. Census was taken in 1790, Blacks (757,000) comprised 19.3% of the total population, the highest percentage they have ever had in America. This included both slaves (92%) and free Blacks (8%). By 1890 (7.5 million) and 1990 (30 mil-

lion), Blacks' percentages were down to about 12%, respectively. However, their actual numbers in the population increased as the American total population increased. Therefore, by the 1990s, Blacks were America's largest minority group (www.blackdemographics .com; http://quickfacts.census.gov/qfd/states/00000 .html; www.census.gov). A few decades later, the 2010 United States Census Bureau reported 42 million black Americans out of a total population of 308.7 million Americans. This number equates to about 14% of the population (www.blackdemographics.com), making them the second largest minority group, following Hispanics, who make up about 16% of the total population in the United States (quickfacts.census.gov/qfd/ states/00000.html).

Over the years though, the African American population has mixed with other racial and ethnic groups; mainly Native Americans and white (European) Americans. In fact, nearly all descendants of slaves have some Native American or European American blood. With the exception of the South Carolina and Georgia's Gullah Sea Islands descendants, who are only about 3% ethnically mixed, the average African American is about 17% white. Closer into the mainland of South Carolina, the area known as the Low Country and Charleston, the percentage of Blacks mixed with white blood increased to about 12% (http://www.blackdemographics.com/geography.html).

In other parts of the country, such as southern Louisiana, which was largely colonized by the French and the Spanish, and out West, Blacks have some of the highest percentages of white blood, somewhere between 23–26%. In fact, there are many Blacks in these areas who are more than 50% white. Indeed, some of them could still pass for "white" in society. Further, many Blacks from Louisiana moved to the west coast rather than to the North during the great migrations, where they intermixed even more. Hence, about 10% of African Americans are more than 50% white. As well, there are about 50 million Whites who have at least one black ancestor, and about 70 million Whites who have no black lineage in America (http://www.blackdemographics.com/geography.html).

THE "GOOD"

The "good" or great contributions and achievements by African Americans have been a part of the American society for many years. Blacks have been among the great inventors, as well as travelled into space. For example, at age 23, Benjamin Banneker designed and built the first clock in the colonies in 1754, before America was even a country. In addition, he and his friend George Ellicott, a Quaker, chose the site for the nation's Capitol and the White House, as well as laid out malls, avenues, circles, and parks in Washington, DC. Banneker was also an astronomer who published an Almanac for farmers which contained useful seasonal information, tide tables, and weather predictions (Potter and Claytor 1994).

Other inventors included Thomas L. Jennings, who owned a dry cleaning business in New York City, and who became the first black to patent an invention for a dry-cleaning process called "dry scouring," in 1821. Next, Norbert Rillieux received a patent for an invention that refined sugar, which revolutionized the sugar industry in 1843. Likewise, Sarah Goode, a furniture store owner in Chicago received a patent for her invention of the "folding cabinet bed," in 1885, which was similar to the current folding bed from a couch. As

well, Sarah Boone invented and patented the ironing board that could be collapsed for storage in 1892 (Potter and Claytor 1994).

Further, great African American inventors continued to contribute significantly to the American society. In 1894, George Washington Carver became the first black graduate of Iowa State College (University). In his honor, a building on the campus of Iowa State University is named for him, and a statue of him is displayed in the building's lobby (http://www.fpm.iastate.edu/maps/building.asp?id=20). However, Carver is most known for his work with the peanut and sweet potato. He found more than 300 ways to use the peanut, and discovered 118 ways to use the sweet potato in creating many products from soap to vinegar. In 1953, he became the first African American to have a National Monument in his honor. As well, in 1914 Garrett A. Morgan invented the "Safety Hood," which was used for breathing, and later became the gas mask. In 1923, he patented the first automatic traffic light (Potter and Claytor 1994).

Of major significance is one of the greatest contributions to medicine made by Dr. Benjamin S. Carson, a pediatric neurosurgeon at Johns Hopkins University Hospital in Baltimore, Maryland. In 1985, he successfully performed a hemispherectomy by removing half of the brain of a 4-year-old girl. Later, in 1987, he successfully headed a team of medical professionals in separating a set of Siamese twins who were joined at the head. This operation was the first in history to be performed by anyone (Potter and Clator 1994).

Blacks have also made contributions to America's space program (NASA). For example, Guion Bluford was the first black astronaut to orbit around the Earth in 1983 in the space shuttle, Challenger. In 1984, Ronald McNair became the second black to orbit the Earth in the space shuttle, Challenger. Unfortunately, he was also aboard the Challenger and killed when it blew up in 1986. In 1992, Mae C. Jemison became the first black female in space aboard the space shuttle, Endeavor. She was also a medical doctor (http://www.vibrationdata.com/space/African.htm).

Sports is another area where "Good" or great contributions and achievements by African Americans have occurred. Nothing can bring racial and ethnic groups together like sports in America, and indeed in the world. Indeed, Blacks have excelled and dominated in most of the playing positions of major spectator sports like football and basketball, and are represented in other sports such as baseball, tennis, boxing, track and field, and golf, as well as others. Yet, they have been mostly shut out of the "power" positions in the sporting arena, such as managers, coaches, and owners (Blackwell 1991).

Black sports super greats such as Michael Jordan and Kareem Abdul-Jabbar have been major inspirations and role models for young black youth, many of whom have hopes and dreams of becoming great athletes, and making a lot of money just like their role models. Unfortunately, these hopes and dreams are a reality for only a few of them. Statistics have shown that less than 10 percent of all college athletes are lucky enough to be drafted by the National Basketball Association (NBA) or the National Football League (NFL). Even bleaker is the number of them who actually get professional contracts, about 2%. Of those who do manage to get into the pros, their professional careers can last anywhere from three to five years in basketball and football, respectively (Blackwell 1991).

In spite of the aforementioned statistics, in any given year, about 75% of the NBA's players are black and about 54% of the NFL's players are black as well as 18% of the Major League baseball players. Many black athletes have done extremely well in their respective sports, earning millions like Michael Jordan in basketball and Dwight Gooden in baseball, and earning additional millions from companies and corporate endorsements (Blackwell 1991).

Still, even in sports where Blacks have made tremendous contributions, racial discrimination against black athletes is present. However, this is more widely seen in football than in basketball. Blacks have literally dominated in all positions in basketball, so little discussion in needed here. However, in football, in terms of the so-called "thinking" positions such as quarterback, racial discrimination is evident. In the past, most quarterbacks were usually white in both college football and the NFL. However, this began to change in the 1980s,

when at least three great black quarterbacks took center stage and led their teams to major victories. These three starting quarterbacks were Doug Williams with the Washington Redskins, Randall Cunningham with the Philadelphia Eagles, and Warren Moon with the Houston Oilers (Blackwell 1991).

In 1988, Doug Williams, a graduate of Grambling State University and a mentee of the great, legendary coach Eddie Robinson, became the first black quarterback to lead the Washington Redskins in winning a Super Bowl game against the Denver Broncos. He was also honored as the Most Valuable Player (MVP) of that game. In 1989, both Randall Cunningham and Warren Moon were the starting quarterbacks in the Pro Bowl game. In that same year in college football, there were black quarterbacks in the Rose Bowl and the Fiesta Bowl games; as well as starting black quarterbacks in other bowl games throughout the country (Blackwell 1991).

Simultaneously and continuously, the black legendary coach Eddie Robinson kept producing great African American football players at Grambling State University in Grambling, Louisiana. He started his coaching career at a time when black athletes were not allowed to play at traditional white colleges and universities. Coach Robinson began and ended his 56-year coaching career at Grambling State University. Although he was not as well-known as Coach Joe Paterno of Penn State, he was just as successful with his football team among HBCUs. He was one of the best coaches the game of football has ever known and he coached some of the NFL's greatest players such as Doug Williams, who became the first black quarterback to win a Super Bowl. He is known as a legend, and won a lot of football games, including 408 wins, 165 losses, and 15 ties. This made him the "winningest" coach in Division I-AA history. Coach Robinson began his career in 1941 and retired in 1997, and was inducted into the College Football Hall of Fame that same year. Unfortunately, he was diagnosed with Alzheimer's disease and died on April 3, 2007 (http://collegefootball.about.com/od/coachinggreats/a/Eddie-Robinson.htm).

Despite the success of black players in both football and basketball, Blacks have not fared well in the upper level power positions off of the courts and fields. For the most part, they were excluded from coaching, managing, and owning teams in the NFL and the NBA. It was in the late 1980s, in fact 1989, before this barrier was broken when Berteam Lee and Peter Bynoe bought the Denver Nuggets basketball team. In that same year, Art Shell became the head football coach of the Los Angeles Raiders football team. The situation was worse for Blacks in baseball, although it was the first major sport to be integrated in 1947 with Jackie Robinson, who was an all-around athlete (Blackwell 1991).

However, baseball still had not progressed very far since the time of racial integration in 1947. Recognizing this flaw, in 1987, Baseball Commissioner Peter Uberroth hired Dr. Harry Edwards, a renowned black sociologist with a specialty in the Sociology of Sport, to develop strategies to hire more Blacks in top level positions in baseball. By the next year, the commissioner reported an increase (from 2% to 10%) in employment of Blacks in baseball. Regardless of this increase, the commissioner's report was criticized by Hank Aaron, an amazing baseball great, who broke Babe Ruth's record. Aaron stated that the report did not show an increase in meaningful higher level positions for Blacks (Blackwell 1991).

Nevertheless, despite racial discrimination in sports, whether subtle or blatant, some of the world's greatest athletes are African American. The great sports tradition of Blacks began in the late 1890s, when John Arthur "Jack" Johnson became the first black heavyweight boxing champion in America. Jack defeated every white opponent he faced, even when one of his opponent's managers was the referee for the fight. Hence, Whites were outraged and searched desperately for a "great white hope," to defeat Johnson. To their dismay, none could be found, as Johnson defeated all who dared to face off with him in the ring. When he defeated Jim Jeffries, who came out of retirement to fight Johnson in 1910, race riots broke out all over America, as white mobs attacked Blacks leaving 19 dead and 251 injured. Subsequently, several states passed laws forbidding interracial boxing. Later, in 1979, James Earl Jones portrayed Jack Johnson's life in the movie, "The Great White Hope" (Altman 1997).

Other African American boxers followed Jack Johnson, such as Joseph "Joe" Frazier ("Billy Boy") and Muhammad Ali (Cassius Clay), two of the greatest boxers in United States history, who also faced racial strife. Ali was active in the Civil Rights and Black Power Movements, and refused to go into the military, stating that he was never called a nigger by a Vietcong. Frazier also left his hometown, Beaufort, South Carolina, and went north to avoid racial confrontations which seemed inevitable had he remained. Nonetheless, these two heavyweight boxers had a lot in common, but were each other's greatest foe in the boxing ring. They both became professional boxers after winning Olympic Gold Medals; Ali in 1960 and Frazier in 1964. Ali referred to himself as "The Greatest," and said he floated like a butterfly and stung like a bee. Whereas Frazier was known as "Smoking Joe," and had an incredible, powerful left hook; this accounted for most of his "knock-outs" (Altman 1997; http://www.joefrazier.com/).

The Frazier-Ali fights have been some of the most electrifying matches in the world. In the three matches between the two, Ali took the first win, followed by the "Fight of the Century," which Frazier won, and their final fight was held in Manila, Philippines, in what was dubbed the "Thrilla in Manila," in which they nearly killed each other with Ali taking the title at the end. Retirements left Ali with 56 wins and 3 losses and Frazier with 37 wins and 4 losses (Altman 1997; http://www.joefrazier.com/).

However, since Jack Johnson's classic "racism" case, another classic sporting event involving racism occurred during the 1936 Berlin, Germany, Olympics. James "Jesse" Cleveland Owens, a United States African American track and field athlete, won four gold medals, and set a record that remained for 40 years. His outstanding performance came at a time when Adolph Hitler, ruler of Germany during the Olympics, outwardly expressed racism toward any race that was not German, "the master white race" (Potter and Claytor 1994).

Unfortunately, perhaps the most controversial Olympics track and field event occurred in 1968 in Mexico (http://www.historylearningsite.co.uk/Mexico_

1968.htm). That year was also a turbulent time for race relations in the United States as the Civil Rights Movement and the Black Power Movement were full-blown in the country (*Ebony* 1971). Sadly, despite the achievements of African American athletes in the Olympics in Mexico, in America, Blacks were still struggling for basic human rights that were given to them after the Civil War but never really granted to them. In fact, the American society still treated black athletes as second class, inferior citizens, no matter what they achieved. This included repeatedly repre-senting the country in Olympic events against the rest of the world (http://www.historylearningsite.co.uk/Mexico_1968.htm).

However, two courageous African American athletes, Tommie Smith and John Carlos, at the 1968 Olympics in Mexico decided to display a symbol of black pride in America by raising their gloved fists, a human rights gesture, when they received their medals. They were also supported by their Australian competitor, Peter Norman, who wore a human rights badge. When the winners left the podium, the crowd booed them. The raised fists gesture was intended to raise the hope of having America respect the contributions of black ath-letes, and indeed all people in America. Instead, the salute was interpreted as a negative, militant gesture; a black power salute, which resulted in ostracism for the two athletes, and negative publicity by popular media such as *Time* magazine. As a result, they and their fam-ilies even received death threats back home in America. Unfortunately, Peter Norman, their white Australian supporter was also ostracized in his country. Smith later stated that if he won, he would be "American," but if he lost, he would be a "Negro." In 2008, Smith and Car-los received an Arthur Ashe Courage Award at the ESPY Awards for their courageous action in 1968 (http://www.historylearningsite.co.uk/Mexico_1968.htm).

Not surprisingly, African American athletes who won Olympic gold medals were not treated fairly in Amer-ica. Once black athletic winners returned home, they were treated with the same disrespect and racism that they confronted before they went to the Olympics. They were still treated as inferior and as second class citizens, just as if they had not done anything worthy for America. Apparently, it seemed that Blacks were never going to be treated any better than an advance slave in America, no matter what they did for the coun-try (*Ebony* 1971).

Nevertheless, black women have also excelled in sports and at the Olympics. For example, Wilma Goldean Rudolph, named the "Lady Gazelle" and "The Black Pearl" became the first American woman to win three gold medals in track at the Rome Olympics in 1960 (Altman 1997). By the turn of the next century, the Williams sisters, Venus and Serena, dominated the pro-fessional tennis courts. Serena is considered the great-est female tennis player in the twenty-first century. She has held all four Grand Slam singles titles at the same time and has won more major titles than any other ten-nis player. Serena has won two Olympic gold medals. Venus has won three gold medals, which is the most won by any female tennis player. In 2002, she became the first black woman to become the World Number 1. In that same year, Venus also became the second player to win Olympic gold medals in singles and doubles at the same Olympics. The sisters have played each other professionally 23 times with Serena having the edge with the most wins—13 (http://www.williamssisters.org/).

African Americans have also excelled in other sports such as golf. Eldrick Tont "Tiger" Woods, a profes-sional golfer is one of the most successful golfers in his-tory. He won the 1997 Masters one year after becoming a professional golfer. Throughout the begin-ning of the twenty-first century, Tiger was the World Number 1 for a longer period than any other golfer. He has also broken numerous golf records and continues to be one of the wealthiest athletes in the world (http://web.tigerwoods.com/aboutTiger/bio).

THE "BAD"

One of the many "Bad" things impacting African Americans is being the victims of environmental racism; many times without even realizing this fact. This is not surprising given the fact that many people take the environment and its impact upon their lives for granted; this is true as well in the black community.

However, African American Environmental sociologists, Dr. Robert Bullard, known as the "Father of Environmental Justice," and the director of the Environmental Justice Resource Center at Clark Atlanta University in Atlanta, Georgia, and Dr. Beverly Wright, director of the Deep South Center for Environmental Justice at Dillard University in New Orleans, Louisiana, are two pioneers who have made tremendous contributions in addressing the social and health problems of deadly toxins in the environment and their impact upon black communities. Bullard and Wright have spent their careers researching this issue and have provided some very significant facts that are, at the least, very distasteful to the well-being of Blacks and other minorities (http://www.dscej.org/; www.ejrc.cau.edu/).

Bullard and Wright both have found that minority neighborhoods have literally been "dumping grounds" for toxic waste and solid waste that have threatened their health and lives. Specifically, minority neighborhoods have been "sacrifice zones" and minorities have been victims of environmental racism. In fact, Bullard stated that he first became aware of the unequal and unfair treatment of minorities while conducting research in Houston, Texas, in the late 1970s. There he noticed that garbage dumps in black neighborhoods uncovered a systematic pattern of injustice. His book, *Dumping in Dixie,* was the first to really take a serious look at this issue in America. In it, he thoroughly explained the concept of "environmental justice," which was subsequently used to explain environmental racism in America (http://www.drrobertbullard.com/).

Further, as a very young child, the author vividly remembers the "dump" in her own black neighborhood in the 1960s. However, the impression of the dump by her family and neighbors was that it was an event of which they looked forward to each week, and saw nothing wrong with having it in their neighborhood. It was viewed as a type of "outside mall." Residents of her neighborhood would watch for the dump truck and then would rush to the dump to dig for goods that they thought were useful such as old clothes, appliances, and furniture. They would go to the dump each week and would take home loads of "goods" of which they then replaced their current items with or supplemented

items that they already had. They seemed totally oblivious to the environmental hazards that the remaining "dumped mess" would pose to their health. This dump remained for many years and the author is unsure when the dump actually disappeared, but eventually it did.

Another "Bad" impacting African Americans is being homeless in America. Although homelessness has been an issue in America for more than a hundred years, it is now a national problem, and like other problems in America, it is profound for Blacks. African Americans comprised about 47% of the homeless population in society in 2007. In addition, the average homeless family is composed of a black, female headed, single parent household. This dismal statistic also varies by geographical location. For example, according to the Chicago Coalition for the Homeless, 77% of its total homeless population is black (http://www.nationalhomeless.org/factsheets/minorities.html).

Further, another "Bad" impacting the lives of African Americans in society is drugs. The so-called "war on drugs" appears to be a witch hunt for African American males, who make up about 14% of known drug users, but are disproportionately arrested for drug offenses, as a result of law enforcement racism. Although all races use and sell drugs, African Americans are more likely than any other racial or ethnic group to be thoroughly processed through the criminal justice system from arrest to imprisonment for violating drug laws (http://www.drugpolicy.org/issues/race-and-drug-war).

Moreover, higher rates of arrest and imprisonment of Blacks for drugs do not necessarily mean that they are the majority users and sellers in America. Rather, it is the reality of law enforcement officers targeting black neighborhoods and racially profiling Blacks as drug users and sellers. Therefore, they are more likely to arrest them for drug laws violations than they are to arrest Whites, who are not racially profiled. The Drug Policy Alliance stated that the mass criminalization of young black males in America is just as much a system of racial control as were the Jim Crow laws during the Civil Rights years of the mid-1960s. Thus, the purpose of the Drug Policy Alliance is to expose the drug war racism and to put an end to the "so-called" war on drugs' assault against African Americans (http://www.drugpolicy.org/issues/race-and-drug-war).

Closely related to the disparate treatment of Blacks in regard to drugs in America is the final "Bad" that will be discussed in this section, crime. Crime has always been an issue in American society even before the country was born. In the beginning, England sent its undesirables such as criminals and mentally ill individuals to America, who then became Americans (Hraba 1979). Yet, over the years crime has become overly associated with African Americans, and it appears that a stint with the criminal justice system is a "rites of passage" for black males. In the end, "justice denied" appears to be their only destiny in America.

From slavery to the twenty-first century, Blacks have been denied justice in the United States at some level. When Blacks first arrived in this country as slaves and for much of their experiences throughout the years, there have been "special" laws that were intended just for African Americans. In slavery, there were the "Black Codes," which were a legal set of codes intended to "keep slaves in their place." Although slaves did not have "any" rights, not even as human beings in America, they could still be held liable for violating these codes. Violations of the codes or any other violation by slaves meant more severe punishments for slaves than for Whites for the same violation (Stampp 1965; *Ebony* 1971). It seems that this trend has not changed much for Blacks even in the twenty-first century.

Some examples of violations of the "Black Codes" were that slaves could not point at Whites, use bad language, hit back when hit by a white person, have guns or liquor. In some cases if slaves did not stop when ordered by white men, the white men were obligated to legally shoot them. Slaves could not testify against Whites, and could only be witnesses if the case involved other slaves. Free Blacks were also subjected to some of these "Black Codes" (Stampp 1965; *Ebony* 1971). It is apparent that social class did not matter in slavery and slightly mattered centuries later in regard to being "black in America." However, without a doubt, race still matters in America, as middle-class Blacks are treated very similar to lower-class Blacks when first confronted by some law enforcement officials.

Slaves also endured other types of punishments such as imprisonment, branding, and mutilation. However, imprisonment was rarely used, as it meant the slave master would be missing out on the slave labor on the plantations. Although there were stiff penalties for Whites who murdered slaves, most were never convicted for doing so. Undoubtedly, the slaves' fate was the death penalty for any violent offense like murder, robbery, and of course rape or attempted rape of white women. This punishment was usually a public lynching but slaves were also publicly burned alive (Stampp 1965; *Ebony* 1971). This trend, too, has remained relatively unchanged since the time of slavery and can still be seen in the criminal justice system today (Shepard, Persaud, and Hughes 2009). Remnants of the "Black Codes" still seem to exist in the American Criminal Justice System, even in the twenty-first century.

After slavery and during Reconstruction, Whites cleverly found a new way to keep Blacks enslaved; the prison system. It seemed clear that the institution of slavery was replaced by the institution of incarceration. The prisons were literally used as warehouses for storing a supply of cheap labor that could be leased out to former slave masters who were desperate for "free" labor. Whenever an ex-slave was accused of a crime, justice was automatically denied, in that the judges were ex-confederates who favored the re-enslavement of Blacks one way or another. These judges always convicted Blacks, whether they were guilty or not, creating a wealth of new "free" labor. This new supply of cheap and expendable "free" laborers could be used much like the slaves were in revitalizing the southern plantations (Carter 2008).

The plot to convict as many Blacks as possible in order to exploit them via a convict leasing plan was slavery in a mask. The plan involved the practice of arresting as many Blacks as possible on any charge, minor or major, such as vagrancy, theft, or talking back to Whites, or in some cases, anything that could be trumped-up of which to convict them. Regardless of the charge, Blacks were given long, inhumane, and unreasonable sentences. While at the same time, prison wardens, backed by the states, leased black men, women, and children to any person who could afford to lease them. Convict leasing then was big business during Reconstruction just as slaves were big business in the antebellum South (before the Civil War). The only difference though, was that a slave was more valuable than a leased convict, who was expendable at any time. A slave was valuable property and could be sold for a major profit (Carter 2008).

Several of the current southern state penitentiaries were old slave plantations or had ties to slavery such as the Mississippi State Penitentiary at Parchman Farm, and the Angola Prison Farm in Angola, Louisiana. In fact, Angola was actually named for the West African country Angola, from which the slaves were taken to make the miserable "middle passage" voyage to America. These two farms specifically went from slave plantations to prisons. Once incarcerated, there seemed to be no way out of the second bondage, and many Blacks stayed in prison until they died, never seeing freedom again (Carter 2008). Sadly, they went from chattel slavery of white masters to chattel prisoners of the states, and many were undoubtedly guilty of nothing more than just being "Black in America."

The current situation for black males in prison has not changed much since Reconstruction. Black men in their early thirties (30–34) have the highest rates of incarceration than any other racial or ethnic group in America. Black males in general represent the largest percentage of the more than two million male inmates, with 35% being in jails or prisons (Blackdemographics .com). This historic trend shows no sign of changing as many Blacks, both male and female, now feel afraid and unsafe just driving period, referring to this phenomenon as "driving while black." Aware that history has taught them that they are the "favored" sons and daughters of the American Criminal Justice System, and that life behind bars is just not the same without "Blacks."

THE "UGLY"

Like the "Good," and the "Bad," the "Ugly" also exists and impacts African Americans in the United States. This section describes the "Ugly" by first examining the social psychological impact of the turbulence Blacks have experienced in America since their capturing in

Africa and right up to their present condition. As a result of these horrid times, intra-racial issues, such as self-hatred continue to haunt the black community. Thus, the psyche of the average African American has been scarred leaving him or her in a social psychological state that must be understood to further understand the African American experience in society.

The social psychological impact of slavery has handicapped a whole nation; specifically black and white Americans. Both have undergone a socialization process that would have to be totally overturned in order to repair their misunderstanding of Blacks in America. Hence, they both must "imagine and understand" slavery and its impact on both races. Until this unpleasant endeavor occurs, slavery will continue to paralyze the "mental" capacity of both races, which will continue to impact the physical treatment of African Americans, based on stereotypes such as Blacks' inferiority to Whites.

The re-socialization of Blacks, Whites, and others must include the fact that Blacks started out in America at a terrible disadvantage; stripped of everything from their names to their mere existence of being considered less than human. No other race or ethnic group in America has ever had to endure something so unimaginable. Blacks never had a fair chance "to catch up" in America. Their struggle was so incredible and so devastating that they are still behind as a race. Unlike other Americans, who were not enslaved and who, for the most part, voluntarily came to America, most Blacks were forced involuntarily into coming to America for a life of servitude. They never had "boot straps" to help pull them up instead they had "chains" that pushed them down.

Consequently, African Americans suffer from what the author describes as the social psychological "pull-push-pull" syndrome experienced from both Whites and Blacks. This includes the irony that every time Blacks try to "pull" themselves out of a hole Whites try to "push" them back into the hole. At the same time, sadly, Blacks too will "pull" other Blacks back into the hole, thereby assisting Whites in keeping Blacks down and in "their place in society." Therefore, those Blacks who try to help themselves are then sandwiched between both Whites and other Blacks who want to defeat their efforts. The Blacks who assist Whites in keeping other Blacks in the hole, are thought to suffer from the mental deformity of not wanting to see other Blacks get ahead; "the crabs in a bucket" syndrome.

Ironically, Whites still do not understand why Blacks cannot seem to "pull" themselves out of the hole on their own; the way other Americans did. Some Whites do not have a clue as to why this is so hard for Blacks to do, and those that do have a clue, sometimes tend to ignore it. Most Whites simply do not fully "understand" their privileged status in America and how it came about through racism. Unfortunately, some Whites do not understand racism and how it works to their advantage in America. Some just know that it works, and in their favor. Subsequently, this "misunderstanding" of racism continues to feed the negative racial stereotypes they possess of Blacks. Deplorably, it is so hard to change stereotypes when people have been socialized for generations to "think" they are true. These negative mental thoughts can become so deeply internalized by both Whites and Blacks that Blacks begin to believe them as well. This internalization of stereotypes can then manifest into self-hatred among Blacks and into continued hatred of Blacks among Whites.

Slavery and racism, the "Negro/Black Problems," have made Blacks socially and psychologically impaired in America. Blacks are confused, frustrated, distrustful, enraged, and full of self-hatred. These emotions have led to many intra-racial and interracial issues that have continued to stunt the positive movement of the race. Experiencing these emotions, some at the same time, can really manifest into a number of negative thoughts and behaviors among Blacks. For example, the frustrations of just being "BLACK" in America on a daily basis and all of the pain and suffering which caused the frustration over the years, have enraged some Blacks to a point of not valuing each other's lives, which may lead to black-on-black violence. They scapegoat, or blame each other and then take out their frustrations on one another, rather than the true source of the frustration.

Frustration among Blacks is further exacerbated as they fumble through the maze of being "Black" in America. They often are confused on what to think, how to be-

have, what to do, when to do it, where to go, who they are, why they are, what to believe, who to trust, when to trust, and the confusion goes on and on. Complicating matters is their general distrust of Whites, which obviously originated in Africa when Blacks were tricked, kidnapped, lied to, and stolen from their homeland and forced into slavery in America. Over their treacherous and disappointing experiences in America, they have continued to experience the trickery and lies by Whites over and over again. This perception of Whites has been ingrained into the psyche of Blacks through socialization and the realization that "nothing Whites say can be trusted."

African Americans also have been brainwashed into thinking that "black is bad." As a result, some dislike their natural "bad" hair that is usually coarse, thick, and bushy. Some then prefer to straighten or lengthen their natural hair by either getting a perm or a weave to turn their "bad hair" into "good hair" that is similar to white hair. However, many are pleased with their natural hair and wear natural or braided hair styles. Some have even reverted back to wearing afros.

However, the "colors" of the black race skin tones are and always have been both an intra-racial issue and an interracial issue in America. The skin tones of African Americans range from being jet black to near white. This "color" issue has been around since the time of slavery when some of the house servants, especially the lighter complexioned ones, thought they were much better than the field hands and looked down upon the slaves who worked the fields. Whites too, thought that the light-skinned Blacks were better than the dark-skinned Blacks, perhaps because of the way they became light-skinned; mostly through rapes of slave women who gave birth to half-white babies (*Ebony* 1971). As a result, light-skinned Blacks received more opportunities for advancement than dark-skinned Blacks. This is still evident in some cases even in the twenty-first century, and unfortunately among both Whites and Blacks. Unfortunately, some brainwashed Blacks still believe that light-skinned Blacks are better than dark-skinned Blacks.

The negative effect of African Americans' skin color has manifested itself in a number of ways in America.

Hence, some Blacks who could pass for Whites tried their very best to do so. For example, some prominent Blacks such as Jean Toomer, author of the book, *Cane*, and Dr. William Augustus Hinton, a prominent Harvard University medical doctor, both tried to deny their black heritage. Toomer rejected his "blackness" and left the black community to live as a "white" person. He was married twice to white women (http://www.poets .org/poet.php/prmPID/71). Similarly, Hinton declined to accept the NAACP's Spingarn Medal in 1938, fearing the exposure to the world that he was black. He thought that having the award would have been more detrimental to his career than not having it (Potter and Claytor 1994).

The "skin color" issue has also caused low self-concept and low self-esteem among some very dark-skinned Blacks who have suffered from being teased and ignored by other Blacks as well as being taunted by Whites. This constant teasing and taunting have made many very dark-skinned Blacks hate themselves for being so dark, and the realization that there is nothing they can do about it. This reality has lowered their self-concepts and self-esteems and they feel like they will never get ahead in America because of the "actual" color of their skin. This is especially acute when other Blacks tend to view very dark-skinned Blacks as less than they are. Yet, "Black is Beautiful."

THE MAGNIFICENT

The "Good," the "Bad," and the "Ugly" have all impacted African Americans over the years in America. Yet, some magnificent contributions by Blacks have been a part of the American society for many years, whether recognized or not. One of these magnificent contributions has been the tradition of "quilting" among African American women. In slavery, like old Negro spirituals, quilt patterns were also used to give coded messages to slaves, particularly those planning to escape. Since it was common to see quilts placed over fences on plantations, they did not arouse any suspicion among slave masters and overseers. However, each quilt's pattern cleverly displayed a different message to the slaves, which included patterns of stars and wagon wheels (Carter 2008). Nonetheless, black

women made quilts by hand and continued this laborious tradition until this day. However, the distinct patterns of slavery symbols may or may not be a specific part of the quilt. The actual process of quilting is described in the highlight box.

Courtesy of author

ELBERTHA DUNBAR GRAY, A MASTERMIND OF *QUILTING*

When I was a very young child, my sisters and I would observe our mother sitting at a table making a quilt for our family. Back then, I had no idea of the significance of this art form in the black community, dating all the way back to slavery in America. My mother would gather scraps from old clothing: pants, jeans, dresses, old work uniforms, sheets, or wherever she could find them. She kept them in a barrel and would pull them out and literally hand-sew each piece together until she had enough for one side of the quilt. She would make two individual sides of the quilt and then join them together. These quilts were the most amazingly warm covers we ever had! They were so very unique! She was the most patient woman I knew. I am not sure how she developed that skill, but unfortunately, it was not passed down the gene pool to any of her eight daughters! Needless to say, none of us ever mustered the patience or mastered the skill to continue in her footsteps. Today, some of her masterpieces still remain within her immediate and extended family. She was indeed, a "Mastermind" of Quilting!!!!

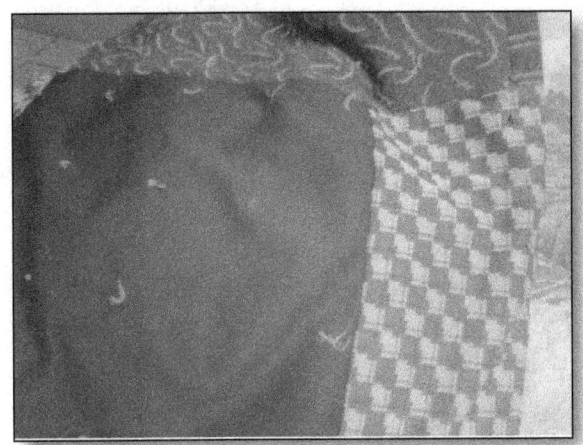

Quilt

The Gullah nation is another magnificent part of African culture that has been well preserved since the time of slavery. The African Americans who are known as Gullah or Geechees are mostly found along the South Carolina and Georgia coastlines on a string of Sea Islands including Charleston, Hilton Head, and Beaufort, South Carolina, and Savannah, Georgia. The African slaves who were brought to these islands were mostly rice farmers from Sierra Leone, and today rice continues to be a staple in the diet of the Gullah people. These slaves outnumbered Whites by the thousands and were therefore able to retain some of their Africanisms (elements of the African culture), which can be heard in their distinct dialect of combining the English language with languages of West and Central Africa, and seen in their unique, and highly artistic sweet grass basket weaving (Carter 2008).

Some of the words in the Gullah language that the author grew up hearing from time to time by individuals from the Sea Islands near her hometown of Beaufort (Burton), South Carolina, include: *eh* (you, he, she, it, them, they); *dem* (them, they); *uh* (I); *da* (the); *dat* (that); *kum ba yah* (come by here); *ketch* (catch); *chillun* (children); *dey* (there); *fuh* (would, will, for); *haffuh* (have to); *du'um* (do it); *enny* (aren't they); *we* (our); *wid* (with); *mo* (more); *waay* (where); *buckrah* (white men); *git* (get); *cha* (here); *kum* (come); *yah* (here); *all two* (both); *a* (of); *ta* (to); *cay* (carry, take); *fo* (before); *u* (you); *sto* (store). Some of the sentences she remembered hearing from one of her brother-in-laws, who is from Scott Island, one of the Sea Islands in South Car-

olina include: Bally, du dat now fo uh haffuh du'um masef (Bally, do that now before I have to do it myself). Other sentences heard include: Eh alwaays cum ya wid all dem bad chillun (They always come over here with their bad children); Eh need ta cay dem chillun some waay an git em sum mannas (They need to take the children somewhere and get them some manners); and Kum ba yah fo u go ta da sto (Come by here before you go to the store).

The Sea Islands is also home to Penn Center, located on St. Helena Island, a Gullah community in Beaufort County, South Carolina. Penn Center is one of the oldest schools for Blacks in America, which began functioning as a school for the newly freed slaves. Charlotte Forten was the first black teacher at Penn Center, which began operating during the early years of the Civil War in 1862. She is also considered the first to formally teach black history to her students in America. The Gullah nation is a testament in opposition to the notion that slavery was so devastating that no African culture could have survived it (Carter 2008).

The Daufuskie Island, a remote island only accessible by ferry off of the Hilton Head Island coast in South Carolina, is another distinct Gullah island with a rich African American history. Bravely, the slaves remained and survived on the island when the slave masters abandoned them and their plantations during the Civil War. Subsequently, the slaves were able to keep many of their African traditions, including language and dialect. Some of the original buildings from the time of slavery still remain on Daufuskie Island including an old church and several houses. The remoteness of the island aided the former slave residents in retaining their Africanisms. Their Gullah dialect is so unique that one will likely not hear it anywhere else in the world. Moreover, the movie "Conrack" was about Pat Conroy's experiences as a white teacher on Daufuskie in the late 1960s (http://www.hiltonheadisland.org/daufuskie-island/history-and-culture; http://www.thedaufuskiecompany.com/index.php? page=history).

Other magnificent parts of the black community include a lot of unique sayings, icons, behaviors, thoughts, and urban legends. For example, the letters CPT refers to "colored people time," which means that an individual does not have to be on time for an event; if it begins at 9 PM, then some Blacks will interpret this to mean that it starts around 9:30 PM or even 10 PM. It refers to the opinion that Blacks are never on time for anything and that they are usually late for everything. So, Blacks should be told that that an event starts at least 30 minutes earlier, if they are expected to be there on time. A second set of letters, HNIC means "head niggah in charge," which refers to a black person who is in charge of something of which Blacks are normally not in charge; or a high ranking position over a lot of white employees.

The "n-word" has different meanings and reactions depending on who is using the word, when it is used, and with whom it is used. "Nigger," is still the derogatory word that many Blacks have chosen to remove from their vocabulary because of the ugly connation and link that it has to slavery. However, many Blacks have given it a whole different meaning and spelling and use it quite frequently among only them. The new word is "Niggah," and usually used as a term of endearment or to show unity among sub groups of Blacks. It is used quite often among some African Americans, and no one thinks anything of it. However, if a white person uses either word, "nigger" or "niggah," they immediately take on the original derogatory meaning associated with slavery.

The term "picnic" is also thought to have a negative, horrible meaning in the black community and is thought to be an urban legend, originating from some unknown source, but appearing to be true. The term "picnic" or "pick a nigger," has been associated with the lynching of a black person, sometimes chosen randomly and for no reason other than the amusement of Whites, who would gather to watch the lynching and then celebrate by eating food on the grass where the lynching took place (http://www.ferris.edu/jimcrow/question/jan04.htm). Therefore, Blacks have been socialized to use the term "cook out" rather than "picnic."

Other peculiar notions in the black community include the terms "self-help" and "unity." They suggest that Blacks should unite and help each other every chance they get and should support black businesses and professionals whenever possible. Yet, some Blacks still prefer to have a white physician or a white lawyer; feeling that the black physician or lawyer may not "be good or smart enough" to help them, or hoping that they would be in a better position to be treated with more respect. Some Blacks also feel that black service providers would not do as good a job for them as they would for Whites who might use the black service providers. Others complain that black businesses sell their products or services higher than white businesses, so they prefer to consume goods and services from white-owned businesses.

Closely related to consumer choice is the fact that many Blacks are criticized for spending a high percentage of their income on clothes, cars, and other materialistic items, while renting a place to live for years, and shying away from financial planning and investments. Blacks have also been criticized for inheriting and owning a lot of land, paying taxes on it for many decades, and just letting it sit. Much of this land was acquired right after the Civil War when Whites abandoned their plantations and left the slaves on the land. Land can stay as heirs' property for years but no one will take the initiative to sell it or develop it.

Still, icons exist in the black community that are uniquely black, such as an HBCU marching band, whose performance is more affectionately known as the "fifth quarter," at a football game. Known for their high stepping, dancing, and music prowess, all at the same time, nothing can compare to the HBCU marching band at halftime. No one leaves his or her seat and all eyes are on the field at halftime. In fact, some HBCU bands have performed at major events such as presidential inaugurations and Super Bowl games. Some have even done endorsements for major corporations. They are indeed the highlight of any HBCU football game. Nonetheless, names will not be mentioned so that no wars are started. Of course the games are also important!

Another icon in the black community is the infamous "Family Reunion," which usually takes place throughout the summer months. This is a major event comprised of many activities over a three- or four-day period where extended family members come together from all over the country. During the reunion, family members usually wear a specially designed t-shirt, eat deliciously prepared food, and enjoy great fun activities. Sometimes family members meet new members for the first time; which could occur at each subsequent reunion. It is also a time to learn family history that can usually date back as far as the eldest living relative can remember.

Sadly and unfortunately, most Blacks can only trace their family history a few generations back and only in the United States due to the way they were stolen and thrown into society, never to see their African family members again. Most Blacks can only dream of knowing their African roots and African ancestors since as slaves they were forbidden to keep any ties to Africa. It is unlikely that the average African American knows exactly where his or her family roots are in Africa. All they know is that they are "in" Africa. So, the family reunion is extremely important in the black community, and family members are always glad to meet and greet each other.

Courtesy of author

Family Reunion

SOCIOLOGY OF THE BLACK EXPERIENCE REVISITED

The Sociological Imagination is most helpful to the understanding of the "Sociology of the Black Experience" in the United States. Further, the sociological imagination enables one to understand the events, painful or not, of personal troubles within the larger context of society. It enables one to understand the effect of social forces such as slavery on people's lives, and then allows for the understanding of how social forces shape people's perspectives and experiences. Thus, Sociology allows one to question "taken for granted" assumptions and realities, and then replaces subsequent misconceptions and misinterpretations with more accurate data and explanations (Shepard et al. 2009).

The sociological imagination or the ability to see one's own life and the lives of others as part of a larger social structure and a larger human condition (Shepard et al. 2009; Henslin 2011) is the main conceptualization for the "Sociology of the Black Experience." Once an individual develops this critical way of thinking, he/she will be less likely to explain others' behavior through their "race" and will begin to examine the social structures and social forces which determine behavior such as slavery and racism.

Therefore, it is evident that sociology and the sociological imagination are most useful to the understanding of the "Sociology of the Black Experience" in the United States. Historically, this experience has been very excruciatingly painful for Black Americans, as is evident in their lives from slavery to the present and everything in between. Hence, Americans cannot ignore the fact that "race" still matters in this society. Without a doubt, most would argue and many would agree that the African American experience has been the worst, although most unique in the United States. In spite of all of this, there are no other human creations in the world that are parallel to black Americans. They are a unique creation, "created" by white Americans and "made" in America. It is the hope that this book has aided the reader in developing a "Sociological Imagination."

"inner strength"

© *Sonja Griffin Evans*

"I am a man"

© *Sonja Griffin Evans*

1. REFLECTIONS II: "WHO AM I NOW?"

    Prepare a one *full* page reflection of "you" and your black experience.

    Each student should write a *1-page* paper on "your" black experience after this class. You can reflect on anything you desire, as long as it relates to the Sociology of the Black Experience. Who were you? Who are you now? Why? What was the most interesting part of the course and what can you readily identify with now that you were not aware of before? Should everyone be required to take this course or a course like this? What was the overall impact of this course on you? Use specific examples or scenarios. You may use opinions for this paper!!!!!!!!!!!!!!!!!!

TEN THOUGHTS ACTIVITY

1. List 10 thoughts on what comes to mind when you think of the "Good" in the black community.

    _____

    _____

    _____

    _____

    _____

    _____

    _____

    _____

    _____

    _____

2. List 10 thoughts on what comes to mind when you think of the "Bad" in the black community.

    _____

    _____

    _____

    _____

    _____

    _____

    _____

    _____

    _____

    _____

3. List 10 thoughts on what comes to mind when you think of the "Ugly" in the black community.

_____

_____

_____

_____

_____

_____

_____

_____

_____

_____

4. List 10 thoughts on what comes to mind when you think of the "Magnificent" in the black community.

_____

_____

_____

_____

_____

_____

_____

_____

_____

_____

5. List 10 thoughts on what comes to mind when you think of "The Black Experience in America."

_____

_____

_____

_____

_____

_____

_____

_____

_____

_____

SOCIOLOGY OF THE BLACK EXPERIENCE

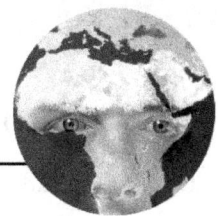

BLACK FACTS (BLACK HISTORY MONTH) RESEARCH PAPER

First, discuss the origins and founder of Black History Month, then:

1. For the month of February (1–28, any year), each student will prepare a chronicle of black history. No two chronicles should be the same.***

2. For *each day of the month* of February, research and document a meaningful and significant fact relating to black history (throughout the diaspora). ***Explain the significance of little known facts** for example, research significant facts that occurred on February 1 (state the year that it occurred), and continue this format until you reach February 28. You may also include February 29. Your selected fact must have occurred on the actual date in *February*.

3. Do not use opinions for this paper. You must use and **CITE ALL FACTS.**

4. Consult your "Tools for Assignments" section of your syllabus to format and structure your paper. You should use bullets for each fact instead of paragraphs. Approximately 5 pages should be sufficient, no more than 7 pages maximum.

5. ENJOY THIS ASSIGNMENT WHILE YOU LEARN ABOUT THE BLACK EXPERIENCE AND DIASPORA!!!!!!!!!!!!!!!!!!

BLACK FACTS RESEARCH PAPER

1. Each student will research and prepare a document of black history. No two documents should be the same. ****

2. Research and document 30 meaningful and significant facts relating to black history (throughout the diaspora). Your document should include a variety of facts; not all facts should be on sports or entertainers, instead, include inventors and ordinary people. Be sure to include little known facts.

3. Do not use opinions for this paper. You must USE and CITE ALL FACTS.

4. Consult your "Tools for Assignments" section of your syllabus to format and structure your paper. List and number each fact. Five full pages should be sufficient, no more than 7 pages maximum.

5. ENJOY THIS ASSIGNMENT WHILE YOU LEARN ABOUT THE BLACK EXPERIENCE AND DIASPORA!!!!!!!!!!!!!!!!!!

CLASS PROJECT: AFRICAN DIASPORA DAY

"Celebrate Africa: Motherland of All Mankind"

1. To celebrate Africa and all of her people, small groups of students will be assigned a different aspect of black culture and history to research and present/perform on "Diaspora Day."

2. Selections include:

    *   Black cultural artifacts (items representative of any dimension of the diaspora including black power symbols, afro picks, art, etc.)

    *   Ethnic foods and non-alcoholic beverages (prepare and bring), also bring paperware (cups, napkins, plates, forks, etc.)

    *   Ethnic music (perform or bring Jazz, Reggae, Gospel, Soul, etc.)

    *   Ethnic talents (dance, soul train line, sing, poetry reading, etc.)

    *   Ethnic fashions (wear '50s, '60s, '70s, and beyond; including hairstyles)

    *   Actors/Actresses (typical day/experience as a black person skit; anything from Juneteenth to Boyz N da hood)

    *   Recitation of literature, and other black expressions

    *   Representatives from the Caribbean Islands, discuss at least 5 Islands with predominantly black inhabitants (basic facts and anything unique about the Islands)

    *   Other Diaspora Jewels such as sports and inventions

3. Each group is to prepare a 2- to 3-page paper on your selection. You must cite ALL FACTS.

4. Consult your "Tools for Assignments" section of your syllabus to format and structure your paper.

5. ENJOY THIS ASSIGNMENT WHILE YOU LEARN ABOUT THE BLACK EXPERIENCE AND DIASPORA!!!!!!!!!!!!!!!!!!

REFERENCES

Altman, Susan. 1997. *The Encyclopedia of African-American Heritage*. New York: Facts on File, Inc.

Blackwell, James E. 1991. *The Black Community Diversity and Unity*, 3rd ed. New York: Harper Collins, Publisher.

Carter, Cynthia Jacobs. 2008. *Freedom in My Heart: Voices from the United States National Slavery Museum*. Washington, DC: The National Geographic Society.

Ebony Pictorial History of Black America, Volume 1. 1971. Nashville, TN: The Southwestern Company.

Henslin, James M. 2011. *Essentials of Sociology*, 9th ed. Boston: Allyn and Bacon.

Hraba, Joseph. 1979. *American Ethnicity*. Itasca, IL: F. E. Peacock.

http://collegefootball.about.com/od/coachinggreats/a/Eddie-Robinson.htm

http://quickfacts.census.gov/qfd/states/00000.html

http://web.tigerwoods.com/aboutTiger/bio

http://www.blackdemographics.com

http://www.blackdemographics.com/geography.html

http://www.census.gov

http://www.drrobertbullard.com/

http://www.drugpolicy.org/issues/race-and-drug-war

http://www.dscej.org/

http://www.ferris.edu/jimcrow/question/jan04.htm

http://www.fpm.iastate.edu/maps/building.asp?id=20

http://www.hiltonheadisland.org/daufuskie-island/history-and-culture

http://www.historylearningsite.co.uk/Mexico_1968.htm

http://www.joefrazier.com/

http://www.nationalhomeless.org/factsheets/minorities.html

http://www.poets.org/poet.php/prmPID/71

http://www.thedaufuskiecompany.com/index.php?page=history

http://www.vibrationdata.com/space/African.htm

http://www.williamssisters.org/

Potter, Joan and Constance Claytor. 1994. *African American Firsts*. New York: Pinto Press.

Shepard, Jon M., Narayan Persaud, and Brenda Hughes. 2009. *Sociology*, 10th ed. Thomson/Wadsworth, Publisher.

Stampp, Kenneth. 1965. *The Peculiar Institution: Slavery in the Ante-bellum South*. New York: Alfred A. Knopf, Publisher.

www.ejrc.cau.edu/

CPSIA information can be obtained
at www.ICGtesting.com
Printed in the USA
LVHW022352201119
637959LV00001B/3/P